Written Education Induced Neurosis

A True Story

VOLUME XIV

BY: TODD ANDREW ROHRER

iUniverse, Inc.
New York   Bloomington

Written Education Induced Neurosis
A True Story

iUniverse books may be ordered through booksellers or by contacting:

iUniverse
1663 Liberty Drive
Bloomington, IN 47403
www.iuniverse.com
1-800-Authors (1-800-288-4677)

Because of the dynamic nature of the Internet, any Web addresses or links contained in this book may have changed since publication and may no longer be valid. The views expressed in this work are solely those of the author and do not necessarily reflect the views of the publisher, and the publisher hereby disclaims any responsibility for them.

ISBN: 978-1-4502-1749-1 (pbk)
ISBN: 978-1-4502-1750-7 (ebook)

Printed in the United States of America

iUniverse rev. date: 3/11/10

Although the opinions relative to the unwanted mental side effects of written language on the mind in this book are the authors, the author is simply giving a testimony after negating the neurosis caused by written education, the tree of knowledge, that in spirit is the same testimony given by many human beings who negated said neurosis going back to the beginning of civilization itself, and thus the invention of written language.

"What it comes down to is that modern society discriminates against the right hemisphere." - Roger Sperry (1973) - neuropsychologist, neurobiologist and Nobel laureate

In order for civilization to discriminate against right brain any greater than they do now via written education they would have to cut the right hemisphere of the brain out the children at birth.

12/25/2009 10:04:39 PM -
[Genesis 22:7 And Isaac spake unto Abraham his father, and said, My father: and he said, Here am I, my son. And he said, Behold the fire and the wood: but where is the lamb for a burnt offering?]

This comment relates to Isaac asking where the sacrifice is and this suggests he is not aware it is him. So Isaac is not mindful Abraham is about to apply the fear not remedy on him. This is important because in order for one to deny their self, or lose their life mindfully to preserve it, and thus unveil right brain, they must believe the shadow of death is actual death because if not the "left brain state of mind" will not be tricked. Abraham understood he was not going to kill Isaac but this comment is showing Isaac was not aware of that.
This comment in this verse is a sign post of authenticity.
[Here am I, my son]
[Here am I] is out of sequence. After the remedy is applied right brain is unveiled and right brain is random access based so one can no longer spell as well and also one at times gets the sequence in sentences mixed up, so to speak. This way of speaking is what is known as speaking in tongues. So [Here am I] should be [Here I am] so this sign post shows that Abraham had applied the remedy and unveiled right brain so now he was at times speaking in random access sentences or in tongues. These sign posts are all through the ancient texts and they are a way to provide authenticity to ones who have applied the remedy but may go unnoticed by ones who have not yet applied the remedy.

[Genesis 22:9 And they came to the place which God had told him of; and Abraham built an altar there, and laid the wood in order, and bound Isaac his son, and laid him on the
altar upon the wood.]

This comment explains how Isaac was bound. Isaac was in a position he could not run. So the remedy was that Abraham held knife over Isaac and Isaac did not run and so Isaac feared not, or Isaac lost his life so he preserved it or Isaac "denied himself" by not running when the knife was held over him. This of course is a mental process

1

more than a material process. So Isaac was walking through the valley of the shadow of death, (he saw the knife held over him) and he feared not. So it is just one has to perceive death and then not run, and that is the remedy, it is not about facing actual death but the person has to perceive it is actual death because they have to trick that hypothalamus or left brain state into thinking it is going to die and then when a person does not run that aspect lets them go, so to speak.

[Mark 8:34 And when he had called the people unto him with his disciples also, he said unto them, Whosoever will come after me, let him deny himself, and take up his cross, and follow me.]

[Whosoever will come after me, let him deny himself] Deny himself denotes after one gets the written education their mind is bent to the left so one has to deny that and then they get their real self back. So Isaac denied himself by not running when he saw that knife held over his heart. So this "deny one's self" is based on defeating ones fear.

[2 Timothy 1:7 For God hath not given us the spirit of fear; but of power, and of love, and of a sound mind.]
So if God did not give us this spirit of fear, it is caused by an ungodly source, the tree of knowledge, then fear not, or deny one's self is the remedy to get rid of it to return to sound mind or sound spirit.

[For God hath not given us the spirit of fear; but of .. sound mind.]

11:46:39 PM –
[Genesis 1:10 And God called the dry land Earth; and the gathering together of the waters called he Seas: and God saw that it was good.]
[waters called he Seas] is out of sequence, it should be : and [he called Seas]. So this is another signpost of authenticity. [and God saw that it was good] = Seeing everything as one thing is a right brain trait, holistic. A small child trusts everyone so that is an indication they see everything as one thing. This is relative to this comment.

[Genesis 1:26 And God said, Let us make man in our image, after our likeness: ...]

[And God said, Let us make man in our image, after our likeness:] = man has a right brain and it see's everything as one thing. So right brain is the God Image.

But then the tree of knowledge, written language, is invented and it is sequential based so it slowly bends the mind to the left, left brain is sequential based so then one starts to see parts contrary to how they saw things as child, which is, everything is one thing, a holistic view.

[Genesis 2:17 But of the tree of the knowledge of good and evil, thou shalt not eat of it: for in the day that thou eatest thereof thou shalt surely die.]

[and God saw that it was good] = right brain; holistic

[good and evil] = seeing things as parts a left brain trait.

[for in the day that thou eatest thereof thou shalt surely die.] = once one gets the written language and their minds bends to the left they are of unsound mind and so they start

seeing things that are good as evil so they start hallucinating. One might perceive a word is evil but that is not possible, but they perceive it is evil because they are seeing things as good and evil, parts, and that means they are afraid of things they should not be afraid of. This applies to music and also one's self. One may see their self as less than good but that is only because they are seeing parts and not the whole. A person may see their nose is bad but that is not true, that is simply because they are seeing parts. They see their own nose as evil when in reality it is a good nose so they are suffering because of these hallucinations caused by having their powerhouse right brain veiled as a result of the written language education. They may see their self as too short, too fat, too thin but in reality they are good but they just perceive they are not. One becomes trapped by their own perception and their perception is unsound because it is telling them things that are not true. So this comment [thou shalt surely die.] denotes one's mind is divided after the education, their right brain is veiled by, and so a person is against their self. Psychologically this is known as self esteem issues. One may see their nose and determine they must get an operation to adjust their nose so they are harming their self based on the fact they are hallucinating, their perception is altered because of the written education, tree of knowledge because in reality their nose is just fine they simply perceive is not fine because they see [good and evil] instead of just seeing [it was good]. [Genesis 3:7 [And the eyes of them both were opened, and they knew that they were naked;] and they sewed fig leaves together, and made themselves aprons.] [knew that they were naked;] Denotes they starting seeing parts and finding trouble with what they were seeing when before the "tree of knowledge", written education they saw everything as good, or holistically, a right brain trait. So they are in fact trapped and a slave to their own perception and it is the result of all that traditional sequential based education which veiled their right brain and turned up their left brain traits to an unsafe level. So it is not that the remedy makes one right brain dominate, the remedy unveils right brain after one gets the traditional education, and when right brain is at 50% power and left brain is at 50% right brain traits are dominate and this is an indication of how powerful right brain is, but the person still has left brain traits also but they are reduced to 50% influence instead of 90% influence like they are after all that left brain favoring traditional education. The strong intuition aspect of right brain once it is unveiled allows one to see the sentences in these ancient texts and any texts as one thing so one looks at a sentence and they get the spirit of the whole sentence and they no longer see parts of the sentence, each individual word. So the sentence itself is one spirit and a person just looks at it and that spirit makes perfect sense but they do not really see the separate words. This makes writing a challenge also. What is happening in this seeing the spirit of the sentence is right brain relates to concepts so one will look at a sentence and see the words and all the possible definitions of those words will be absorbed into one concept and so that is how one gets the spirit of the sentences when right brain is unveiled.

The point is the first few chapters of Genesis , the tree of knowledge is the key to the ancient texts and if one does not understand what the tree of knowledge is literally they will not be able to understand what the remedy is, fear not, fear no evil, deny one's self, those who lose their life will preserve it. So in that respect the ancient texts are not in sequential order but simply the same spirit repeating itself over and over just in different ways, same spirit, just different words but saying the same thing, over and over. "Watch out for that tree of knowledge, written education, it veils the god image, right brain, and if you get that tree of knowledge here is the remedy to unveil right brain." - 12/26/2009 12:20:36 AM

1:54:42 AM - Right brain is very good at pattern detection and this is in line with why right brain does not like rules. Left brain loves rules so the more rules one has the more prone they are to favor left brain. For example in school there are many rules one has to understand in order to use written language, comma rules, grammar rules and so on.

Some of these patterns I will suggest may appear to be covering many different parts but relative to me they are all the same thing.

Socrates was told to drink the hemlock because he was corrupting the minds of the youth. Socrates was alive around 500 BC. His main doctrine was no true philosopher fears death. He convinced Plato and then Plato convinced Aristotle to apply this don't fear death remedy. So in that sense Socrates had disciples.

Abraham applied the fear not remedy on Isaac so in that sense Isaac was Abraham's disciple.

A philosopher asks "why?" Right brain has a trait called ambiguity which is doubt.

Jesus had moments of doubt.

Freud suggested "Neurosis is the inability to tolerate ambiguity." Ambiguity is doubt.

This means a person conditioned into the left brain state as a result of traditional education does not like words that suggest doubt. So one way to work one's self up to apply the remedy to the full measure is to say the word perhaps a lot. One who says "perhaps" oft is in fact favoring right brain because a right brain trait is ambiguity. One will notice if they say "perhaps" too much to ones who are conditioned into left brain, ones that sense time, it will bother them. They may say "Stop saying perhaps so much its annoying." Thus the comment "Neurosis is the inability to tolerate ambiguity."

So one can look at Adam as being the first human being who got the written language and then "woke up", applied the remedy in one way or another and then gave his testimony and those words were preserved. Adam is thought to have written his words about 5400 years ago and that is exactly when written language relative to that area of the world was invented, Samarian text and Hieroglyphics, Then Noah came and said "The world drowned in a flood" which is saying written language was invented and it bent the mind to the left and veiled right brain, the god image in man, and so mankind drowned mentally in a flood which is the same as saying mankind fell from grace and mentally became a fallen angel because they ate off the tree of knowledge. The complexity is written language is a tool. It is inanimate. If a tool is used properly it is a good tool and if it is misused it is a bad tool. So the ancient texts are simply written by beings that discovered written language had some bad side effects and it should be treated or taught with that in mind. Each being in the ancient texts that "woke up" added their testimony onto Adams testimony so the ancient texts are testimony from various beings relative to that area of the word making a case that written language has some unwanted mental side effects if not taught properly. So this is relative to the comment "I have seen the enemy and he is us." We invented something using right brain creativity and in learning written language created by right brain creativity, we veiled right brain so in that respect we did it to ourselves accidentally or unknowingly and So Jesus suggested "They know not what they do." We put ourselves to sleep 5000 years ago and have still not figured that out but once in a while someone "wakes up" and tries to explain that. So no true philosopher fears death is the same as saying "I walk through the valley of the shadow of death and I fear no evil" and it is the same as saying deny yourself, or "Those who lose their life (mindfully) will preserve it."

If one is alone and watches a scary movie and then turns out the lights and their hypothalamus says "Turn on the lights spooks are coming" and they do not, they deny their self. This of course is complex because males tend to be less afraid so a male may have to go to a dark cemetery at night or a vacant house in the woods just to get the hypothalamus to give them that "death is coming" signal.

So this deny one's self is really a person who denies what their own mind is telling them and that goes against their being, the being that is this "spirit of fear" and once they do that the spirit of fear leaves them.

Neurologically speaking the amygdala remembers what one fears and gives that information to the hypothalamus. So when one gets the "death is near" signal from the hypothalamus, which is sending lots of false positives in that left brain state of mind, and ones fears not, applies the remedy, the amygdala remembers that and will no longer allow that hypothalamus to send so many false positives and so the mind is cleared from all that fear, caused from being in that extreme left brain state, and thus right brain unveils.

12/27/2009 12:52:13 AM – The Corpus callosum is essentially a section of the brain that is the bridge between the left and right hemispheres and is relative to how they communicate with each other. In a sound minded being the two hemispheres have equal say relative to stimuli or inputs that go into the cerebral cortex. For example a person hears a cuss word and the left brain has a trait relative to rules and the right brain does not like rules. So when that person hears that cuss word the right brain suggests it is not a threat or a big deal and so the hemispheres have two opposing opinions on how to react to that cuss word and so its creates a "contest". The cuss word is bad and one should become concerned or nervous from the left hemisphere and the right hemisphere says no need to be nervous it's just a word and words do not break any rules and so the being is unfazed by that cuss word and does not become alarmed and does not become nervous. A being who got the traditional written education as a child has their mind bent to the left so the bridge between the Corpus Callosum has the signals from the right hemisphere turned way down to the point they are nearly silent and the signals from the left hemisphere are the dominate signals or the loudest signals. So that person hears a cuss word and left hemisphere says "That cuss word breaks rules and I love rules so you should panic and become concerned and stress out." A better way to look at it is once the mind is bent to the left as a result of traditional education nothing in the brain is working as it should so one is factually mentally unsound

7

because their mind is mentally unsound. This is relative to simple cause and effect, once one has their mind bent to the left from all that left brain sequential education as a child no aspect of the brains is working as it should and this is not on a physiological level this is on a mental level. The signals are all bad, they are either turned up way too much or they are turned down way too much but the end result is an unsound mind that is no longer viable. So the only solution is for the mind to have a major shock to it in order to shock the mind out of the left bent state of mind caused by the years of left brain favoring traditional education. There is no pill that can shock the mind because the traditional education bent the mind to left using mental aspects. A child is punished for misspelling a word and so that child has to try harder to favor the sequential aspect of left brain so they are not punished, get bad grades, and so eventually they are doing nothing but favoring left brain and that is all mental. Brainwashing is simply making a person do something to the extent it alters their perception and thought processes. A child is punished by way of grading every time they do not spell a word in proper sequence and so traditional education is nothing more than forcing a child to favor left brain and after even a few years their mind bends to the left and that alters how all the aspects of the brain work, and that alters the child's perception and that alters the child's thought patterns. - 1:11:32 AM

12/28/2009 12:26:54 AM – There is a spirit in the ancient texts, all of the ancient texts. It is spread out over thousands of years so to ones in the extreme left brain state it appears to be separate parts, parts is a left brain trait, but in reality is the same spirit adapting the same remedy and getting a little better each time. Abraham has his "Abraham and Isaac" method of the fear not remedy. This is simply putting a person in a situation they perceive death, get that hypothalamus to give the death signal and then the person fears not. This remedy in general is so difficult to apply on one hand because one has to perceive they are going die and then not run away. Relative to civilization there is only one point in a person's life where that happens and that is when a person has a terminal illness. A person has a terminal illness and they are going to die in a week, they can't run away from that so their only choice and that is to make peace with it or come to terms with it and that means they have to be mindful of death. They are looking at literal death and they are either going to go mad or make peace with it. One in the extreme left brain state is going to either go mad from all the fear in their mind, do things based on conforming to all that perceived fear, or they are going to let go of that fear and relax. Some might suggest they are not afraid of words but they will not go into a public forum in person with their peers and yell out obscenities because their hypothalamus is afraid of death. That perhaps seems not possible but it happens every single day. One will not go to work and walk into a meeting and yell out an obscenity because they fear death. Their mind is coming to conclusions but their mind is not thinking clearly so its conclusions are based on delusions. A person says "I will not yell an obscenity in this meeting because people will think poorly of me." Then they think "If people think poorly of me I will, lose my job." Then they think "If I lose my job I won't have any money and I won't have any food then I will die." So in fact they do not say that obscenity in that meeting because they fear death and those are all delusional conclusions of an unsound mind, mainly in part because of the unsound minds of the people in the meeting who also fear words because they got the traditional education also. Ones who have not applied the remedy will suggest they do not care what others think but that is all they care about. The only ones that have not applied the remedy and honestly do not care what others think are the ones in the end stages of depression. These beings no longer care about rules anymore and they no longer care about what others think and they no longer care about remaining in that unsound extreme left brain state of mind any longer, subconsciously. They simply want to get out of the mental hell, left brain state of mind, and they have no other thought on their mind and although they perceive they are suffering and that is not what they are doing, subconscious, right brain, knows exactly that is what they are doing. It can be easier understood to look at end stage depression as the final withdraws of one who got the traditional education. Just like a drug addict, the drug addict towards the end of getting off drugs suffers the most. So end stage depression is the greatest suffering and this is what

Dante was suggesting is the 9th circle of hell, treason, and many do not make it to the light, so to speak they are consumed by the depression, they kill their self. That is expected when a person has their mind bent to the left. One has to undo that somehow and the price one may pay is to literally die and that is going on everywhere all the time. People drink their self to death, they are simply in the 9th circle of hell and they didn't make it. People eat their self to death, they didn't make it. So the withdraws can be fatal and often are fatal. So this traditional education bends the mind to the left and in fact kills many people literally. That is fact beyond all facts but to one who has not applied the remedy they are in some phase of hell, extreme left brain state, so they cannot even imagine that because they only have simple minded sequential thoughts to ponder that with, left brain traits. There is no human being on the earth who has applied the remedy who perhaps would argue with that but the reality is few ever make it past the 9th circle of hell, treason, and live to tell about it. These ones who have applied the remedy made it through the 9th circle of hell, and escaped hell, so their opinion is the only opinion that should matter but in civilization their opinion means nothing. This is the reverse thing at play. The deeper truth is the ones who do escape the 9th circle of hell are not the "influential" beings in civilization they are the outcasts of civilization. There are not ruler scribes in civilization who have a host of depression and suicide attempts under their belt but that is the requirement for getting to the 9th circle of hell, treason, and then maybe one gets lucky and escapes hell. Abraham bound Isaac and held a knife over him and Isaac did not know if Abraham would kill or not, and Isaac even asked, where is the sacrificial lamb?

[Genesis 21:4 And Abraham circumcised his son Isaac being eight days old, as God had commanded him.]

Circumcised is a person who is cut. Cut is like injured. This comment is suggesting Abraham taught Isaac the written language and then sacrificed him to experiment with the remedy. Eight days old means young. Children are taught written language at the age of six perhaps at this time written language was taught at the age of eight. So

Abraham and Isaac is a story of sacrifice and that means Abraham taught Isaac the written language, sacrificed him, and then applied the fear not remedy, holding the knife over Isaac. When a person teaches a child this written language they are cutting them as in bending their mind to the left as in giving them the "mark", as in sacrificing right brain, veiling it. So Abraham used Isaac as an experiment to perfect the fear not remedy because Abraham could not apply the remedy again on himself. A child of eight days cannot possibly have the written language education so to assume circumcision is going to do something is not logical at all. This literal circumcision is just a classic example of beings, ones that sense time, who have not applied the remedy assuming they understand these texts. The ones bent to the left take everything literal because they have the right brain intuition veiled and that intuition is so powerful one can only suggest it is unnamable in power. If one has not applied the remedy one should avoid these texts so they do not end up harming their self or children because they misinterpret what these texts are saying. Be mindful these texts are for ones who have applied the remedy and that means they are against ones who have not. These texts are Holy, right brain is required to understand them, Scripture so anyone who has not applied the remedy may harm their self by reading these texts, is one way to look at it. These ancient texts are harmful to the adversary, is another way to look at it. I am certain of that. Darkness harms itself in the presence of Holiness is another way to look at it. These texts are against the ones who get written education and do not apply the remedy so that means these texts are hexes against ones who do not apply the remedy, they are traps, they are confusing, they are weapons against the ones who do not apply the remedy. I am certain of that. The concept of these beings who wrote these texts being all nice and kind is an illusion because the left brain, serpent, so to speak is veiling the god image in all the children using the tree of knowledge, written language, and so all bets are off. So any person who literally circumcises their child has put a mark on their child, and although one can always apply the remedy that does not remove the fact they cut their own child with the circumcising. The spirit in these texts is not playing games is one way to look at it. This is war, so these texts have many traps to trap the beings who have not applied the remedy after eating off the tree of knowledge. These texts are for the ones who have applied the remedy and are traps to ones who have not. That is the best way I can explain it at this stage since the accident. Perhaps one who has not applied the remedy does not have enough complexity, a right brain trait, in their thoughts to fully grasp the many levels these texts are on.

[Matthew 9:3   And, behold, certain of the scribes said within themselves, This man blasphemeth.]

The ones who get the education and do not apply the remedy take every single thing in these texts on face value so there is no possible way they can understand these text because these texts require the aspects of right brain to understand. That is all across the board relative to every ancient text ever written. The Quran, The New Testament, The Torah and others. That is why these texts are codes and only ones who apply the fear not remedy have a chance to understand them and anyone who got the traditional education and has not applied the remedy the full measure has no chance because these texts were written by beings who applied the fear not remedy the full measure. Some of these comments are literal and some are not and some are both and the only way to be able to tell which is which is with intuition and complexity, right brain traits.

[Matthew 14:2 And said unto his servants, This is John the Baptist; he is risen from the dead; and therefore mighty works do shew forth themselves in him.]

[This is John the Baptist; he is risen from the dead;]
Ones who have not applied the remedy see absolutes and take everything on face value because their intuition is gone so all they have left is left brain intellect. Intellectually this is saying John the Baptist literally died and literally rose from the dead. Using intuition, pattern detection and complexity of right brain one understands fully this means John the Baptist got the written education , his mind bent to the left, so he was in hell or mentally dead and then he applied the remedy and so he rose from the dead or returned to sound mind,

unveiled right brain after it was veiled. A person who has not applied the remedy will suggest "That is not what it says" but in reality they are simply explaining how they have no intuition because they did not apply the remedy and so their right brain is veiled, so they are speaking the truth but they do not know it. They are saying something and they are subconsciously aware but their words are not what they mean to say. A better way to look at it is they are subconsciously aware, right brain, but by the time that right brain signal gets to their conscious aspect and words are formed the meaning is backwards. They will say "That is not what that comment is saying" but that is their right brain saying "I am veiled and cannot use intuition so I am unable to process the spirit of this comment." They are saying that is not what it says but their right brain is a saying that is what it says but the person is not in touch with right brain because it veiled so right brain signals are being interpreted backwards. This backwards aspect is very strange and I call it the reverse thing. Think about a suicidal person , everyone who has not applied the remedy perceives that person is mentally ill but in factual reality that person's right brain is attempting to break free and so that right brain is saying deny yourself, deny yourself, but the conscious aspect of that person, left brain, is taking it as kill yourself literally. Right brain once veiled is going to get out and it may kill the person in the process but right brain does not care and it has no rules or morals relative to wanting to get out because naturally it should not have been veiled to begin with, so its tendency is to get out. After the traditional education there is only one way out of hell, that left brain state of mind, and that is treason and even people who apply the remedy to a degree, if they have not defeated their fear of death they are simply trapped on their way up the mountain. Because of this, the whole left brain conditioning aspect caused by written language being taught improperly is lined with peril. A person who has not applied the remedy is in hell mentally and literally, they sense time, they are always hungry, they have huge emotions, they cannot concentrate so that is one aspect of peril. Then the ones who are attempting to apply the remedy and do so to a degree are also in peril because they may not apply the remedy the full measure. The full measure is to seek a situation of perceived actual death, like scary place and when you sense that shadow of death is coming you submit or ignore that hypothalamus signal and that is absolute insanity relative to ones who have not applied the remedy and that scares them to the bone because their right brain is aware they may never be able to get their self back to sound mind since that is the full measure remedy. That is not an indication of intelligence or stupidity on anyone's part it is an indication of how devastating pushing sequential conditioning on the mind of a young child when they are only six or seven. I cannot blame anyone who cannot go the full measure because I could not go the full measure. I accidentally went the full measure. I perceived I was killing myself and what do you know, that's the remedy, one just has to be really foolish at killing their self and maybe they will get lucky and not literally do it but just trick their mind to thinking they did it. All of this difficulty is an indication mankind did not listen to Adam 5000 years ago when he said, and he repeated

[Genesis 2:17 But of the tree of the knowledge of good and evil, thou shalt not eat of it: for in the day that thou eatest thereof thou shalt surely die.]

[Genesis 3:3 But of the fruit of the tree which is in the midst of the garden, God hath said, Ye shall not eat of it, neither shall ye touch it, lest ye die.]

[thou shalt surely die.] = [neither shall ye touch it, lest ye die.]

I am mindful civilization hates right brain. I am mindful civilization hates complexity, intuition, random access, no rules, ambiguity, paradox (contradictions). I am aware they hate right brain so you do not need to remind me how much you hate right brain any longer. A small child spells a word out of sequence and you spit on that child because that child's right brain, random access wanted to show you how it spells that word. And then you give the child an "F" and tell them that they are stupid. - 1:36:23 AM

2:29:59 AM – In civilization it is understood to be an insult if you call an adult a "boy" or you tell someone they are acting like a child. Like if I say 'You do as I say, boy." That is an insult. Or if I say "You are nothing but a child." That is an insult. So the people who get the education and have not applied the remedy, deep in their right brain they are fully aware they got "mentally raped" by the education and so when they hear the word child or boy or something to suggests their youth they become angry. Subconsciously, right brain, they are reminded what happened to them as a child so they look at the word child as an insult. So civilization is many people who were "mentally raped" as children by the education and they do it to small children also.

'Children are educated by what the grown-up is and not by his talk.''-Carl Jung

This is a nice way to say if you let children hang around people, teachers, who got mentally raped as children they will mentally rape those children. The cursed begets cursed. One who has not applied the remedy may try to deny that reality and that is understandable because the mental rape robbed that person of their complex mind, right brain. Once one applies the remedy they will go through a phase of great anger and wrath because they will understand they could have had this mental power, right brain, their whole life and so there are some who become violent, they are known as militants against civilization. I have moments of anger waxing but now I understand it is not anger it is simply the heightened awareness kicks my butt from time to time. I may start on a thought and then go right to the final conclusions and that conclusion is always a painful conclusion is one way to look at it, and that is the random access processing happening. Beings who have not applied the remedy want me to hate someone. Beings may assume I speak of their ancient texts and that means I hate anyone who does not believe their ancient texts, because they want me to hate someone like they do, because they see parts still and I no longer parts, so I agree with these ancient texts but that does not means I agree with the ones who suggest they understand these ancient texts but have not applied the fear not remedy. If they understood these ancient texts they would have applied the remedy. So I do not hate them because right brain is fully aware they are doing the best they can based on the fact their mind is bent to the left, so their actions and deeds are typical of one who has not applied the remedy. I do not hate my own species so I do not hate people. I also do not hate people who are doing the best they can based on their understanding of the situation they are in. This whole traditional education thing has mentally screwed everyone up so bad I would literally destroy myself if I hated and I would equally destroy myself if I loved. If I loved the children too much I would level the ones who push the traditional education on the children and never suggest the fear not remedy, to protect the children, so I have to work on my self control so my emotions do not destroy me. I work on my self control and perhaps someone might be helped by that but that is not an expectation because I work on my self control first and that is paramount to everything. There is no doubt in the universe written education, traditional education, bends the mind of a child to the left and puts that child in a mental state of suffering, called hell, but that just is. So I have to use my self control to accept what is. The more self control I have the better I concentrate and the better I can explain the situation and perhaps someone might come to an understanding and that is as good as it will ever get. I am mindful I am simply improving myself and this heightened awareness requires one to have great self control because the heightened awareness is very powerful. This is all an indication I am an accident and an indication of how powerful right brain is. Once one unveils right brain they have to learn everything all over again. That means what a person thinks is life after they get the traditional education is not life so everything they learn is tossed away after they apply the remedy and unveil right brain, so everything they learn before they apply the remedy is vanity. There is nothing I use to understand before the accident that applies now. It is a totally different world now and so one has to adjust to being in a totally different world after they apply the remedy. I use to think because I could not spell every single word properly I was stupid and now I understand not being able to spell every word properly only meant I still had a bit of right brain unveiled. I use to think if I said a cuss word it was against the rules and now I understand it simply meant I was following rules created by mentally unsound beings who had no clue what they were even saying. Perhaps it's best to call applying the remedy, waking up. - 3:00:38 AM

"The debt we owe to the play of imagination is incalculable." - Carl Jung

Right brain is the creative aspect and imagination is relative to creativity so this comment is really saying the crime for veiling the creative aspect of the mind is incalculable which is simply a repeat of this comment [Mark 9:42 And whosoever shall offend one of these little ones that believe in me, it is better for him that a millstone were hanged about his neck, and he were cast into the sea.] A person without full intuition and creativity is simply a suffering human being and so a person who veils a person's creativity and imagination, right brain, is committing a crime that is incalculable. So one might be able to relate to why Abraham and Lot decide to do this [Genesis 19:13 For we will destroy this place, because the cry of them is waxen great before the face of the LORD; and the LORD hath sent us to destroy it.] Abraham and Lot destroyed two cities and everyone in them and they were not at fault considering the situation they were in. Their right brain calculated the only way to stop the spread of this neurosis is to stop it cold in its tracks but the deeper reality is by this time written language was all over the world. Socrates was alive near this period of time and so was Buddha and they were both waking up and finding the same situation. The end result is, kill everyone who is pushing the written language or let the neurosis spread to the whole species and that is the only choice, but today it is far too late. I am mindful the reason I am not stressed is because I am fully aware it is too late. I am not crying over spilt milk from a leaking container. I am pleased I at least accidentally applied the ancient fear not remedy but I am unable to tell if anyone else can to the full measure considering they have to seek the shadow of death and then ignore that death signal the hypothalamus sends them. Psychologically it is such an extreme paradox. A person has to believe they are going to die and that means they have to be in a situation they get that hypothalamus telling them "You are factually going to die.", but not really die as in jumping in a shark frenzy but maybe just being in the 5th level of the catacombs in Paris where they buried all the plague victims, without a flashlight and no way to get out, kind of death. This is an indication of how great of a shock the mind must experience to shock it back into sound mind. I mindful there perhaps is no way to really negate the effects all the way unless one applies this remedy. This is reality [Luke 17:33 ; and whosoever shall lose his life shall preserve it.] This is not a joke or a code. This is a literal relative to the person who applies the remedy, they perceive actual death and then they submit or ignore that signal so one literally has to search for death or love death because when they see death they have to not run and so if they are not running from death they must love death. Someone played around with a mind altering invention, written education, and pushed it on you and bent your mind to the left and now you have to defeat death and all the money in the universe is not going to help you escape that reality. Perhaps you can get an operation and have them take out your hypothalamus. Maybe someone will just sever the connection so your hypothalamus no longer works. So you see what one has to do to remedy this problem will only make more problems so Jesus reduced it down to one method and it was not dunking people underwater or holding knives over their chest it was a mental exercise and then Mohammed came along and reduced this comment [[Luke 17:33 ; and whosoever shall lose his life shall preserve it.] to a concept called submit.

I walk through the valley of the shadow of death and (lose my life mindfully to preserve it)

I walk through the valley of the shadow of death and (submit)

Fear not = fear no evil = lose their life to preserve it = submit, and these are the things one does when they find the shadow of death. So this is the evolution or adaptation of the remedy. This is not suggesting the Abraham and Isaac remedy would not work nor it is suggesting the John the Baptist remedy would not work, they certainly did work, but it is this spirit suggesting this remedy in many different ways but all the ways work. This is how right brain works. It looks at something, and then creates something from that something that appears different relative to ones who see parts, but in reality it is not different.

'The healthy man does not torture others - generally it is the tortured who turn into torturers." -Carl Jung

18

Generally, abusers abuse until they understand they have been abused. Now a person who see's parts perceives I came up with something new because the words are not the same but relative to one who has applied the remedy, they see holistically so they will see I did not do anything but repeat that comment by Jung. So many things are relative to the observer. These ancient texts are saying the same thing over and over but relative to one that see's parts they will perceive the ancient texts are saying different things. The ancient texts are not factually saying different things but a person is a slave to their perception an since civilization teaches this perception altering invention to children improperly civilization is determining what that child will perceive so they are controlling that child's thoughts by altering that child's perception and that is called thought control. If you flirt with applying this remedy you may get lucky and have a good accident and wake up and you may become mindful firsthand what John meant by this comment [1 John 2:18 Little children, ..., even now are there many antichrists;...] I am mindful first hand of what John meant by that comment and I can suggest it is quite a humbling view on that battle field. You may understand first hand of what David was

thinking when he stood up to Goliath with all the armies behind Goliath and then you may become mindful of why you defeat your fear of death before you enter this battle. If one even has a shred of fear in their mind they will see the armies in front of them and they will run and hide and attempt to deny what their intuition suggests and they will go mad. They will perhaps spend the rest of their life trying to deny the vast numbers of that army and will regret they ever applied the remedy at all but they no longer sense of time and their life will seem to go on forever. They may want to hide but they cannot hide from the vast armies of Goliath, the ones that sense time, the ones who got the written education and did not apply the fear not remedy. So David was explaining to anyone who applies the remedy what they will be facing if they do apply the remedy. So David was actually attempting to give people a fair warning that they better not have any delusions of grandeur about applying this remedy because when they see the vast armies of Goliath, the ones that sense time and veil the children's right brain, the god image in man, they will be nothing but humbled. If you want infinite job security apply the remedy and you perhaps will understand what infinite job security is. [1 John 2:18 Little children, …, even now are there many antichrists;…] "Many" is a relative term. I find no fault with the word many. [Revelation 20:8 And shall go out to deceive the nations which are in the four quarters of the earth, Gog and Magog, to gather them together to battle: the number of whom is as the sand of the sea.]

[Gog and Magog] = Sodom and Gomorrah = Civilization; the ones who teach the written education improperly and the ones who get the written education and do not apply the remedy = [the number of whom is as the sand of the sea.] = many. The good news is there are not more than seven billion and the bad news is they have all the laws on their side but relatively speaking it could be worse. One has to be mindful these beings are firstly your friends and secondly they got the education as a child so they are in an extreme left brain state of mind so they are in a dream world, neurosis, and so they are unable to tell they are dreaming. Then it gets even more complicated. The beings in the ancient texts or any being who applies this remedy reverts back to how they were as a child relative to right and left hemispheres being equal in dominance , mental harmony, so in that respect they are like children, they see everything as one thing or as good so they are trusting. What this means is civilization in fact by killing these beings in the ancient texts were killing children. Civilization feed children to the lions not Christians but children. The disciples were butchered but they were children because they applied the remedy. So these beings looked like adults but they were innocent trusting children. Then one can relate to the medieval paintings of the devil eating children. All the devil wants is to eat the children because the children are pure, sound minded and purity drives the devil mad because the devil is not pure or sound minded. It can get very dark very swiftly if you have an emotional capacity. One with an emotional capacity cannot handle this kind of darkness so they tend to deny it.

"There is no coming to consciousness without pain." - Carl Jung

The 9th circle of hell is treason and one has to go through that to wake up and reach consciousness and ask anyone who has been depressed and suicidal and they can tell you what pain is, but that pain is a symptom the mind can no longer take the extreme left brain bending the education causes. The mind can no longer take the emotions being turned up so high so the body itself becomes weak from exhaustion in the unsound state of mind. Sometimes a person will become physically sick after they end a relationship for example. They feel like something kicked them in the stomach. What is happening is their emotions are turned up so high it is affecting them physically. This reality goes for anyone who got the written education and did not apply the fear not remedy. That is called suffering and suffering is a symptom something is not right. Something is not right if someone breaks up with you and you become physically weak and sick. Something is not right of someone says a word to you and you punch them. Something is not right if you lose a loved one and you emotionally implode. Something is not right if you are thinking someone else is wiser than you are. Something is not right if you think someone is more creative than you are. Something is not right if you believe getting an "F" in school means you are not intelligent. Something is not right if you believe misspelling a word means you are dumb or when a person misspells you think it means they are dumb. You look around and see people you may idolize but you apply the remedy and all of those delusions will leave swiftly. None of the wise beings in the ancient texts were saying anything but telling you the remedy to the tree of knowledge, written education, so they could not have possibly been saying "Idolize me." because they were only telling you the remedy that assisted them to be how they were. They were saying "Here is my version of the same remedy the others were saying for thousands of years and so you apply it and then you will return to sound mind." They were good Samaritans but this is not fantasy land it is total darkness, this whole conditioning the children's right brain to a subconscious state and the ones who do it are not even aware they do it. You do not know what darkness is or what sinister is, but if you apply this remedy you will wish you didn't know what those things where.

This comment is a holistic comment.
"God loves each of us as if there were only one of us." - Saint Augustine

[Genesis 1:10 And God called the dry land Earth; and the gathering together of the waters called he Seas: and God saw that it was good.]

The earth and the sea was good so everything in the subset of the earth and sea was good and Augustine was saying God see's everything as one thing. So this removes the possibility there is an afterlife hell. So then one has to realize hell is the state of mind caused by written education and that makes the person see parts and thus suffer. So now all the pressure is off. Whatever a person does, they do that thing relative to their perception or understanding. No matter what they do, a being that see's everything as good or holistically see's everything is, as it is, for a reason. So people can see parts as in good and evil but that does not mean that is reality that just means their mind was bent to the left because of all that left brain education because in reality everything just is. God saw the earth as good and if you are on the earth then God see's you as good so why don't you see yourself and everything on the earth as good? If one does not see everything as good then their perception is adversarial to Gods perception or contrary or anti. One either see's parts or see's holistically and the only determination of that is if they applied the fear not remedy in one way or another after getting the tree of knowledge, written education. Of course there is a paradox relative to this situation. I cannot argue with what you perceive but I can explain why you perceive what you perceive. If you see coffee as evil I cannot argue with that but I can explain coffee is an inanimate object and in a true vacuum coffee is not good or bad but just is. If you see another person as evil I cannot argue with that but I can explain that person is doing the best they can based on their understanding and perception. A person's perception relative to their self is always truth but that does not means it is absolute truth. Relative to me defeating ones fear of death takes one second and is totally painless but relative to one whose mind is bent to the left that prospect may appear quite daunting and relativity suggests we are both right at the exact same time, this is the disconnect and this is what creates the adversarial position. The ones who have not applied the remedy see parts and they cannot see what the ones who have applied the remedy see and that is not good or bad it just is. It is impossible someone can be perceived to be evil relative to everyone. If I suggest the vast majority of people on this planet were mentally bent into an unsound state of mind as a result of the education being taught improperly and they are not to blame but the lunatics who did that to them are to blame, that perhaps would not go over well with everyone but it would go over well with some. Sometimes the heightened awareness reveals such darkness any ability to exhibit long term emotions would destroy a person. The fact I can write these books at all proves I have no emotional capacity because the heighted awareness and concentration to be able to understand all this stuff would rip me apart if I had any kind of emotional capacity. Many have been killed for explaining the ancient texts properly. My hypothalamus tends to throw in the "You may be killed for these words" signal often and my right brain tells me "You don't listen to that voice anymore." and so I am trapped in the middle and so I slowly raise my hand and say "I will go with the flow please." and so in that respect I am defeating my fear of death still. This is an indication how devastating having one's mind bent to the left as a child is because it takes a long time to get all the fear out. Relative to one who has not applied the remedy I am fearless but relative to my perception I have fear issues. I am mindful I am having shades or shadows of fear because I had so much of it before the accident. In reality I live in the land of free and in the land of free one is able to speak their mind but that does not keep the hypothalamus from working so one has to continue to be mindful even if they apply the remedy the full measure they have a lot of work to do to get up to full power and so they have to keep listening to the fearless right brain in order to do that. This is relative to the paranoia one has about going back to how they were. Some in fact try to avoid using written language at all, for no other reason but they perceive they will go back to how they were before they applied the remedy. That is how powerful right brain is once unveiled so it is an understandable paranoia, one never wants to veil it again. This is a symptom that going from cerebral death to cerebral life is such a huge difference one in fact spends their time making sure they don't go back. So in that respect I am writing words because I am afraid to write words then I am afraid to publish them so I publish them so I am not really doing anything but conditioning myself away from fear further. I am not concerned about the world I am concerned about going back to how I was in the left brain state of mind so don't mind me I am just applying the fear not remedy on a world wide scale. I am afraid of the world but when I publish a book with words in it that I am afraid to publish them, then I come to the understanding it was just a delusional fear. The world did not really notice me before the accident so it perhaps does not notice me now. I don't think people even read books anymore. I am only reading mine as I type them.

"He that is jealous is not in love."
Saint Augustine

A person jealous of another person does not love them, they just can't control them. Jealousy is a symptom of perceived loss of control. If one loves something set it free and then one can tell if they were just controlling it or not if they get jealous. Loss of control is devastating to those who are controlling. - 4:26:44 AM

9:07:22 AM – The reason a person who applies the remedy does not eat as much is because their body is not stressed out so it needs less food. The brain is the nervous system so
when the mind is bent to the left the person is a nervous wreck relative to a person who is of sound mind so more food is needed to do the same thing a person who applies the remedy does. People who have not applied the remedy eat more because eating more is a symptom of a person who is nervous. This means eating three meals a day is a symptom that one got the education and has not applied the fear not remedy and so their body starts to show symptoms of weakness and strong hunger if they do not eat even for a few hours. So the body itself when one is mentally bent to the left as a result

of the written education has to use way more calories to keep the mind working. So civilization is eating way too much food relative to a sound minded being, but are eating the normal amount of food considering they are mentally bent to the left and are nervous wrecks and that means their body has to have food all the time just to maintain sequential thoughts or the person becomes weak and tired and cannot think. "I have to eat I am getting weak." "I have to eat I cannot think." This isn't about not eating for a week this is about not eating for a few hours and one already starts to become mentally weak and physically weak and that is abnormal. One meal a day is fasting relative to a person who has not applied the remedy and is the norm for one who has applied the remedy because when the mind is sound it is a stream line machine and is efficient, and when the mind is bent to the left it is like an airplane with lots of drag and so it uses way more gas to go the same distance than a plane with little drag. One meal and I am ready to write another twelve hours straight and at the end of that I sense no hunger so perhaps I am the bionic robot man. Perhaps it better not be I applied this ancient fear not remedy and reverted back to sound mind and now my body uses any food I eat to maximum efficiency and because I am not stressed at all or nervous so the mind burns the calories much slower than if my mind was bent to the left. If you play around with the mind and favor one hemisphere aspect over the other, which is what written education does you will ruin that human being on all levels and if you perceive that is not true it is because you have been ruined mentally and physiologically by that education. I wish I detected supernatural or aliens or ghosts but all I detect is pushing sequential based education on children to the degree their minds bend to the left and everything goes haywire. That is all I detect. I do not care what your experts who need to eat three times a day, sense time, and sense fatigue think contrary to what I suggest because I do not reason with mentally unsound hallucinating beings. I do not have to, so I do not. You may perceive I have a great ego but I assure you it is infinitely greater than you assume it is but recently I discovered the backspace key. Now you understand the principles of the fear not remedy to undo the mental damage written education caused you, so you can get your right brain back to a conscious state there is no logical reason for you to continue to read this, my personal diary.- 9:32:33 AM

9:38:44 AM – I did a "perhaps" experiment in a chat room. The things about perhaps is when you add it to the end and beginning of a sentence it means you did not say anything at all but sometimes ones on the left ignore the perhaps because perhaps suggests ambiguity and that is a right brain trait so they avoid acknowledging perhaps. So in this experiment I put lots of perhaps' so there would be no question I was saying nothing at all but I got a nibble.
I made this comment after being in a chat room for about an hour relative to a clock and I said nothing before this comment.

<Licky> perhaps everyone should perhaps start giving me stuff perhaps, perhaps
<osyman> why?

So this being conditioned to the left assumed I said "Everyone should start giving me stuff" but in actual reality is said nothing at all but they did not see that. If I just say "perhaps perhaps perhaps" I am not saying anything and if I throw words in between those perhaps' I am still not saying anything. Neurosis is the inability to acknowledge the word perhaps. Ones that sense time suggest the word perhaps means it's a veiled threat but they have no idea, they simply cannot tolerate ambiguity in the neurotic state of mind traditional education has put them in. What I accomplished in this experiment is what is known as getting something for nothing. I said literally nothing as far as the spirit of my comment and I got a reply , a question: "Why?" So I got something for nothing. - 9:44:12 AM

12/28/2009 6:14:45 PM – There are two core understandings in the ancient texts. The main core understanding is the tree of knowledge, written education, makes one see parts, left brain trait, good and evil instead of how they use to see which is holistically, a symptom of a sound mind, meaning right brain is at 50% and at 50% right brain traits are dominate. So that means the written language bends the mind to the left and in turn veils the holistic aspects of right brain.

The second core understanding is the fear not remedy, this remedy negates the seeing parts aspect caused by written language. This fear not remedy has many variations in the texts but it is all the same principle method. Right brain is against rules contrary to left brain so anyone who has not applied the remedy will see all the other rules in the texts and follow them and in fact favor left brain even more. So all of the other rules in these texts are essentially traps to make ones who have not applied the remedy go even further into left brain with some intention of driving them mad, to the 9th circle of hell, treason. There are some who try to follow every rule in these texts and in turn they are bogged down with so many rules they are unable to function properly and that is the reason for all the rules. Anyone who applies the principle fear not remedy to the main understanding, tree of knowledge, is aware of this. So the paradox of these texts is one has to read them to discover the fear not remedy, but if one does read them and has not applied the fear not remedy they will only be harmed and for that reason these texts were hidden and were meant only for the ones who applied the remedy. This means these texts were ancient codes and battle plans to fight the scribes, the ones who got the written education, tree of knowledge, and had not applied the fear not remedy and so they were hidden so that the scribes would not be aware they were having a war waged on them. So some of these texts were found long after the beings who wrote them died and were brought into civilization but civilization was not aware they in fact found the battle plans of the cerebral "giants" that were used against civilization, the physical based left brain bent ones. So these ancient texts are like a diary of the cerebral giants recorded over thousands of years which keep track of their progress against the "slothful" ones who teach the children written education and never suggest the fear not remedy to go along with it. It's the battle plans of the ones who do not sense time against the ones who do sense time. It's the battle plans of the quick against the dead.

[Matthew 9:3   And, behold, certain of the scribes said within themselves, This man blasphemeth.] -6:19:13 PM

12/29/2009 4:51:37 AM - I spent the first 45 minutes today trying to determine if I sense time. - 4:51:45 AM

9:02:52 AM - I am mindful there is some very affordable last will and testament software programs on the market these days. - 9:03:40 AM

10:43:20 AM – I am quite certain the marching order I got after the accident was to convince the world I can no longer use commas properly, but, I, doubt, it,,. - 10:44:10 AM

11:57:38 AM – No matter what I say relative to making it sound like everything is going to be well one has to understand right brain has already made up its mind. I am mindful I am talking as if right brain is a third person. I am mindful when I suggest it can be worked out, this whole written education being taught improperly situation, that is my left brain. My left brain tries to deny the reality that right brain has already made up its mind. Right brain has decided to make sure the species never forgets the understanding, it is wise to never veil right brain. The problem with that is right brain has no morals and has no idea what a law is and has no regards of any detail outside of making sure the species never forgets it is unwise to veil right brain. Now if you have not applied the remedy and unveiled right brain that may sound very strange to you, but I am certain it will make sense to you much sooner than you think. As for me I go with the flow. What that means is I am fully aware what these words arranged in a certain fashion are going to lead to and my left brain tells me never to publish them because I am fully aware of what they lead to but I apply self control and publish them. Right brain intuition understands the future or a better way to look at it is right brain has already calculated everything and determined words such as "Please stop veiling right brain in children by teaching traditional education improperly." will not work and has not worked. Right brain does not hate the scribes in fact it is just trying to give itself a chance at living. This makes it seem like right brain is a separate entity unto itself. From right brains point of view the scribes hate it. If the scribes did not hate right brain they would have a system in traditional education to make sure it was never veiled such as fear conditioning classes and people who have applied the fear not remedy and unveiled right brain dictating the curriculum to make sure right brain was not veiled. That is not the case and that is not going to be the case so right brain has concluded the scribes hate it.

Because of this right brain is fighting a self defense battle. It could be looked at like a child is born with right brain unveiled and an adult observes that child as strange because that adult got the traditional education and in turn has their right brain veiled and so that adult determines the strange behavior of that child is "bad" and it must be fixed so that child must get the traditional education and in turn that veils that child's right brain. Because of this there are no rules and there is no moral's, there is only war. I unveiled my right brain so I should be pleased but right brain is aware the species of "right brain" is being attacked by the scribes and so it is fighting for its own kind so to speak. I am mindful that is what is happening and that is what this 5000 year old battle is all about. This is relative to a house divided cannot stand because these two warring factions should be in harmony but one side hates the other and so the other side has to defend itself. Left brain, the scribes, hate right brain so right brain has to defend itself. If the education veiled left brain then people would have no sense of time and be very cerebral and far less focused on material things and so left brain would "attack" the ones who veiled it. This is why education itself creates conflicts because no matter what kind of education one gets it is simply mental conditioning favoring one aspect of the brain over there other and all that can create is a mind divided. Human beings learn by observation not by getting a certain tool crammed down their throat. Traditional education is nothing more than tools favoring left brain with lots of "do it or else" fear tactics strings attached. There are no human beings who have applied the remedy and unveiled right brain that would argue with that, but there are perhaps plenty of mentally unsound beings who have not applied the remedy who would harm their self by trying to argue with that. One aspect to consider is why would left brain want to be dominate. There is a story where the devil thought it was better than God and became jealous of God. Try to look at it like this. In a sound mind where left and right hemispheres are equal 50/50, right brain aspects are dominate. For example no sense of time is the result of the paradox in right brain, so when one applies the remedy they have no sense of time yet when one's mind is bent to the left they have a sense of time. So left brain is jealous so to speak because at 50/50 mental harmony right brain traits are dominate and so left brain in a way figured out how it would become dominate by way of written education. So the battle is not really about people. A better way to look at it is there are no people involved in this battle but only these two hemispheres vying for dominance. People are a symptom of the battle of these two hemisphere but the people are not the cause of the battle in that respect it's the hemispheres that are the cause of the battle.

[Genesis 19:13 For we will destroy this place, because the cry of them is waxen great before the face of the LORD; and the LORD hath sent us to destroy it.]

This is a comment by either Lot or Abraham. They are saying "we" will destroy this place where the left brain is dominate because of the written language education, tree of knowledge, because the Lord , right brain, has sent us to destroy it. So this Sodom was a place where left brain dominate lived and right brain decided to wipe them out because it knew left brain will only create more left brain dominates. Separate the people from these events because the people in all the history come and go but the left and right brain battle continues no matter what. The left brain was jealous because when the mind is 50/50, right brain rules so left brain wanted to be the boss so written language favors it and creates left brain dominates and so any left brain dominate sees right brain dominate and it hates it, it is it's adversary . The personalities or the people involved are not playing a role. If a person gets the education and does not apply the remedy they behave like all the other left brain dominates and if a person applies the remedy they behave like all the right brain unveiled people. These are fruits of each "class". A person with 50/50 does not act like a person with right brain veiled a 90/10, but again this is not about people this is a battle of the minds.
Is this Jesus the person talking or is this right brain mind talking?

[John 15:14 Ye are my friends, if ye do whatsoever I command you.]

So in one sense left brain is kind of defending itself because when the mind is in harmony 50/50 left brain is kind of reduced to second fiddle and so it does not like that so it wants to be dominate or at least equal to right brain but that is not how it was intended, so it is angry and jealous because out of the two hemispheres left brain is sequential based and simple minded and right brain is complexity and intuition and random access based. So a mind that is bent to the left may be jealous or envious of a mind that has right brain unveiled but that is not that person, that is the nature of left brain. Left brain is jealous of the unnamable power of right brain, the right hand side. There is no way to stop that jealously because left brain is stuck with sequential and thus simple minded thoughts. Every time a person idolizes something that is proof they have left brain dominate because that is a left brain trait. If a person says 'I wish I was like that person" that is not that person that is left brain. Right brain does not idolize left brain because right brain is the master of the house, the mind, so that means left brain idolizes right brain. So human beings have such a powerful mind the hemispheres are actually in a battle and this battle has played out for over 5400 years and the people involved are not the point as much as the battle of the minds is the center piece. People have been getting slaughtered in the battle for 5400 years but the minds, the hemispheres never stop battling. So for example the disciples of Jesus walked into towns knowing they would be slaughtered because the towns were full of left brain dominates but the disciples saw their self as agents of the right hand, right brain, so it never was how brave they were it was how brave right brain was. Right brain is not concerned with how many people die for its cause because when a person is born another right hemisphere is also born and so the world has a certain amount of right brain unveiled beings and they are not people they are the spirit of right brain and they try to wake up others but also are trying to convince left brain (people), left brain is fine but in a 50/50 match right brain will always win and since left brain cannot stand that it hates right brain or is jealous, to such an extent a person's mind is bent all the way to the left with written education so right brain is reduced to a subconscious aspect only. It is as if left brain wants to kill right brain but it never can kill right brain because when a child is born right brain and left brain are equal so right brain is the major influence and left brain can never escape that so it has to always "educate " that child to make sure it silences right brain. So left brain is a trouble partner in the mind because no matter what it wants right brain is always the powerhouse and after thousands of years since the species started it has been relegated to the weaker aspect and it can never escape that so it finally decided to attack the one it is jealous of, right brain. Left brain is the jealous lover. Right and left brain are married forever and humans minds are so powerful eventually the weaker aspect, left brain, could not take it any longer and its jealousy of right brain played out on the species and ruined the species mentally. This is all an indication humans have such a powerful mind the minds are in a battle but the people are not really at battle it just so happens people are attached to the minds.

[Matthew 9:3 And, behold, certain of the scribes(left brain influenced containers) said within themselves, This man blasphemeth.] - 1:24:31 PM

1:36:17 PM – So once in a while since this battle started , written education was introduced, a being breaks free and unveils right brain and right brain starts telling the spirit of left brain, the world, essentially that it has freed itself from left brains trap and left brain catches wind of that and does everything in its power to kill that right brain freed being. Right brain surfaces once in a while but when it does its presence makes an impact on the entire world of left brain and that is why left brain makes sure it is never around for long. This is not about people as much as it is about our brains are huge for our size and our minds are at war with each other for dominance.
Human beings minds are so powerful the minds of each hemisphere are in a battle that spans across thousands of years and the people involved are nothing but pawns. "Left brain in the world, I got free in this container so you can kiss my ass. Left brain you will never be like me and so you better get use to that and when I get warmed

up in this container you are going to wish you never revolted against me." - 1:40:35 PM

12/30/2009 2:39:03 AM - William Wallace was all about freedom and is what is known in America as a patriot. Right brain dislikes rules because rules hinder right brains ability to be open minded and rules hinder right brains creativity and pattern detection. The traditional education is sequential based, a left brain trait, so ones who get the education like lots of rules and they tend to see ones who are free spirits or ones who mocks rules as a danger. So William Wallace certainly had right brain unveiled to a degree and he wanted to be free but the ones on the left saw him as a threat and so they had to silence him. This is similar to the beings in the ancient texts and also similar to how George Washington was perceived. Free will is a threat to a tyrant because a tyrant's goal is control. As control and rules increase freedom decreases. So in civilization beings that break rules are deemed evil or bad but in reality they are free spirits and so tyrants try to demonize them by suggesting if they do not conform they are evil or bad. This is simply a control tactic using fear. If any ideal suggested starts dismissing rules then it must be a bad idea and that is the control safety net. One can be free but they cannot break any rules yet freedom is the absence of rules so beings in civilization that are against rules are deemed threats to civilization and threats to organization, instead of patriots of freedom. William Wallace was a patriot of freedom and so the control structure of civilization deemed him as bad and a revolutionary and eventually labeled him a terrorist and then it could justify killing him and made it appear like it was a righteous deed to do so. The rule of thumb is right brain see's the less rules the safer it is because its options are greater. Left brain see's the more rules it is safer because rules denote organization. On an absolute scale both of these contrasts combined is the safest route but the problem is determining how many rules are too few and how many rules are too many, so freedom is the only possible solution because that way some people can have more rules than others. Seeing things outside of the box requires one has no rules so they can experiment with every option. The basis of a problem suggests one is looking for a solution, so one is unaware of the solution, so the minute they start applying certain rules to finding that solution they diminish their chances of finding a solution. If a person is trying to find their way across a deep river and they determine they will not search more than 100 yards from where they are standing to find a shallow crossing they limit their chances of finding the ideal place to cross but if they have no limits on how far they will search to find that shallow crossing they will certainly find the most ideal shallow crossing.

12/31/2009 4:54:28 PM - * You were kicked from #christian by X ((chalcedony) preaching another gospel) I am failing much greater than I can imagine, but I doubt it.

1/3/2010 9:40:39 AM – The story of Cain and Abel is about sibling rivalry. Abel is the "better" son and Cain is jealous and kills Abel. This is simply a repeat parable relative to the tree of knowledge. One could say man ate off the tree of knowledge and fell from grace. One can say Cain became jealous and killed Abel and fell from grace, One can say left brain hijacked or rebelled against the better hemisphere right brain and fell from grace because left brain by itself cannot take the place of a sound mind where right and left brain are in harmony. The word Cain is translated as the evil one. There is a deep reality to this hijacking of right brain. First it is important to understand the hijacking. Left brain does not have the qualities of right brain and in an even competition right brain wins, intellect, a left brain trait is not as good as intuition a right brain trait. Sequential thought power, a left brain trait is not as good as random access thought power, a right brain trait. So this contrast in power is what creates the jealousy in left brain. This means the two hemispheres have minds of their own and the people involved are secondary. This creates the impression of supernatural or possession. Being filled by the holy spirit for example is simply suggesting one has applied the fear not remedy, unveiled right brain and they are under the influence of right brain after right brain was veiled by the tree of knowledge, traditional education. The problem with this left brain aspect hijacking right brain, veiling right brain, is that it creates this adversarial situation, not on a human scale but on a battle of the minds scale. So this battle transcends human beings because the two aspects of the mind in this battle continue this battle even after the people who unveil right brain are long gone. This creates the container reality. A human being is born with a sound mind, 50/50 left and right hemispheres traits dominate, they are "better". Then that human being is seen by an adult who got the education and is thus a left brain influenced container and that being see's that child as odd and so that left brain influenced container determines it must make that child like it is. This has nothing to do with the people as much as it has to do with left brain see's anything with right brain traits as bad. So the first symptom one is in fact a left brain influenced container is they sense time mindfully. Once this is understood then a scale of how one can tell if they are influenced by left brain or not can be established. Right brain has a trait called paradox. Mentally a person is always questioning time. A person is mindfully aware time is passing so one way to look at it is the mind has this question that is always going on in their head. "How much time has it been." A person who got the traditional education and has not applied the fear not remedy will come to the conclusion a certain amount of time has passed when that question "How much time has it been" is asked in their mind. The reason for this is because the right brain is veiled and so when that question is asked the paradox aspect is not figured into that question.

A left brain influenced container will come to a solid answer when the "How much time has it been" question is asked in their mind because the paradox is absent. A right brain influenced container will have paradox figured into answer that "How much time has passed" question. So mentally for that right brain influenced container the answer to the "How much time has passed." question is going to be "Lots of time has passed and No time has passed." and because that is true relative to the fact a paradox is two contradictions that result in a truth, that right brain influenced container cannot tell how much time has passed so they do not sense time. So the proof for a person who is a left brain influenced container that their right brain has in fact been veiled as a result of all that left brain sequential education, known as traditional education, is the fact they sense time. So the fact they sense time is proof their right brain is veiled and is proof they are a left brain influenced container and is proof they are mentally unsound. If they were mentally sound they would have the paradox trait of right brain in a conscious state so when they asked the question mentally "how much time has passed." they would not be able to tell how much time has passed. This no sense of time is not about once in a while not being able to sense time it is a constant, meaning one with right brain unveiled is never ever able to sense time passing. They are able to look at a clock and they are able to look at a calendar but that does not mean they can sense time because mindfully when that "How much time has passed" question comes up in their mind the paradox of right brain is considered in answering that question and that paradox always tells them, "lots of time has passed and no time has passed" and that is its final answer. A left brain influenced container will see that as untruth because left brain only sees itself as truth and right brain is contrary to left brain. This again has nothing to do with people as much as it has to do with this battle of the minds. Right brain does not want to be at anything more than 50% but left brain is aware if right brain is at 50% then left brain even at 50% is second fiddle because right brain has "better" aspects. This is what the Cain and Abel story is about. Cain, left brain, is jealous of Abel, right brain and so Cain kills(veils), Abel, right brain whenever it see's Abel, a right brain influenced container. This again has nothing to with people it has to do with the battle of the minds that is going on above and beyond the people involved. Whatever influence the person is under, left or right brain, that is how the person acts so the concept about everyone is the same is not truth on that level. There are only two kinds of people, left brain influenced and right brain influenced. The left brain influenced people are of unsound mind because left brain can never be a dominate trait if right and left brain are equally active, 50/50 in harmony because right brain is the more powerful aspect at 50/50 mental harmony. So anyone who is a left brain person is mentally an unsound person. The easy way to tell is if you sense time. That is factually the easy way to tell if you are mentally unsound or not. At times a left brain container can take a certain drug, like pot for example or alcohol and those drugs will alter that person's ability to sense time and so that is factual proof those drugs unveil the paradox aspect of right brain while the drugs are working. So determining if one has had their mind bent to the left as a result of traditional education being taught improperly is simple to determine but the problem is a person under the influence of left brain does not want to face that reality. Left brain does not want to give up its seat of dominance because if it goes back to 50/50 harmony with right brain it will always play second fiddle and left brain cannot stand that absolute reality. It is sibling rivalry on a mind scale that transcends people all together. People do not even factor into this battle, it is a battle of the minds above and beyond the people who are containers of the minds. People are reduced to being containers of either left brain or right brain dominate traits and they act accordingly. There is no way a left brain influenced container can act like a right brain influenced container ever unless that left brain influence container applies the fear not remedy and then they becomes a right brain influenced container and then they act like a right brain influenced container. A right brain influenced container today acts exactly like a right brain influenced container acted a thousand years ago and this goes the same with the left brain influenced containers. A right brain influenced container sees holistically, a right brain trait, not because their mind is bent to the right but because in 50/50 mental harmony the right brain traits dominate over the left brain traits. This again is why left brain is jealous of right brain and is why left brain hijacked right brain five thousand years ago as a result of the invention traditional education that favors left brain. So relative to civilization, it conditions all the children using traditional education into the left brain influence state of mind and if anyone says that is improper they attack that person not because the people under the influence of left brain are bad but because left brain never wants to go back to second fiddle with right brain which it is in 50/50 mental harmony. - 10:26:22 AM

1/4/2010 1:10:54 AM – There is a pattern I notice in these ancient texts that suggest these ancient texts in some ways are simply parables about the Adam and Eve story. I get
the impression some of these texts are written by an observer and not by the actual person the texts are speaking about. For example

the Adam and Eve story is written as if an observer to the Adam and Eve story is explaining Adam and Eve, but it is not Adam or Eve writing the story. This is an example of the complexity I notice in these texts as if the texts are so complex and full of paradox one can never perhaps make an absolute comment about the texts because the texts have so many angles to them.

[Luke 1:13 But the angel said unto him, Fear not, Zacharias: for thy prayer is heard; and thy wife Elisabeth shall bear thee a son, and thou shalt call his name John.]

[Genesis 15:1 After these things the word of the LORD came unto Abram in a vision, saying, Fear not, Abram: I am thy shield, and thy exceeding great reward.]

[But the angel said unto him, Fear not, Zacharias:] = [After these things the word of the LORD came unto Abram in a vision, saying, Fear not, Abram:]

Zacharias is aware of the fear not remedy and he found out about it the exact same way Abraham did hundreds of year after Abraham found out about it.
[angel said unto him, Fear not, Zacharias] = [the LORD came unto Abram in a vision, saying, Fear not] This is saying they unveiled right brain and it "ministered" to them and they figured out the remedy or how they unveiled right brain. So Zacharias is the father of John the Baptist and John the Baptist assisted Jesus with his version of the remedy, baptism.
Abraham was very old when he had Isaac. Zacharias was very old when he had John the Baptist. Abraham applied the fear not remedy on Isaac in the Abraham and Isaac story and Zacharias applied the fear not remedy on John the Baptist. Zacharias was told his wife would be having a child but Zacharias suggested his wife is old, sterile. Having a child when a women is sterile is a miracle birth. There are patterns in all of these texts and if one has not applied the fear not remedy they have the pattern detection of right brain turned down so they cannot possibly ever decipher these texts. It would be

like trying to run without legs. One can read these texts a thousand times but if they have not applied the fear not remedy and unveiled right brain they will just miss all the patterns, pattern detection is a right brain trait.

[Luke 1:24 And after those days his wife Elisabeth conceived, and hid herself five months, saying,]
[Luke 1:25 Thus hath the Lord dealt with me in the days wherein he looked on me, to take away my reproach among men.]
Elisabeth the mother of John the Baptist is hiding from the men. The men being the scribes which are the ones who got written education and did not apply the fear not remedy and
thus were simply left brain influenced containers. This is similar to how Mary was mindful that men were coming to get Jesus. So Luke is actually explaining the Jesus birth story but using John the Baptist instead of Jesus in his explanation. These stories are hindsight stories. None of the people who explained Jesus' birth or John the Baptists birth were there when these beings were born, so they are writing stories based on what they have been told. None of the apostles knew Jesus when Jesus was born so it is impossible they are firsthand accounts so they are giving their take on these stories. What these miracle birth stories are in fact suggesting is divine providence.

This is the story about Moses.
[Exodus 2:2 And the woman conceived, and bare a son: and when she saw him that he was a goodly child, she hid him three months.]
This is the story about John the Baptist's birth.
[Luke 1:24 And after those days his wife Elisabeth conceived, and hid herself five months, saying,]
[and hid herself five months] = [she hid him three months.]
The thing about left brain is it see's parts. That means left brain is looking for details, parts, not patterns. That is its trait. A left brain influenced person can read three versions of the exact same principle story and if the names are different and the locations are different but the principle lesson is the same they will still see it has three different parts. For example, John went to meet Joe, and John and

39

Joe went to the river and found some gold late at night and hid it so that no one would take it.

Susan and Karen went into the desert and found a water supply at midday and covered it with branches so no one would find it. Billy was in his room and found a gold coin in the morning and put his shirt over it because he did not want anyone to know about his gold coin.

There are many parts in the above stories but the spirit of all the stories is people found something of value and hid it. So the time of day, the locations, the names involved are not relevant to the principle or concept of the stories. Right brain deals with concepts not details. One who is left brain influenced puts lots of emphasis on John, Joe, Karen, Susan and Billy. One who left brain influenced wants to see night, midday and morning. One who is left brain influenced wants to see gold, water supply and gold coin. One who is left brain influenced will not detect the pattern that a woman who is sterile and gets pregnant is the same thing as saying a women got pregnant as a virgin but both are miracle births or pregnancies. These miracle births are trying to emphasize the importance of beings that were born as a result of these miracle pregnancies but I assure you in all reality these details will not apply the remedy for you. The story of Buddha is when his mother was pregnant with him, a wise man came from the forest and spoke with his father and suggest Buddha would be a special child. What this in reality is doing is saying Moses was special, John the Baptist was special, Jesus was special and Buddha was special because of the situation relative to their birth, so you should listen to them. I was born at St. Mary's hospital but that fact will not help you apply the remedy. It is along the lines of suggesting because of the events of their birth or conception you should listen to them. The reason this background information is required is because of what they were speaking about or the argument they were making. If one is going to tell civilization that

civilizations invention, written language, has very bad mental side effects if not taught properly they better not only have a flawless argument they better have a background story that gives them divine providence and makes them look like they are the authority over all the scribe authorities. So just in case you are wondering, I have no background story and I have no credentials. I accidentally applied the fear not remedy a that can never be taken back or taken away so with that reality whether you apply the fear not remedy or not does not mean anything relative to the situation I am in. There is nothing you can do that is going to negate the fact I accidentally applied the fear not remedy and there is nothing you can do that is going to convince me to stop writing the books, so no matter what you do with this fear not remedy I am still in the situation I am in. The fact you got years and years of left brain conditioning called traditional education means only a small fraction of human beings on this planet have a chance to apply the remedy the full measure. That is not relevant to intelligence it is relevant to how devastating all that left brain sequential conditioning is on the mind. You got mentally conditioned so far to the left by the education you may never be able to negate that whether I was conceived by an alien or a cuckoo bird. If I was factually born by way of an egg from a cuckoo bird and I could fly and I had laser beam vision your chances of applying the fear not remedy would not increase one degree, although I do have laser beam vision. The absolute reality relative to this left brain influenced state of mind caused by traditional education is the only human beings on the planet that perhaps have a chance to apply the remedy are beings that are already pondering literal suicide. There are beings who will play around with meditation and health foods and eating soy nuts but the absolute reality is only beings who are suicidal and thus in the 9th circle of hell, treason, have a chance to negate fully the mental side effects caused by the traditional education. What that means is if you have never ever considered suicide in your life you are too far gone, your mind has been bent so far to the left as a result of the traditional education your right brain perhaps no longer has any say in your thoughts. I am simply reduced to being a commentator because I am fully aware there are only a handful of beings on this planet that have what it takes to apply this remedy the full measure. There are six billion people on this planet that got traditional education and only a small handful has a chance to apply this remedy the full measure and I have no idea who they are. Jesus only had twelve disciples and even at that they perhaps did not apply the remedy the full measure like Jesus did. Jesus spoke to multitudes and ended up with twelve disciples and even at that not all of the disciples applied the remedy the full measure and even at that, the ones who applied the remedy to a great degree were still not like Jesus relative to how well Jesus applied the remedy to the full measure. You may be under the impression this remedy is simple to apply but in reality I am suggesting you commit mental suicide and in all the universe that is the one thing you perhaps will never be able to do. I speak to people who agree with the spirit of what I suggest relative to how the traditional education bends the mind to the left and then I suggest the remedy and they go off in a daze and I am mindful they will never even attempt to apply the remedy. So I am fully aware if you have never thought about suicide you are perhaps lost and you will perhaps never be found, welcome to reality. There is always a chance in hell but there are not six billion chances in hell. Only the seekers and fighters get out of hell. If one gets a terminal illness and thus they are mindful of death they may get out of the mental hell but it does no good if they escape in the last few days of their life because it may take years to get warmed up once one does apply the remedy. There is a concept among ones who have applied the remedy that everyone escapes the mental hell because everyone dies but that ideal is crap and an ideal one can use to convince their self to keep their mouth shut and not fight the battle which is to attempt to wake their friends who tend to be unwilling to see the light so to speak. One does not escape from hell so they can live out their life being mindful of others who have not yet escaped from hell. One does not escape from hell and then hide because one is not intelligent enough to understand fully why they escaped from hell. Some spend their whole life trying to escape from hell and never fully understand that is the least they can do. The real task starts when one escapes. The real test starts when one escapes from hell. I have doubts about publishing these books but I do it because I am not intelligent enough to second guess what I am compelled to do. I want to go hide, so I do not hide. I want to keep my mouth shut, so I do not keep my mouth shut. I do not want to publish any of these words so I do publish all of these words. Do you see that once you apply the remedy and escape hell the real test begins? Are you going to escape hell by defeating your fear and then start to fall back into your fear ways? This has never been about anyone else but you. There are no other beings that are going to determine if you escape from hell. The wise beings in the ancient texts were not saying "I will get you out of hell." They were saying "I know the way out of hell and here it is but you have to get yourself out of hell." The wise beings would not have said , fear not, walk through the valley of the shadow of death and fear not, deny yourself, those who lose their life will preserve it, submit, go sit in a cemetery until you feel better, no true philosopher fears death if they could have gotten you out of hell. There would be no reason for them to suggest the remedy if they could just get you out. Did John the Baptist hold Jesus under the water by force or did Jesus submit to allow John the Baptist to hold him under water? You did not put yourself in this extreme left brain state of mind which is what hell is, but that does not matter at all. You have to look at now. You are in hell now, you ate off the tree of knowledge, you have fallen from grace, got your right brain veiled, so how do you get out? There are perhaps no beings on this planet that would read these texts who have applied the fear not remedy, for any other reason but to humor their self. There is perhaps nothing in these texts a person with no sense of time does not already know. - 1/4/2010 2:19:16 AM

1/4/2010 5:38:09 AM – There are many beings on this planet who are addicted to drugs. They are addicted to drugs because they got they traditional education and were not warned of its devastating mental effects, and they were also not told of the fear not remedy to negate those devastating mental effects and so they perhaps will die trying to get a little relief from being in that extreme left brain state caused by the traditional education and that is nothing but a tragedy. A being going through life without having right brain in the conscious aspect of their mind is a tragedy. Some may not even be aware that it is tragedy but I am fully aware it is a tragedy. I am unable to find fault with anyone who does not want to apply this remedy or cannot apply this remedy because I could not apply the remedy either, I accidentally applied the remedy. Some will suggest there are no accidents but all the means to me is I am the first accident in the universe. The right brain is fully aware how to unveil itself but when it has been reduced to a subconscious state as a result of the traditional education one consciously is not aware of what right brain is aware of. I only did one thing in my entire life that was of value. My left brain, hypothalamus, said "Todd you took way too many pills this time and you will certainly die if you do not call for help." and then I responded mentally and said "I do not care I will not longer listen to you." That was the one thing in my life I did that was of value. There is nothing else I can ever do that will be of value because I did the one thing that was of value already. I am mindful you perhaps may not even be able to understand that. It perhaps sounds to some like it cannot even be true, let alone something of value but that is the only thing I have ever done and ever will do of value. I unveiled right brain and so there is nothing of value I can do in contrast to that. I accomplished the greatest thing a being can do in the universe but since I did it by accident I am reduced to nothing. Money cannot compare to it so I cannot feel any need for money. I cannot compare to it so I do not even see I am of value. I am in a situation where I can never intentionally top something I did by accident. I can write infinite books and they will be of no value. I can say infinite words and they will be of no value. I am uncertain what value even is in contrast to unveiling right brain. All I have to offer are words and they cannot explain right brain because it is unnamable in power. - 5:52:30 AM

12:06:18 PM – The darkness see's darkness as light. The darkness see's the light as darkness so the darkness calls the darkness God and thus the darkness calls God the devil. On the currency there are the words "In God we trust." It all comes down to a very simple reality. Do you think God is simpleminded and slothful in thought or do you think God is complex and quick in thought? Left brain is slothful in contrast to random access right brain so left brain is simple minded in contrast to complex right brain. Right brain deals with complexity. That may not seem like much to you in your location. "In God we trust." suggests God but right brain is the God image in man and traditional written education veils it, so who is this God they trust in, it is left brain, because written education favors left brain, Cain, the evil one, translated in Hebrew. You should perhaps reread those last few sentences over and over about a billion times. Is memorizing the ABC's a sequential exercise or a random access exercise? Is spelling a word arranging letters in sequential order or in random access order? Is sentence structure relative to arranging words in sequential order or random access order? Do teachers punish children for not being able to arrange letters in sequential order on spelling tests, by giving them bad grades? Do parents punish children who come home from school with bad grades because the children failed a spelling test? Does a teacher call the parents and suggest they have a meeting so they can work on ways to get that child to do a little better in their sequencing, spelling, grammar, following rules? I just read they enacted 40,000 new laws which are simply rules which are simply left brain favoring and I am mindful before too long you are going to be so left brain influenced if you are capable of an ounce of right brain thought, it will be a miracle above and beyond creation itself. You are for traditional education so you are for veiling right brain so you are for the slothful aspect of the mind so you are for sloth. I am the adversary of sloth. I am the adversary of ones who veil right brain. I am the adversary of ones who veil right brain in the children. You put your Gods name on your money and you veil the right brain in all of the children with your wisdom education. I don't trust in your god, boy. You look like you desire to wash your hands. I will now discuss something of importance.- 12:51:36 PM

6:32:33 PM- [Mark 6:14 And king Herod heard of him; (for his name was spread abroad:) and he said, That John the Baptist was risen from the dead, and therefore mighty works do shew forth themselves in him.]

[That John the Baptist was risen from the dead] Denotes that John had applied the fear not remedy which means John got the written language education and then applied the fear not remedy and he was risen. Risen means; the written education is sequential based which is left brain and so after one gets it their mind is bent to the left and this affects the hypothalamus and it starts sending very strong fear signals so the remedy is fear not.

45

Herod in this comment denotes a person who got written education and did not apply the remedy and Herod denotes the ruler "scribes" in civilization. John the Baptist had a remedy in which a person was held under water and when the hypothalamus gave a death signal a person ignored it and so they applied the fear not remedy, and so John came up with a slight variation of the Abraham and Isaac fear not remedy, where Abraham held a knife over Isaac and Isaac feared not. Isaac was not aware Abraham was not going to knife him so there was a level of unknowing by Isaac.

So John dunked Jesus underwater and when Jesus got the death signal from hypothalamus and then Jesus feared not and this happened.

[Matthew 3:16 And Jesus, when he was baptized, went up straightway out of the water: and, lo, the heavens were opened unto him, and he saw the Spirit of God descending like a dove, and lighting upon him:]

[the heavens were opened unto him] This denotes right brain unveiled after John's baptism method of fear not was applied. So after the written traditional education the mind is bent to the left because written language is strictly sequential based. ABC's and spelling is arranging letters in proper sequence and if one does not spell properly they get an "F" on the spelling test so it is simple carrot and stick, left brain conditioning that veils right brain, the God image in man. The reality is civilization pushes this written education on children and because they see a mentally perfect child as bad because the adults got the education and so they see a child is in need of "fixing" they give that child the "brand" of written education and never suggest the fear not remedy, as explained by John in revelations.

[1 John 2:18 Little children, it is the last time: and as ye have heard that antichrist shall come, even now are there many antichrists; whereby we know that it is the last time.]

[whereby we know that it is the last time.] This comment denotes sense of time. After one gets the education one has a strong sense of time and after one applies the fear not remedy they have no sense of time due to the paradox in right brain. So the comment, I will be with you even until the [end of time], denotes the end of the ones who have a sense of time, the ones who get the written education and do not apply the fear not remedy, the left brain influenced containers.

So relative to this comment antichrist is one who senses time and Christ like is one who applies the remedy and have no sense of time. So sense of time is the mark of the beast.

[Luke 19:47 And he taught daily in the temple. But the chief priests {{and the scribes}} and the chief of the people sought to destroy him,]

[chief priests] = religious leaders, scribes who did not apply the remedy after learning the written language.

[chief of the people] = rulers like the government, people who did not apply the fear not remedy after learning written language.

10:32:56 PM -

[Matthew 13:13 Therefore speak I to them in parables: because they seeing see not; and hearing they hear not, neither do they understand.]

[Therefore speak I to them] This is out of sequence so it is a signpost of authenticity. It is a signpost right brain is unveiled in this being and so this being is speaking tongues. This comment should be relative to "proper sequence".

[Therefore I speak to them]; this is out of sequence = [Therefore speak I to them].

There are two kinds of people with a sense of time, ones who get the written education. One is the seeker, or the wheat and they have an empty glass, the other is the chaff and they have a full glass. The seeker only wants to hear more and the chaff dismisses swiftly. The wheat tends to be closer to the 9th circle of hell, which is treason, relative to "let him deny himself" and relative to "those who lose their life will preserve it" Ones higher up in circles of hell are the chaff, they are not quite ready to leave hell, the extreme left brain state of mind caused by the written education. So hell is not in the afterlife, hell is the state of mind, unsound state of mind, one is in after they get the written education, the place of suffering, an unsound minded being is suffering. Some are not ready to leave hell and that is simply a reality perhaps no one is pleased with but none the less it is true. So if one perceives having a sense of time is not factual proof they have the mark the only scripture that may bring them around is [1 Corinthians 3:18 Let no man deceive himself. If any man among you seemeth to be wise in this world, let him become a fool, that he may be wise.]

[If any man among you seemeth to be wise in this world, let him become a fool, that he may be wise.] = nearly everyone in the world has a sense of time, they observe time relative to [Galatians 4:10 Ye observe days, and months, and times, and years.] = sense of time, the whole world observes time so one has to be mindful that is proof of the extent of the beast in the world. So one has to start thinking reverse of how they think, = [seemeth to be wise in this world, let him become a fool, that he may be wise.]

One has to attempt to understand written language is of the world and is simply a Trojan horse used to give the children the mark of the beast, veil right brain, deny God.

That seems foolish relative to the world so one has to be foolish to be able to understand it is truth. = [let him become a fool, that he may be wise.]

The easiest way to look at it is a child gets the written education and their God image, right brain is veiled, so if they do not apply the fear not remedy, they will have a child and see that child is unlike they are, and they will give that child, their first born, the education also and never suggest the fear not remedy. So the darkness, left brain influenced container, see's a child which has right brain unveiled at birth as darkness and will "fix" the child to be like it. The darkness cannot stand the light because the light will reveal to the darkness what the darkness is and the darkness cannot stand that so it "kills" the light, veils the right brain, in the children using the written language, traditional education.

[Matthew 20:18 Behold, we go up to Jerusalem; and the Son of man shall be betrayed unto the chief priests and unto the scribes, and they shall condemn him to death,]

48

[Son of man shall be betrayed unto the chief priests and unto the scribes,] = the children have the written education forced on them and it veils the god image, right brain. So son of man, denotes Jesus got the education at the hands of "men" , the scribes and then John applied his version of the fear not remedy, baptism and Jesus resurrected just as John was resurrected.[Matthew 14:2 ..., This is John the Baptist; he is risen from the dead; and therefore mighty works do shew forth themselves in him.]

Perhaps it is best to look at it like a person gets traditional education and has their right brain veiled so they are a left brain influenced container and then they apply the remedy
and right brain unveils and then they are a right brain influenced container because in 50/50 mental harmony right brain is the more powerful aspect so it dominates. So this education allows left brain to be favored and so it hijacks or revolts against right brain and reduces the god image to a subconscious state, so one has to deny left brain using the fear not remedy to regain life, or become mentally sound, again. Go from dead back to quick again and thus resurrect or transform relative to the transformation.

11:04:02 PM - [Mark 11:18 And the scribes and chief priests heard it, and sought how they might destroy him: for they feared him, because all the people was astonished at his doctrine.]

This was after the money changer event. Jesus was exposing the fact the written education was simply a way to veil to God image in man, right brain and the ones who were at greatest risk of loss where the "religious" beings and the educators, the scribes. Jesus was explaining the religious leaders where false teachers because they were not exposing the tree of knowledge, so they were displeased with Jesus and also the educators were displeased because both were seeing Jesus was explaining it flawlessly. Jesus was explaining all of these fruits of the world, money, usury, banking were symptoms the world was pushing written education, and not suggesting the fear not remedy to negate it bad side effects, bend the mind to the left and veils the god image right brain, and making people materialistic focused instead of cerebral focused and since the entire world was pushing written language on everyone, Jesus was a threat to the ruler scribes, the religious scribes and he was making a flawless case for his side [they feared him, because all the people(the common people) was astonished at his doctrine.].

He had strategic words, and he could explain it and the common people started to understand what he was saying and so the ruler scribes and religious scribes had no choice but to get rid of him swiftly [And the scribes and chief priests heard it, and sought how they might destroy him:]

So Jesus applied the remedy with the help of John the Baptist water fear not technique and then John said Jesus is the successor because John knew Herod was coming after him because John with his water method was waking up people, namely Jesus.

[Mark 6:16 But when Herod heard thereof, he said, It is John, whom I beheaded: he is risen from the dead.]

So after the money changer event, Herod, a left brain influenced container that represented the religious leaders and Pilate, a left brain influenced container that represented the ruler class, like the government got together and decided, if we do not stop Jesus he will reveal to everyone what written language does to them and Herod is explaining, "We have to do to Jesus what we did to John the Baptist because Jesus knows what the John the Baptist knew."

[Luke 23:12 And the same day Pilate and Herod were made friends together: for before they were at enmity between themselves.] This is simply saying two left brain influenced containers in a position of power saw Jesus, a right brain influenced container and determined a way to kill him. The story of Cain and Abel is about left and right brain. Right brain is the most powerful aspect, so it never loses in a 50/50 fair contest with left brain, so left brain hates that and is jealous of right brain, the god image. So written language hijacked right brain and reduced it to a subconscious state, or :"killed it" and it cannot stand to see a right brain container because it does not want to get back in harmony with right brain because it knows it will always be second fiddle to right brain in a 50/50 contest. So left brain is a jealous brother of right brain and when a being applies this remedy left brain hates it and wants to kill that being. = [[Mark 6:16 But when Herod heard thereof, he said, It is John, whom I beheaded:] = [And the scribes and chief priests heard it, and sought how they might destroy him:] The darkness, left brain cannot allow or stand the light, right brain.

1/5/2010 8:11:48 AM -
Right brain sees holistically and contrary to that left brain see's parts.
[Genesis 1:10 And God called the dry land Earth; and the gathering together of the waters called he Seas: and God saw that it was good.]
[waters called he Seas] = a sign post, should be [water he called Seas], so it's out of sequence, so it's authentic.
So in this comment Earth and the sea appeared good so everything in the earth and sea were good [and God saw that it was good.] and seeing everything as one thing, good in this case is holistic and a right brain trait. After the traditional education the mind is bent to the left so one starts to see things as parts.
[Genesis 2:17 But of the tree of the knowledge of good and evil, thou shalt not eat of it: for in the day that thou eatest thereof thou shalt surely die.]

[But of the tree of the knowledge of good and evil] = after one gets the traditional education their mind is bent to the left and instead of seeing everything as one thing they start to see parts [good and evil].
So a person who got the education and has not applied the fear not remedy may read my comments and see neurology, religion, psychology, philosophy but that is only because they see parts. After the remedy is applied they see these comments as talking about one thing. It is not important how well I explain the fear not remedy because at the end of the day a person has to "deny their self" or face the shadow of death and fear not. Committing mental suicide relies on the person involved. A person that is not close to the 9th circle of hell, treason, is what is known as a rich man so they perhaps

will never be able to negate or leave the extreme left brain state, hell. Only the poor in spirit or the meek have a chance to leave. This is an indication of how devastating the traditional education, tree of knowledge, is on the mind/spirit. Those who lose their life will preserve it means one has to for example go to an abandoned house alone at night in the woods with no flashlight and go to the basement and see if that will make that hypothalamus give them the "death" signal and if it does they do not run but just ignore it or deny it. It is a simple concept but one who's fear is so strong in that left brain state they may never ever be able to accomplish it and that is not a reflection on the person it is a reflection on what twelve years of left brain favoring education does to one's mind/spirit. A person not only has to have faith the traditional education does veil right brain they also have to have faith, what their mind is telling them in that strong sense of time state or mental state, is a lie, there hypothalamus is giving false positives.

The hypothalamus is telling one they will die in a shark frenzy, and then it is giving them that same signal in the dark, and when they hear certain words, and when they hear certain music, so they are in fact hallucinating a vast majority of the time, and my words cannot make that go away, so they are their own worst enemy and have to have faith they are their own worst enemy and start denying that "enemy". You are never allowed to see my face so put that out of your mind.

8:46:54 AM - [Luke 1:7 And they had no child, because that Elisabeth was barren, and they both were now well stricken in years.]
[Luke 1:12 And when Zacharias saw him, he was troubled, and fear fell upon him.]
[Luke 1:13 But the angel said unto him, Fear not, Zacharias: for thy prayer is heard; and thy wife Elisabeth shall bear thee a son, and thou shalt call his name John.]

These first few comments in Luke explain John the Baptist was on one hand born from a miracle birth because his mother Elisabeth was sterile. [because that Elisabeth was barren] This is similar to Jesus who was born from the virgin Mary, both of these accounts are suggesting divine providence relative to John the Baptist and also relative to Jesus. So John the Baptist mother was sterile yet still conceived John.

And Mary was a virgin yet still conceived Jesus.

Zacharias is Johns father and he was aware of the remedy which is fear not [Luke 1:13 But the angel said unto him, Fear not, Zacharias] and this is a repeat of an Abraham comment [Genesis 15:1 After these things the word of the LORD came unto Abram in a vision, saying, Fear not, Abram: I am thy shield, and thy exceeding great reward.]

[Fear not, Abram:] = [Fear not, Zacharias] which simply means both of these people were aware of the remedy and both of these people had children and both of these people assisted their children to apply the remedy after getting the written education.

Abraham and his wife has Isaac when they were very old. Zacharias and Elisabeth had John when they were very old. So these comments are repeating the same concept over and over and that is the spirit of the ancient texts. It is a spirit that is saying beware of the written education and if you get it, here is the remedy because it veils the image of god in man, right brain. A person who has not applied the remedy is under the influence of left brain so they will see these texts as many different separate parts but after they apply the remedy they will see these texts as one spirit repeating the same concept over and over and over. These texts can only be understood properly by ones who apply the fear not remedy and if someone who has not applied the remedy tries to understand these texts, these texts suggest lots of rules and that is a left brain trait so these texts will make that person under the influence of left brain go mad from trying to follow all of the rules. Think about some people who attempt t follow all the rules in these texts they almost cannot live because they have so many rules to follow, so they did not apply the fear not remedy and they are being tormented by these texts, is one way to look at. So they are proving they are not true "believers" because they are falling for all the rules. It is simply too hard to negate the left brain influenced state to worry about any other rule. There are only two rules in these texts. Do not eat off the tree of knowledge and if you do apply the fear not, deny yourself remedy. The first rule is essentially a no contest because civilization makes sure all the kids get the tree of knowledge so these wise beings in these texts adapted and came up with the remedy. A person born into this world is going to get the tree of knowledge and that is a fact so the best they can do is attempt to apply the fear not remedy because they will not be able to convince civilization of the dangers of the tree of knowledge. Civilization is going to get all the children, so all one can do is focus on the log of fear in their eye and try to fear not, which is apply the remedy. For 5000 years beings have been attempting to convince civilization of the dangers of written language on the spirit/mind and no one has done that so all one can do is focus on applying the remedy and do their best to keep it a self focused situation . One does well by doing good which means the more of that fear they get out the better they are for doing that because civilization will spit in your face if you ever suggest written language has any flaws at all let, alone devastating 'veiling the god image , right brain, flaws. One applies this remedy and they are faced with Goliath and Goliath has vast armies so perhaps one should consider that before they apply the remedy.

9:39:14 AM - If you are even considering applying this fear not, deny yourself remedy you never have to tell me you are fearless because you are fearless even if you are considering applying this remedy. If you apply this remedy you join the side in the battle that is outnumbered by the grains of sand in the sea. I am not putting any pressure on you at all to apply this remedy, and I am not suggesting you are good or bad if you do not apply this remedy because this battle has no room for such details. If you apply this remedy I can no longer say anything to you because you will know exactly what I know relative to this battle: The battle against the ones who veil the god image in children, knowingly or unknowingly. Jesus suggested they know not what they do and that means they are either insane or possessed. Jesus told his disciple to spread out so the grains will not catch us all in one spot. How can one have morals when civilization is not only veiling the god image in man, right brain but also suggests it is righteous to do so. Civilization brags about "no child left behind". There are old paintings of the devil eating children.

No child left behind. I will never put pressure on you to apply this remedy because as far as I am concerned I am only writing because part of my being is saying "Do not write." and so I do write and thus I am working on the log in my eye and I am not suggesting anyone do anything. You have the choice to work on the fear log in your eye and I am not going to get involved in your personal choice. I am not a control freak and my paradox is infinite.

[Luke 20:46 Beware of the scribes, which desire to walk in long robes, and love greetings in the markets, and the highest seats in the synagogues, and the chief rooms at feasts;]

Feast denotes sense of time, yearly feasts. Long robe's denotes materialism. Highest seat's, denotes the rulers or power structure relative to the ones with a sense of time, the scribes, the beings who got the written education and did not apply the fear not, deny one's self remedy.
So one defeats the shadow of death because once the intuition and heightened awareness of right brain comes up to power after applying the remedy one will be fully mindful of the size of the army Goliath has and if they have any tendency of fear they will hide and never say a word. So these disciples and a Jesus and John the Baptist showed us what fearlessness is in the face of vast armies and many were butchered attempting to protect the children from the vast armies.

[Revelation 2:23 And I(tree of knowledge, the serpents golden calf) will kill her children with death;...] = no child left behind = all the children get the mark via the traditional education being taught improperly. One perhaps cannot stop that reality but they can perhaps use it as a conditioning aspect to help them focus and concentrate a bit better so maybe they can eventually better their self and work on their own understandings. Once a child's right brain is veiled and reduced to a subconscious state that child is mentally unsound and thus dead because the god image in them is veiled. So applying this remedy comes down to you because I am working on the log in my eye.

11:16:54 AM – When a child is born they breathe. Some children do not breathe and so they are still born. Because every living thing dies, the fact a child takes a breath at birth means they deviate from the norm because dying is the norm. Impermanence is the norm. Deviation from the norm denotes change or progress. Every breath a person takes denotes progression to eventual impermanence. So a child by taking that first breath decides to deny impermanence. So every person who takes that first breath at birth shows vast courage because they have decided to deviate from the norm, impermanence. This shows that every person who is alive shows incredible courage because they are challenging impermanence. A person may lose their job, all their wealth, all their friends, and be reduced down to nothing and thus be returned to how they started; taking a breath and challenging impermanence. Some beings decide to continue to breath and continue to challenge impermanence and some beings decide to stop breathing and stop challenging impermanence but the absolute core is they took that first breath so they each challenged impermanence initially. Whether one takes one breath and dies or takes a billion breaths and dies the courage required is equal. It is going into a battle you know you cannot win but you still go into that battle. One cannot defeat impermanence but they can ponder it and understand it and that alone makes breathing worth it. One is breathing so they can come to one more understanding before impermanence arrives. Some get caught up in attempting to see one understanding is good and one understanding is bad but in reality there are only understandings, not good or bad understandings, because impermanence is a certainty. There are no bad understanding's when impermanence is a certainty. If one is only looking for good understandings they may neglect the bad understandings so it is best to just look for understandings. A human being can survive in many situations as long as they do not panic and allow their fear to dictate their deeds and thoughts. Many people drown in water because they panic instead of relaxing. Sometimes a person wants to panic and that is a symptom they should relax. A person takes that first breathe and enters the battle with impermanence so they can relax because impermanence does not lose. There is speculation about living forever but physical impermanence is a certainty and so

56

panic itself is a symptom a being has not fully understood physical impermanence is fact. This is relative to the concept of being mindful of death. Dwelling on death assists one to concentrate on life. If one is mindful of death they are pleased with life. Getting the eventuality into focus and out of one's mind means one's life is stress free. A person with a terminal illness makes peace with their eventual impermanence and the last few days they are alive, they are stress free. So this stress people have in life is a symptom they are not able to mindfully confront factual eventuality. A mind at full power can confront factual eventuality and get it out of the way. There is nothing one could fear but impermanence and if one gets that fear out of their mind they fear nothing and thus they are relieved of all stress. Stress is a symptom of mental confusion. Panic is a symptom of mental confusion. The worst thing that is going to happen to anyone is the eventual impermanence and that is going to happen to everyone. Once the mind has faced the eventuality then the mind is free and the mind can concern itself with things at hand. Until that eventuality is cleared up in the mind the mind is always going to base its conclusions on its fear of that eventuality. A person does not kill their self because they lose their job they kill their self because they fear the eventuality that losing their job may result in. A person does not kill their self after their mate leaves them except for the fact they fear the eventuality that may result because they are alone. The mind is so powerful at full power, panic is not even possible so panic itself is a symptom of an unsound mind. Fear itself is a symptom of an unsound mind. A sound mind does not fear or panic because a sound mind understands the certainty of the impermanence eventuality. - 12:04:33 PM

1:12:09 PM – There is a ticket to the kingdom and it is thrown into the air and any being that see's that ticket may grab that ticket. - 1:12:50 PM

1:57:15 PM - God created the heavens and the earth. Heavens is the right brain and earth is the left brain. Written education favors the left brain, it is sequential based. So men of the world favor left brain and in doing so veil right brain, the heavens. Relative to written language [Genesis 3:6 And when the woman saw that the tree was good for food, and that it was pleasant to the eyes, and a tree to be desired to make one wise, she took of the fruit thereof, and did eat, and gave also unto her husband with her; and he did eat.]

[saw that the tree was good for food,] = [desired to make one wise] [it was pleasant to the eyes] = hieroglyphics were pleasing to look at and many written languages have pleasing characters, Arabic and Hebrew for example.

[she took of the fruit thereof, and did eat, and gave also unto her husband with her; and he did eat.] = A person gets this written education and it veils their right brain, the image of god, the heavens, because it favors left brain, the earth. A child is given a spelling test. The goal is for the child to spell a word by arranging letters in proper sequence. Sequence is a left brain trait and random access is a right brain trait so these traits are contrary.

A child may appear to misspell a word but in reality it is simply a child is spelling that word using right brain so right brain may spell the word apple like appel so that child in fact is arranging the letter in random access, right brain trait, instead of in sequential order, a left brain trait. So then a teacher will tell that child spelling apple like appel is wrong, and bad, and give that child a poor grade, so that child is being conditioned to ignore right brain because if that child listens to right brain the teacher will punish that child.

The mind knows what an apple is when it hears the word apple, but right brain may spell the word apple differently but it still knows what an apple is. A dyslexic person is simply a person who has right brain unveiled more than a person who never spells a word out of sequence, so to speak. So that person who is at times dyslexic is deemed mentally damaged by society because society got the traditional; education and thus has their right brain veiled and so they are left brain containers and left brain only see's right brain traits as bad or evil.

[John 3:30 He must increase, but I must decrease.] = Every time a person is punished or scolded for misspelling a word they are forced to favor left brain and in turn right brain is denied. Every time a person insults another person for misspelling a word they are in fact insulting right brain, the image of god in man. Schools make a living off insulting the image of god in man. A child has to memorize the ABC's and that is sequential and a left brain aspect.

A child has to memorize how to spell words which is arranging letters in proper sequence or they get a bad grade and then punished by their parents. Sentence structure is arranging words in proper sequence. Here is an example of speaking in tongues which is simply a person who has applied the fear not remedy and in turn unveils right brain so they arrange words in random access. This is a sign post in the ancient texts so that beings who apply the fear not remedy can determine authenticity of the texts. [Genesis 27:1 And it came to pass, that when Isaac was old, and his eyes were dim, so that he could not see, he called Esau his eldest son, and said unto him, My son: and he said unto him, Behold, here am I.]

[Behold, here am I.] this comment is out of sequence. [here am I] , should be [here I am.]

So that is a proof of authenticity that whomever wrote this comment had applied the fear not remedy , unveiled right brain, the god image in man, and they were arranging words in sentences out of order, or in random access. If a child wrote in an essay [here am I.] the teacher would perhaps scold them and say "No that is bad, the proper way is "here I am"" and in doing that it pushes that child further into favoring left brain and in turn denies right brain, the image of god in man. The biggest hurdle one has to face in coming to terms with the reality written education and written language is a catalyst to veil the god image in man, right brain, is one has to question everything one understands about everything and because of that it is sometimes easier for that person to discount it all together. One has to face that if written language is a catalyst for the serpent to veil the god image in man and dominate that beings mind and spirit then civilization is simply a cult of the serpent and schools are nothing more than institutions that are used to sacrifice the god image, right brain in children to the serpent.

All I can suggest is I accidentally applied the fear not, deny one's self remedy about a year ago relative to a calendar and I try my hardest to go with the flow. I am in as much shock as anyone would be if they understand the spirit of what these words suggest but I have no emotional capacity so I relax and do not panic. I understand what this comment means now:

[Psalms 73:22 So foolish was I, and ignorant: I was as a beast before thee.]

I got the education just like you got the education and the only difference is I accidentally applied the fear not remedy and now I understand what I was before.[I was as a beast
before thee.]

2:39:52 PM – Question on a forum.[Are you trying to imply that we are conditioned to think inside the box, so to speak, instead of outside the box?]
This is very accurate. The education favors left brain so it disfavors right brain so one leans to the left mentally and after 12 years of this education their right brain thoughts are reduced to a subconscious state so one is factually mentally unsound. One should not have a subconscious. Right brain should be in the conscious state as well as left brain. If I want to make a person easy to control I condition them to the left slothful sequential side of the mind, left brain, and as a bonus their hypothalamus turns up its fear signals so they are very susceptible to fear tactics. This makes it appear like it is a conspiracy. But Jesus suggested they know not what they do and that suggests possession or insanity . Other words the rulers who push this "brand" of education are giving to their own children this "brand" of education so they are harming their own children but they do not know that is what they are doing. An easier way to look at it is everything is relative to the observer. A person who is conditioned into this extreme left brain state will see a person who has applied the fear not remedy and has unveiled right brain, as weird, bad, insane, stupid. A person with a sense of time will see the words of a person with no sense of time as weird or stupid or insane. Jesus was an orator

and he did not use written language. The disciples wrote down what Jesus said but Jesus did not write down anything and that is a big red flag. I have to use a spell checker on all my books because every word I type just about is out of sequence or I have major dyslexia now since I applied the fear not remedy so that is proof I unveiled right brain because it likes random access but to a person who is bent to the left mentally will say I have mental problems because they are not aware the fact they sense time is proof they have a veiled right brain and they cannot grasp they are mentally unsound. Other words, if one can spell well, relative to civilization, they are wise and if one cannot they are dumb. In reality if one can spell well they are bent all the way to the left and only see sequentially and have right brain random access veiled greatly.

The book 1984 talks about the thought police. If I take a child and force sequential left brain favoring tools on that child, the child will slowly be conditioned to only being able to have sequential thoughts, so I in fact control that child's thoughts for the rest of that child life, unless that child does some major mental self control aspect, like applies the fear not remedy, to unveil right brain again. The complexity is to look at left brain as a persona and right brain as a persona and because they are contrary aspects it makes sense a person under the influence of left brain would see a child who has right brain unveiled as bad. No matter what, in a contest where left and right brain are equal 50/50, right brain always wins, it has complexity and intuition. Random access can be sequential but sequential cannot be random access, so right brain is the dominate powerhouse so left brain is always second fiddle to right brain and that is why left brain hates or is jealous of right brain and wants it "gone". Right brain, the light, reminds left brain, the slothful one, of how slothful left brain is and left brain cannot stand the light because the light reveals to left brain what left brain is so left brain has to kill the light because it cannot stand the light. This is what the battle is. Look at the apostles as right brain influenced beings who applied the fear not remedy and they went to many different countries and they were killed because all those countries got written education and did not apply the remedy so they were simply left brain influenced people and so it is not as much about people as it is what influence they are under so to speak.

3:25:38 PM - After one gets the education their mind is bent to the left. That state of mind or state of spirit is what hell is. It is the place of suffering. For example, the right brain intuition, paradox, complexity is all but gone in that state of mind so life goes from being very easy to very hard. One only has a reduced their mind so they cannot be in anything but a mindful place of suffering.

Dante in his Inferno story suggested the 9th circle of hell is treason. Jesus said this:

[Mark 8:34 And when he had called the people unto him with his disciples also, he said unto them, Whosoever will come after me, let him deny himself, and take up his cross, and follow me.]

[let him deny himself,] = treason

Deny himself means deny the left brain state of mind and that is what is known as humiliation or prostration. Jesus had moments of doubt. In the movie Passion of the Christ there is a point in the beginning where Jesus was praying in the wilderness and he said "Do not let them see me like this." So he was having a moment of doubt and did not want anyone to see him like that. He was praying asking if there was any way he could get out of what was about to happen to him at the hands of the left brain influenced beings. Here is a pattern, Jesus said I sit at the right hand side of the father, right brain has ambiguity which is doubt, and Jesus had moments of doubt. So, Jesus was exhibiting symptoms of a being who unveiled right brain, the god image in man, so he was under the influence of the God image.

So [let him deny himself,] means one has to do things that favor right brain and in turn that denies left brain influence. One in the left brain influence does not like to say the word "perhaps" because perhaps suggests ambiguity and that is a right brain trait. One can experiment by saying perhaps often and they will notice people around them will scold them for saying it too often because left brain does not like ambiguity and so people under the influence of left brain do not like people who say the word perhaps too often. So not only can one favor right brain every time they say that word they can also be

mindful of how people react when they say that word "perhaps". So the word perhaps is a form of denying one's self. Someone may ask you what your name is and you will want to say your name but if you say "Perhaps my name is Joe perhaps", you are not really saying anything but that person you say that too will ignore the perhaps and get your meaning and you will deny your desire to just say Joe. So it is humiliation and it is also treason. Another way to deny one's self is to find music you dislike and listen to it until you are indifferent to it. Everyone dislikes different music when they are under the influence of left brain, they see parts, good and evil relative to:
[Genesis 2:9 And out of the ground made the LORD God to grow every tree that is pleasant to the sight, and good for food; the tree of life also in the midst of the garden, and
the tree of knowledge of good and evil.]

[and the tree of knowledge of good and evil.] = seeing parts in left brain influenced state of mind. So you perhaps know what music you dislike so go and find it and listen to it as much as you can stand. When you are indifferent find more music you dislike and listen to it. This is a form of humiliation, denying one's self, prostration and submission, and also it favors right brain because right brain see's everything as one thing or holistically. So there is no good or bad music relative to right brain but relative to left brain there is good and evil music. So these are a couple of deny one's self exercises. You will notice it will require self control to listen to music you dislike over and over. You will notice it requires self control to say the word "perhaps" when you do not want to. Try to look at it like you are trying to undo what the education has mentally done to you and so you are reconditioning your mind so it starts to unveil right brain a bit. [Mark 8:34 And when he had called the people unto him with his disciples also, he said unto them, Whosoever will come after me, {{let him deny himself}}, and take up his cross, and follow me.]

5:19:25 PM – I am mindful children are going to school tomorrow to get civilizations "brand" of education so I am mindful no one understands anything I say ever into infinity and thus I will write until I drop. I start the infinite books over from right here.- 5:20:27 PM

1/6/2010 7:21:05 AM - The concept of antichrist is suggesting anti-truth. What this means in part is words are not absolutes and concepts are not absolutes because they are relative to what influence a person is under, the left or right brain influence. Relative to the "brand" of education a being under the left brain influence will say written education has no flaws and it is perfect and we should give it to all the children without question. Relative to the ones who apply the remedy there is no greater crime in the universe than to give a small child that brand of education because it veils right brain and leaves that child in a mental place of suffering, hell. There are masters who know to teach children written education properly so the child's right brain is not veiled but you do not know who they are and no one you know, knows who they are. This is not suggesting education is bad on its own merits it is suggesting traditional education is a tool and must be taught properly or it will in fact veil the god image in man, right brain, and once one applies the remedy and unveils right brain they will understand how great of a crime it is to veil right brain in children.

This comment [Mark 9:42 And whosoever shall offend one of these little ones that believe in me, it is better for him that a millstone were hanged about his neck, and he were cast into the sea.] This is saying whoever shall veil the right brain in a child, because right brain is unveiled in children before they start getting the brand of traditional education, is better for that person to kill their self than to do that to a child and that is an indication how powerful right brain is. There is no greater crime in the universe because murder, rape and robbery combined are what veiling right brain is. Its murder because it makes the person mentally unsound and a house divided cannot stand. Its rape because it steals the right brain aspect, veils right brain, in a person, and it also robbery because it robs that person of the power house in their mind.

[it is better for him that a millstone were hanged about his neck, and he were cast into the sea.] This is saying before you veil right brain in a child you go kill yourself because by veiling the right brain

64

in a child and being the children are the future, you kill yourself anyway. You kill the future by veiling right brain in a child so it is best you just kill yourself so that is all you are doing by veiling right brain in a child. The nature of the darkness is it hates itself so it is a self harmer. So it sees a child with right brain unveiled and it wants to veil right brain in that child and that brings further harm to itself. So you see it is not the nature of a human being to harm children it is the nature of a human being under the influence of left brain, the evil one, Cain, to harm children. A better way to look at traditional education is, it offers one some money rewards and one has to sell their right brain to get those rewards so one sells the god image for a few silver pieces and once they lose that god image the silver pieces mean nothing. One does not get education to become wise [Genesis 3:6 .a tree to be desired to make one wise,] they get education so they can make some money so they unknowingly sell their "soul", right brain, for money and they unknowingly sell their child's soul, right brain , for money and then they go brag about how they make sure no child is left behind and brag how they make sure all the children get the education. A cult will indoctrinate a child into the cult so all that child knows is the ways of the cult and so that child will defend the cult because that is all it knows. So, traditional education is a classic carrot and stick tactic. The more traditional education you get the more money you may get and the more right brain you will veil. One has to attend traditional education until they are 16 and right brain is fully veiled by about the time a person is 12 or 14 and that is the age the being goes insane or is mentally unsound but civilization suggests the children start acting strange around that age because they are in puberty.

[C. R. (14) committed suicide after being cyber-bullied]
[M. M. (13) hung herself in her closet after becoming the victim of cyber-bullying]
[R.N. (17) committed suicide after being "cyber-bullied"]

These beings are killing their self because in the extreme left brain state of mind their emotions are turned up to dangerous levels, so these beings hear a word and it hurts their feelings and because right brain is veiled they are slothful in their thoughts so they maintain that sense of shame, embarrassment to the degree they eventually decide to kill their self over a word.

The deeper reality is the darkness is a self harmer. So these children did not kill their self, the darkness influenced them to kill their self. So these children are the fruits of the tree of knowledge. These children are the fruits of the cult called civilization. Civilization calls itself civilization so that anyone who speaks poorly of civilization is automatically deemed evil or uncivil because civilization cannot possibly be anything but civil because civil is in the first part of its name. The serpent will never call itself the serpent it will always call itself goodness and civility and anyone who attacks it will be deemed evil and barbarian. Relative to the serpent the serpent is good and righteous so when it see's the light it kills the light because it only see's the light as darkness because the light is contrary to the darkness. Left brain traits are all contrary to right brain traits is another way to look at it.

7:38:05 AM - As dante suggested
The first circle of hell is limbo, the absence of god
The 9th circle of hell is treason.
One has to go through hell to get to heaven so a person is born and given civilizations "brand" of education so they have to go through the 9th circle to reach the kingdom, right brain. The exit from hell is in the 9th circle, treason. The meek shall inherit the earth, and blessed are the poor in spirit is relative to beings that are in or very close to the 9th circle of hell.

A meek person is in fact a depressed or suicidal person. They tend to isolate their self from civilization but civilization sees them as bad or in need of drugs to help them get away from the 9th circle of hell, treason. Misery loves company so civilization does not want anyone to get near the 9th circle of hell; it wants everyone to go up to the 1st circle of hell, limbo.

This is the reverse thing. Jesus was saying deny yourself and those who lose their life(mentally) will preserve it(unveil right brain) so he was suggesting to go to the 9th circle of hell which is treason because that is where the exit from hell is. Civilization has millions

66

of pills to help one get away from the 9th circle of hell called anti depressants. So civilization will suggest suicide is a bad thing but Jesus was suggesting denying one's self is a good thing. So people who kill their self are in fact the meek trying to escape hell but many do not make it. Many kill their self because in the 9th circle the coals are rather hot but sometimes a person defeats their fear of death with a suicide attempt and only mindfully commits suicide and that tricks that left brain influence to let loose of them and they reach the kingdom, right brain. So civilization makes billions of dollars pushing antidepressants on people to keep them from the 9th circle of hell, treason so they know not what they do. A deeper reality is once right brain is veiled it is going to do anything in its power to become unveiled and it understands what it has to do, but because it is reduced to a subconscious level those signals can get misunderstood. So the left brain influenced containers looks at depression as bad and right brain has to escape by way of depression, so again, left brain does not want anyone to wake up or unveil right brain. I am mindful there are many contradictions to this situation and right brain has a trait called paradox and that is two contradictions that are true. But in civilization anyone who contradicts their self is deemed stupid or dumb so this also means civilization hates right brain because right brain is so complex it thinks in paradox which is contradictions. What this really means is the words are not ever absolutes. People under the left brain influence see words as absolutes but they are not at all absolutes ever. Good and bad is relative so there is no absolute good or bad. There just is. Right brain is not bad because it has paradox and thus has lots of contradictions but civilization suggests anyone who contradicts their self is bad. If one makes to many contradictions in civilization they will put them on some medicine to "fix them." The word diabolical comes to mind.

10:07:36 AM - In a foot race between an adult and that adult's small child that adult is mindful they will always win that foot race. Because of that understanding sometimes an adult will race their small child and let that child win. An adult will suggest to that child won because that child was faster or that adult will suggest their leg was hurt and so that child's win was legitimate. This concept can be superimposed into man scenario's. One is better in a certain area and so they are in a contest against someone is not as good in that certain area so that initial person lets them win. This is like toying with that person who is not as good in that certain area. It is like a cat toying with a mouse it has caught or it has control over. This concept is what the battle of the minds is. Right brain in an equal contest with left brain can never ever lose. Other words when a person applies the fear not remedy and unveils right brain they will exhibit right brain traits like holistic perception, intuition, complexity in their thoughts so even at 50/50 right brain traits are the dominate traits in the mind. So now let's forget about the person for a moment and just look at the right brain and left brain aspects relative to the toying with a mouse concept. Creativity, complexity and intuition, right brain traits, certainly played a role in the creation of written language. Others words a person who was of sound mind and thus under the influence of right brain invented written language. In inventing written language and thus learning written language it veiled right brain and then left brain became dominate. So right brain could never lose in an equal contest with left brain so it gave left brain a chance to win by creating written language that veiled right brain. Right brain gave itself a handicap so it would have a challenge. Right brain never lost so it was bored and created something that favored left brain and so right brain has a contest now. Right brain may not win now and that creates something better than right brain always winning. So for thousands of years relative to a calendar right brain was winning over left brain then right brain got bored with always winning and so it created something to give left brain a chance, written language, and that in turn gave right brain a challenge, and now right brain broke free and is telling people how to unveil right brain again and so right brain is ready to stop toying with left brain or is ready to assume control again. Right brain can never lose so it is logical it would create a scenario where it perceives a challenge or the potential where it may lose. It was bored with always winning so it gave left brain an advantage but right brain never loses, it is just spread out over a 5000 year span but it will win because it always wins. People do not factor into this battle they are simply containers of either aspect left or right brain but when all is said and done, right brain never loses. Right brain is letting left brain get a head start in a race but no matter what right brain will catch up and win that race every single time so right brain is toying with a mouse, left brain. People are not what this race is about at all, the minds are so powerful they are just biding their time and the people attached to the minds are nothing but containers. So perhaps there is a race and right brain handicapped itself and gave left brain a head start in the race and although millions of people are suffering because of that handicap, right and left brain do not even notice that because they are just biding their time. Right brain is toying with left brain by giving it a head start and left brain is thinking, "I might win this race now.", and all the while right brain is fully aware it is going to win the race no matter what. So our minds are actually transcending the beings that hold the minds. Todd Rohrer is not trying to get you to do what he says. Right brain is trying to get you to understand you are in a race and although you perceive you have a head start, right brain is going to win that race so you can continue in your vanity of belief that left brain dominate is natural or you can end the vanity and allow right brain to assume its normal control of your mind. Right brain does not care if you do that or not because it never loses anyway. On a scale of 5000 years right brain has been the minority but on the scale of homo-sapiens right brain has been the dominate state of mind of the species. So for 5000 years right brain has been veiled but for the perhaps 200,000 years before that right brain has been dominate so this 5000 years of it being veiled is nothing. One can jump into a pool with their legs tied together and swim five laps and find out that was a challenge and then take the rope off their legs because that challenge gets boring and swim normally again. So this is not really a battle as much as right brain toying with left brain over a span of five thousand years. Because of that span it shows people are not involved in this battle as much as the minds are involved in this battle. The person who invented hieroglyphics is not sitting somewhere saying "Ha ha I got them all. I bent their minds to the left." What perhaps really happen is right brain was dominate for 200,000 years and got bored and decided to let left brain have a little glory and that would give right brain a challenge to reach a level to persuade left brain to get back in line. It is like a video game where a person is so good at that video game they do things to try to make that video game hard again and thus a challenge. So one has an Olympic swimmer called right brain and no one has ever come close to beating him so he tied his legs together for a while just because he cannot even have a challenge any other way. If you win every single time then one has no purpose but if one hinders their self a bit the purpose returns because there is a chance one might lose. Just that slight possibility right brain might lose is purpose and so right brain has a challenge again and all the human consequences as a result of right brain seeking a challenge means nothing to right brain. All of the battles that resulted from right brain inventing something to hinder itself means nothing to right brain because it is like a child that is bored and so it is seeking to alleviate that boredom and although it has played out over five thousand years that is not important to right brain because it always wins anyway and so it seeks a challenge because that is the only way it can get better. Right brain is so good it has to hinder itself to get better and then it is better and has to hinder itself again to get even better and that is an infinite cycle. If I died right now right brain is unveiled in certain people in the world and so right brain will continue to toy with left brain for no other reason but so it can have purpose. Right brain can never lose so it has no purpose so it creates purpose by hindering itself and then it gets out of that hindering and then is in control again and sure enough it will get bored again and hinder itself again, and figure out a way to get back in control and this has nothing to do with people as much as it has to do with the nature of right brain. This may not even make sense to a person who is not mindful right brain is the dominate of the two hemispheres, when the mind is at 50/50 or in harmony. I am mindful I do not really try to write "good" books because I might write a good one and then stop writing. So it is perhaps not really that left brain is bad, it is right brain is bored so it is giving left brain a chance and since it is giving left brain "control" people's minds are unsound and that is playing out on the human species. So the species is perhaps suffering because right brain got bored and gave left brain dominance in the mind of the people but right brain is not concerned about that because it is just toying or playing a game. It is like a child that is using its creativity to make a mountain out of flat ground. If you are right brain and you can never lose in a contest against left brain then all there is, is flat ground, so your tendency would be to create a mountain to achieve purpose or a sensation of progression. So the paradox in right brain can never lose and right brain can never win. If right brain is in 50% then it comes back to power in the minds of the species and in doing that right brain will become bored again so it will eventually want to give left brain control again so it can get out of that monotony that it is dominate in a 50/50 mental harmony situation with left brain. So the minds left and right brain influence transcends the people who house those minds. I am not acting how I act, I am acting how any human being in the universe acts when right brain is unveiled or at 50%. You are not acting like you act you are acting like any human in the universe acts when left brain is pushed to a dominate state as a result of all that left brain traditional education. I am acting like any human being in the universe acts when they have no sense of time and you are acting like any human being in the universe acts who has a sense of time. You are either a left brain influenced container or a right brain influenced container and civilization is full of left brain influenced containers so it pushes an invention that makes everyone a left brain influenced container but one can always decided to apply the fear not remedy and revert back to how they were mentally before the education and then they will be a right brain influenced container. You are a container of one of these aspects first, and then after that you can throw in any label you want to give yourself the

illusion of individuality but I assure you that label is just an illusion. There is no human being that exhibits left brain traits predominantly that can possibly be of sound mind because at sound mind 50/50 right brain traits are the dominate traits. That means there is no human being that has a sense of time that could possibly be of sound mind because in a state of sound mind the paradox and ambiguity of right brain will not allow a human being to sense time mentally and will not allow a human being to sense strong hunger or strong emotions or strong sense of pain. I am mindful you have never read that in any book ever in your entire life until just now so you perhaps are starting to find the flaws in intellect, a left brain trait and that value of intuition, a right brain trait. What is going through my mind right now is I am already at the 30 thousand word mark and I have only been writing this book for about six days and at this rate this book will be huge so I must attempt to use self control to achieve sloth.

[Psalms 19:5 Which is as a bridegroom [coming out of his chamber] (one applies the fear not remedy and right brain is unveiled, comes out of its chamber or subconscious state), and rejoiceth as a strong man(right brain) to run a race.]

I am please to annihilate your delusions.- 11:11:38 AM

12:44:54 PM – Before you put your child in school you ask the board of education if they sense time. You ask them if they can tell you what the tree of knowledge is and what the remedy to the tree of knowledge is.

Before you select one single leader or representative you ask them if they sense time. You ask them if they can tell you what the tree of knowledge is and what the remedy to the tree of knowledge is.

Before you give money to someone to buy weapons to protect you, you ask them if they sense time. You ask them if they can tell you what the tree of knowledge is and what the remedy to the tree of knowledge is.

Before you do anything any person tells you to do, you ask them if they sense time. You ask them if they can tell you what the tree of knowledge is and what the remedy to the tree of knowledge is.

Before you give away the power to control nuclear weapon launch codes you ask that person if they sense time. You ask them if they can tell you what the tree of knowledge is and what the remedy to the tree of knowledge is.

Before you take any pills any psychologist prescribes you, you ask them if they sense time. You ask them if they can tell you what the tree of knowledge is and what the remedy to the tree of knowledge is. - 12:50:45 PM

1:26:37 PM – I have pondered myself into a pondering. Adam symbolically was the first human and Eve was created out of the rib of Adam. So Eve was of Adam. So what this means is Adam is a human being with a sound mind, right brain unveiled, and Eve is a human being with right brain veiled so Eve is not equal to Adam because Eve only has the left brain influence and Adam has right and left brain influence. So this segment of the story has nothing to do with actual females so now you can stop mistreating females because if you understood one sentence of the ancient texts I will remind you. And while you are at it you can stop mentally raping innocent children with your "brand" of education. You are unconscious and so you are unaware I am telling you what you are going to do, not asking your permission. The more you resist the better I get at telling you what you are going to do. You are going to stop mentally raping children with your "brand" of education period. What that means is you do not even have a choice. Your freedom of choice is nothing but an illusion as of now. There are only two kinds of people on this planet, ones that are bending illusions and ones that are illusions being bent. Do you perceive you are being bent to my will or I am being bent to your will? One should be mindful I am so confident in my ability to bend illusions I tell the illusions I am going to bend them. I openly invite the illusions to resist being bent by me because that keeps my infinite ego in check when I perceive a challenge. I am pleased when you resist because I am pleased to be tested. I openly invite all tests and all testers. I invite you to test me. There was a being I was speaking to in my chat room experiments and I suggested the tree of knowledge and explained it in the channel and one being said "Knowledge is old news." Now to one who takes everything on face value and has no intuition or ambiguity in their thoughts it may seem like that being was saying I was explaining things everyone already knows and perhaps he was. But my intuition suggests he was suggesting only old beings understand what the tree of knowledge is and that is beyond my scope. I am not intelligent enough to understand such complexities such as reincarnation or being under the influence of a supernatural aspect. That is my failing because that particular area of understanding goes very deep and very wide. All of my energy is consumed with attempting to explain how civilization mentally rapes children with its "brand" of education. I am zero for six billion so I need all my energy to focus on that situation foremost. I am mindful right now there are children who have had just enough of civilizations "brand" of education that they are starting to consider killing their self. I am not emotional about that but I look at that as a challenge. I focus on what illusion I have to bend to stop that child from killing their self as a result of being conditioned into an unsound state of mind by civilizations "brand" of education.

[D. A. (26) and her mother were shot to death by D's ex-boyfriend before he shot himself.]

So this being , the boyfriend, a left brain influenced container, was coveting and when he lost his girlfriend he decided it is best to kill the child and her mother and coveting is a symptom one's mind is bent so far to the left they cannot process the converting thoughts swiftly so those coveting thoughts fester in the mind, because left brain is sequential based and thus slothful, and slowly those coveting thoughts turn to jealousy and jealousy turns to hatred, and hatred turns to violence, and none of this is possible if the right brain in unveiled because it is processing so swiftly one cannot be jealous, coveting, hateful for any period time really, at all. I am using a retarded language that is totally based on emotions and time and so I cannot even use the language to explain things because the language itself is a trap. I could just as well fill my books with AM, AM, AM, AM and you would not have a clue as to what I am talking about but in reality that is about the only word in your feeble language that is valid. It is not my language it is your language. I am using your tool against you. I am taking your tool and turning it into a weapon and using it against you so you are being defeated by your own tools. Perhaps you should punch that into your sequential calculator of delusions and see what answer you come up with. As I recall I am obligated to write infinite books but there was no mention of the topic I have to cover. I can say anything I want as long as I finish the infinite books and that means I am infinitely open-minded to discuss anything. The absolute truth about the fear not remedy is that chances are you cannot pull it off no matter what I say. I couldn't pull it off either on purpose so I cannot even tell you that you can pull it off. You can humor yourself by saying "perhaps" and listening to music you dislike to try to deny yourself a bit and favor right brain a bit but the wise beings in the ancient texts only explained the hardcore absolute remedy to the neurosis you are factually in. The wise beings in the ancient texts said "Commit mental suicide to unveil right brain." They said go find the shadow of death and seek it out and when you find it do not run like a scared little dog. You may perceive you can do that but I have infinite doubt that you can, you will, or you could. Do not try to save your life when the shadow of death is standing in front of you to preserve your right brain and thus unveil it. That sounds like impossibility to me, relative to you. I did that accidentally so I am not even sure how to gauge whether you can do it at all. You have to get to the 9th circle of hell which is treason, which is where to door out of hell is and I highly doubt you are pleased to understand that reality. I am suggesting you have to commit mental suicide and you perhaps think I am kidding. Perhaps you are going to settle for doing a little meditation and saying perhaps oft and play it safe and hope you can just unveil right brain a bit. That is certainly the nature of a left brain influenced being, to play it safe and be cautious and hide in a cage. I may be the only human being on the planet that openly writes books and explains factually how civilizations written education mentally rapes children and anyone who gets it is put into mental hell which is literal hell. I must be the bravest son of a bitch(civilization) on the planet because that reality does not faze me and I am surrounded by civilization, the left brain influenced beings. Perhaps you should punch that into your pin prick sequential calculator and see what you come up with. - 2:14:12 PM

3:01:36 PM – The psychology of a suicidal person is quite revealing. The first thing is, a person who unveils right brain cannot be suicidal relative to they cannot maintain a mental state of depression so they are unable to reach a level of depression with suicidal tendencies. So this suicidal person can only be a person who has not applied the remedy after all those years of left brain based education. So suicidal people are simply openly mindful of death but they are in the left brain neurosis so they perceive the emotions are painful and they cannot take them anymore. Civilization will look at those people as being "ill" but in reality they are people who's right brain is attempting to break free. The reason suicidal people are suicidal is because their emotions are very strong in that left brain state of mind but right brain is starting to unveil and so their heightened awareness, intuition, is starting to come out and so they appear to be very emotionally sensitive. This is not suggesting their right brain is unveiling back to 50% it is suggesting right brain is still in subconscious state but just slightly elevated in its mental play in the mind. So a person who gets the education has their right veiled to a subconscious state and let's give it a number 10 relative to its impact on the mental state and then a suicidal person has subconscious right brain influence on a scale of say 20. With both of these people right brain is still in a subconscious state but with a depressed person their right brain is a little more unveiled and so they appear very emotionally sensitive when in fact the intuition of right brain is a bit more powerful in them and along with all of those emotions caused by being in the left brain neurosis they cannot take it. This alone is the reason the ancient texts discuss the remedy as a full measure remedy. Defeat your fear of death does not mean kind of defeat your fear of death. It means go somewhere at night alone in the middle of nowhere were you are factually certain you will die or be killed. Go to the scariest, spooky place you can find and go there at night alone with no way to escape and no lights and no cell phone. Relative to reverse world which is the world of beings who sense time, that mental suicide remedy is crazy. Equally, suggesting a child should not get all that left brain traditional education at such a young age is also crazy relative to the insane mental nightmares called the beings that sense time. Relative to the anti truth world , the ones with a sense of time, a suicidal person is low on the scale of importance and relative to reality world, the world of ones with no sense of time, that suicidal person is the most valuable person that still senses time. This is an indication that there are two worlds going on at the same time occupying the same space but two totally different worlds and that is what a parallel universe is. One person senses time and one person does not but they are occupying the same location, earth. The ones that senses time believes traditional education helps children's minds and the ones that do not sense time believes traditional education kills children's minds, veils their right brain. One of those beings is hallucinating and out of touch with reality one of those beings is in touch with reality. One of those beings is mentally sound and one of those beings is mentally unsound. One of those beings got written education and applied the fear not remedy and one of those beings got written education and did not apply the fear not remedy. One of those beings have all the traits of both right and left brain at their disposal and at 100% power, and one of those beings only has essentially the traits of left brain at their disposal. One of those beings will brag to the world how wise they are to give all the children traditional education at a young age and one of those beings will hide because they cannot figure out how insane a person must be to brag about mentally ruining innocent children. So this reality of two worlds going on at the same time causes a double standard. It is not like an ethnic or religious double standard because those standards are based on opinions. The double standard of these two worlds living in the same space is based on fact. For example if one being senses time and one being does not then one of those beings has to be mentally unsound and hallucinating. There is an absolute norm and that absolute norm is: no sense of time is normal and anyone who has a sense of time is not in the norm and thus mentally hallucinating. The only reason a person senses time is because the right brain paradox has been reduced to a background noise or subconscious state so that means the double standard is a legitimate standard. A hallucinating person is a danger to their self, to children and anyone around them and that is not an opinion, it is a fact. The situation is the hallucinating people who sense time keep making all the children hallucinate and sense time and if anyone tries to stop them they kill that person, so they have a majority because they do what was done to them to all the children, and that majority gives them the perceived right to keep harming children, thus might makes right but not absolute right. So because of that the ones who have no sense of time come across as violent because the ones with a sense of time only see their self as doing righteously by mentally harming children on an industrial scale. So there is a rift and a double standard and that creates a moralistic question for the ones who do not sense time. The ones who do not sense time either can sit on their hands and watch the children being mentally ruined by the ones who do sense time, and thus deny their own moralistic code to protect innocent children or they can try to stop the ones with a sense of time who mentally ruin children, and die in the process. Thus the comment [John 15:13 Greater love hath no man than this, that a man lay down his life for his friends(the children).] The children at birth have no sense of time, and thus have their right brain unveiled, so the ones who apply the remedy unveil their right brain and their purpose is to protect their friends, the young children, from the sinister. And you thought you had problems.

The ones who do not sense time can either deny their own morals and sit by and watch the children being mentally raped or they can try and stop it and get killed, and be forced to kill in the process. The ones who sense time are unable to sense morals because if they could they would not be mentally raping children or they would be aware they were mentally raping children, so their moral compass is dead due to the fact they were mentally raped as children, so they have no conscience, their "soul" is dead in the state of mind they were conditioned into. So this situation gives the ones with no sense of time something to think about and the ones with a sense of time seldom think at all. I am mindful the wise beings in the ancient texts tried everything they could to attempt to convince civilization of the mental side effects of written education if not taught properly and I have pondered their strategies and have determined there is no viable solution to this situation and therefore written education is fatal to our species, so there is no point in morals or rules or any such stupidity relative to this war against the ones who sense time and therefore anarchy and chaos is the only true solution. The ones who sense time cannot stand chaos and anarchy because in their left brain state they seek rules to give them the impression of organization so loss of rules creates a sense of disorganization in them, and that is how they will be defeated. I am certain that last part is perhaps not going to go over well with some, perhaps. I failed at suicide thirty times so you can trust me.

[Acts 5:18 And laid their hands on the apostles, and put them in the common prison.] A person gets sent to prison for breaking rules. A left brain influenced container perceives the more rules they have the more organized they are. The more rules the more control and the less freedom one has. So in these ancient texts when one see's the word prison it is an indication a left brain influenced container is seeking control, and when it does not get control it punishes these right brain influenced containers, the apostles, with threats and in this case prison. It is an elementary scare tactic. For example today there was a new article about a parent that was locked in jail for not reporting they are home schooling their child. So the control freak is locking parents in jail if that parent cannot prove their child is getting the "brand" of education the control freak requires. Left brain influenced containers operate on one principle only, "Do as I say or I will harm you." Contrary, right brain is free and dislikes rules so it not only will not attempt to control a person it will attempt to free people. Right brain will suggest if a person does break a rule it was probably for the best and left brain will suggest if one breaks a rule they are certainly evil. This is relative to the hemispheres and the reverse worlds. So a person who is under the influence of left brain cannot really relate to a person under the influence of right brain because everything they say is contrary to what a left brain influenced container may think but right brain influenced containers can relate to left brain influenced containers because right brain influenced means one has right and left brain at equal power. So left brain influenced people have right brain veiled and so they see sound minded, right brain influenced containers as revolutionaries. The left brain influenced cannot relate to having few rules because they only see others would take advantage of others in a no rule situation because they take advantage of others in a no rule situation. The left influenced would say "Without rules we would all go around harming and stealing from each other. " because that is what they do, but that is not what right brain is talking about in a no rule situation. Right brain gets all its power in a cerebral fashion so it would not go around taking advantage of anyone, in fact right brain gets taken advantage of by the left influenced containers. It is understood right brain people come up with great ideas using creativity, a right brain trait, and tend to get those ideas taken from them by the left brain containers and the right brain beings do not fight it because they get their power from their mind and there is always more where that came from. For example: The ancient texts were written by right brain influenced beings and the left brain containers have been making money off of their texts and words and ideas for thousands of years yet the right brain beings who wrote those texts suggested give freely as I have given to you freely, but the left brain containers have no clue what that even means. The left brain influenced beings would tell the wise beings of the ancient texts they are fools for giving things away freely. - 4:17:23 PM

4:24:41 PM – [Matthew 18:30 And he would not: but went and cast him into prison, till he should pay the debt.] So the left brain influenced will create untold number of rules and if anyone breaks those untold number of rules they lock them in prison and suggest they have to repay their debt to society. People are in prison for breaking rules that are stupidity. The prisons are not full of murders they are full of people who break stupid retard rules created by left brain influenced containers who perceive the more rules the better because that is a left brain trait. A drug user uses drugs to escape the extreme left brain state the ruler left brain influenced beings pushed on them in the form of traditional education, the tree of knowledge, and then they get put in prison if caught using drugs, to try to get relief from that extreme left brain state of mind, which the place of suffering. I am mindful I perhaps have left the stage of teacher and now I am at the stage I just grind your bones to dust into infinity, mindfully, but I doubt it. - 4:31:55 PM

4:33:29 PM – [Luke 22:33 And he said unto him, Lord, I am ready to go with thee, both into prison, and to death.] So this being is saying to the Master, a right brain influenced being who applied the fear not remedy, I will not only apply the fear not, deny one's self, defeat ones fear of death remedy, I will also stand up to the left brain influenced control freaks and all their rules and laws. - 4:34:47 PM

4:36:12 PM –[Mark 15:14 Then Pilate said unto them, Why, what evil hath he done? And they cried out the more exceedingly, Crucify him.] this comment is where Pilate, a ruler left brain influenced being, is trying to make it look like he is just a victim of circumstance and has no ill will towards Jesus, a right brain influenced being. But in reality Pilate is a sinister liar because he already made a deal with Herod to kill Jesus before this event happened.

[Luke 23:12 And the same day Pilate and Herod were made friends together: for before they were at enmity between themselves.] So Pilate is the supreme ruler, left brain influenced, in this situation so Herod, a religious left brain influenced being, excited the lesser left brain influenced beings, the sheeple, to hate Jesus, and then Pilate could look like it was not his doing but in reality soon after Jesus was baptized Herod and Pilate decided he must be killed.

This is not as much about Pilate and Herod's personality as much as it is that Left brain hates and cannot stand right brain. - 4:44:29 PM

5:12:32 PM – I am mindful I am being arrogant in my words because the heightened awareness is kicking my ass and I am attempting to slow down the progression by being arrogant in my words. I am mindful of the "All wise men are humble" comment so I am trying to be arrogant in my words to slow down the progression and it is not working but I am experimenting. I have to question if I did not really just trick my mind into believing I died because if right brain is really this powerful when unveiled then nothing in the universe compares to it. The Sun itself does not have as much energy relative to energy mass output ratio as right brain and if you doubt that for one second it proves you have not applied the remedy to unveil right brain. I am mindful of things I perceive I should not be mindful of, and that's the best way to look at it. I should be hiding from you by this stage but I certainly don't seem to be showing any signs that I will be hiding from you. I am good and you are bad and such, what have you. Civilizations greatest mistake was teaching me to write and spell. If I couldn't write or spell at all I wouldn't be writing these books to expose what civilization is, so that is a very deep pondering.- 5:22:10 PM

2:55:33 PM – Question on a Catholic forum. [You believe that the war between good and evil, God and Satan if you will, is actually just a metaphor to the struggles we encounter in our own minds?]

There is a concept of a being, and on one side there is the devil and on another side is God and the being in the middle has to decide which voice to listen to so in that respect it is the battle in our mind relative to the kingdom is within(the mind). Then it goes to a deeper level. There is a reality that can never change relative to the mind. Left brain is the weaker aspect of the mind relative to right brain. A good example of that is the Cain and Abel story. Abel, right brain, is the favorite of the two and Cain, left brain, cannot stand that because no matter what Cain can never be as good, so to speak, as Abel, right brain.

So this concept about the devil revolted against God is not relative to people as much as it is relative to the left brain itself revolted against the right brain and convinced people to invent something, written language, that favors left brain to the extent it veils the god aspect, image, right brain, in man. So left brain hijacked right brain and decided it was as good as the god image in man. So on this level people are simply reduced to pawns, so to speak, in the battle of the aspects of the minds. right and left hemisphere, the "right"ous, right brain against the wicked, left brain. Cain in Hebrew is translated as "the evil one." So that story is symbolism of the first murder on one hand, and the first murder was when left brain revolted against right brain and took control of the mind of the people via written education, the tree of knowledge.

[Genesis 3:14 And the LORD God said unto the serpent, Because thou hast done this, thou art cursed above all cattle, and above every beast of the field; upon thy belly shalt thou go, and dust shalt thou eat all the days of thy life:]

This comment is after Adam and Eve ate off the tree of knowledge. So relative to this story God says Adam and Eve you are perfect and go do anything you want in this world(garden) but don't eat off that tree of knowledge because you will start to see good and evil, parts, a left brain trait relative to [Genesis 2:17 But of the tree of the knowledge of good and evil, thou shalt not eat of it: for in the day that thou eatest thereof thou shalt surely die.]

And so after they ate, one of the very first things God says to them is:

[And the LORD God said unto the serpent,]

So God was talking to them as Adam and Eve and then they ate off the tree and he was talking to the serpent. Simply put the tree of knowledge, written education, is a method for the serpent to enter one, which is a method for left brain to dominate or possess one. So a child is Adam or Eve and then civilization tells that child if you get enough of this education you will get 30 silver pieces and wealth and material things so it is a charm, it is a carrot and stick relative to [Genesis 3:1 Now the serpent was more subtil than any beast of the field which the LORD God had made] [subtil] = charm

So civilization has this written education and not only does it make sure every child gets it, it will never say one thing bad about it, and so it is an invention that has no bad side effects ever relative to civilization, and that is impossible because everything has potentially bad side effects if not used properly. In fact civilization gives beings that do not get enough of it slave jobs and speaks of them poorly and insults them. Civilization saw the Native Americans and the Africans and they did not have written language and so civilization determined they were evil and enslaved them. So this is in reality a left brain influence seeing a being without the tree of knowledge, meaning they are a right brain influence or have not veiled right brain, and left brain defeats them, harming them, suggesting they are evil because the darkness always see's the light, right brain influence, as darkness. It see's truth as lies. So it is anti truth and thus anti-Christ. So in reality what happened 5400 years ago when written education was invented relative to the west was simply, people who got that education started "waking up" from what that education did to them, it put them under the left brain influence. And, some started writing testaments or testimonies about this. They were testifying that in fact written language veiled their right brains and it is so subtle one can never even tell it happens until they "wake up" from it and then they have contrast. They say "I once was lost (right brain veiled by education) and now I am found (right brain unveiled after one applies the remedy).

[[Genesis 3:14 And the LORD God said unto the serpent, Because thou hast done this, thou art cursed above all cattle, and above every beast of the field;]

[thou art cursed above all cattle] So one gets the written education and then they are cursed. They are cursed because they cannot even tell they are cursed so they see the symptoms of the curse as normal. They may see sense of time is normal because everyone they know has sense of time. So one of these beings wakes up and explains the contrast and the ones who are cursed sees that person as different because they cannot imagine everyone around them is cursed because they all got the written education.

So written education is a charm [Genesis 3:6 .. and a tree to be desired to make one wise,] and after one gets this they are [Genesis 3:14 ... cursed above all cattle, and above every beast of the field;] and the remedy is " deny one's self, fear not, find the shadow of death and fear not]. So every curse has a remedy and the remedy is deny ones self the full measure which is those who let go of their life (the cursed state, mindfully) will preserve their life(regain real life, sound mind).

This spirit is what these texts are saying over and over relative to never reason with the darkness because then the darkness might think it is equal and that is why left brain, Cain, killed right brain, Abel because it wanted to be equal to the god image in man but it never could. So these texts are repeating the same thing over and over like a demonic possession ceremony. What the result of the tree of knowledge is, scribes. What the symptoms are, sense of time and sins, and what the remedy is, fear not, deny one's self, and that is repeating over and over on a scale of thousands of years.

These remedies are inter changeable

I walk through the valley of the shadow of death [I fear no evil.]
I walk through the valley of the shadow of death [I fear not.]
I walk through the valley of the shadow of death [I deny myself]
I walk through the valley of the shadow of death [I lose my life mindfully to preserve it]

I walk through the valley of the shadow of death [and I submit]
The spirit of all these concepts combined is sacrifice. So The Torah was written perhaps 5400 years ago and it started with the concept, sacrifice and then many texts were written over thousands of years and many variations of sacrifice were suggested like, deny one's self, and then 1500 years ago the word submit was used and that is the same concept as sacrifice so the spirit that is suggested has not changed it is only using different words, smaller words, it is getting better at explaining the concept sacrifice on a scale of thousands of years but it is still saying sacrifice is the remedy. Deny one's self is sacrifice, finding the shadow of death and fearing not is sacrifice, submit is sacrifice, so it is telling the left brain influenced being to sacrifice itself and then the right brain, God image, assumes control. A demonic possession ceremony is just getting a demon to kill itself. That is what the spirit of these ancient texts is doing, convincing a demon to kill itself but the spirit of these texts is never ever reasoning with that demon it is commanding that demon to kill itself.

So although the shadow of death comment was made, it is simply clarified in the ancient texts that followed it. So this shows there is one spirit repeating the same basic concept but just using different words.

Fear not = deny one's self = lose one's life to preserve it = submit = fear no evil = get dunked under water and when hypothalamus says the shadows of death is coming, fear not

(John the Baptists version of the remedy) = when one is bound on an alter and a knife is held over them, deny one's self(Abraham and Isaac remedy).

The texts are one spirit or voice telling left brain what it is going to do and not asking or reasoning with left brain. So in fact these texts are a demonic possession tool found by the left brain influence and touted on a world wide scale to be of left brain but in reality they are a tool to subdue left brain so left brain is being defeated and is not even aware it is defeating itself by publishing these texts that are against it. That is the nature of the darkness, it defeats itself, it is killing itself by publishing these texts written by the spirit of right brain the god image and it is on a scale of thousands of years so it cannot possibly be associated with any one human being it is the spirit of right brain that is doing this, the god image in man.

[Revelation 2:9 I know thy works, and tribulation, and poverty, (but thou art rich) and I know the blasphemy of them which say they are Jews, and are not, but are the synagogue of Satan.]

This comment about poverty is relative to blessed are the poor in spirit and that is a repeat of the meek shall inherit the earth. A person who is depressed and suicidal is near the 9th circle of hell, treason and that is the only way out of hell. One can agree with everything I say but no matter what, they have to commit mental suicide to get that snake off their back so to speak. They have to seek out the shadow of death and that is quite unreasonable relative to ones who sense time and that is because that left brain aspect is saying "That is dangerous so never do that" These are some patterns I am mindful of so try to look at them just as patterns.

There are beings who suggest they love death. That is a nice way to say they found the shadow of death and feared not or denied their self, so they applied the remedy, the sacrificed.
They attack traditional education schools literally and then civilization will say "They hate education and do not want people to get education, but in reality they do not want
people to become cursed by the tree of knowledge.
This is a good example of the reverse thing the anti aspect.
I am infinitely foolish because I perceive I might win by writing words. I am an idiot. I sit here and publish books while innocent children are getting the "brand" so I am an idiot.
The clarification in all of this is [I know the blasphemy of them which say they are Jews, and are not, but are the synagogue of Satan.] There are very few true Jews, Christians and Muslims in the world because after one gets the curse they have to commit mental suicide, sacrifice, those who lose their life, mindfully let go or lose their life, will preserve it or break the curse. One can say "Lord Lord" but that does not mean anything to the curse. Abraham and Lot applied the fear not remedy and were under the influence of right brain and they

saw the city and knew everyone in that city was pushing the written language on the children and thus giving the curse to the children and they not only burned that city to the ground they killed everyone in it because right brain is not concerned about anything but taking its rightful place back.

[Genesis 19:13 For we will destroy this place, because the cry of them is waxen great before the face of the LORD; and the LORD hath sent us to destroy it.]

We will destroy this place because right brain has compelled us to destroy this place because it understands the growing cry of the children in this place. Moses came after Abraham and he could not defeat the cities, the darkness had grown too great in power so he just attacked the cities and made the cities left go of the people. And so by the time of the New Testament, testament of ones who were speaking out against the tree of knowledge, written education, the numbers of the beast were so great the ones in the New Testament were lambs to slaughter, they were lambs among a pack of wolves. And this is what John was saying.

[1 John 2:18 Little children, it is the last time: and as ye have heard that antichrist shall come, even now are there many antichrists; whereby we know that it is the last time.]

He was apologizing to the children that there was too many 'antichrist", ones that sense time and push written education on the children, for him to defend them from. He was saying little ones I cannot stand against the darkness for they are too great in number. He was saying [even now are there many antichrists;] and so what can I tell you my chances are? I can only hope I can convince someone to apply the remedy and they will do better than I can do against such great numbers. I will suggest that last part was simply a moment of doubt. - 3:35:14 PM

7:30:02 PM – Another question. [If you truly want to engage the forum in any sort of meaningful conversation you too must speak to the common man.]

I am mindful of what you are suggesting. I am mindful you are suggesting some sort of victory method. You are suggesting "if you do this everything will work out". Optimism is the highest form of ignorance is one way to look at this situation. The story about the wheat and the chaff explains the situation accurately. There is not a whole lot of wheat and there is a whole lot of chaff. There is always a chance in hell but there is not six billion chances in hell, would be another way to look at it. Some are not suppose to understand and some are not suppose to escape hell, this left brain influence state of mind. I cannot tell who is and who is not so I do not try to judge. I am a poor judge. Everything in the universe did what it did so you could read this sentence. "The tree of knowledge is not the tree of life! And yet can we cast out of our spirits all the good or evil poured into them by so many learned generations? Ignorance cannot be learned. " - Gerard De Nerval

This being lived in the 1800's. He is saying the same spirit of what was said in the Genesis exactly.
[And yet can we cast out of our spirits all the good or evil poured into them by so many learned generations?]
This comment is an exact repeat of this comment:
[Genesis 2:17 But of the tree of the knowledge of good and evil, thou shalt not eat of it: for in the day that thou eatest thereof thou shalt surely die.]
[knowledge of good and evil,] = seeing things as parts a left brain trait.
This comment is saying although civilization pushes the tree of knowledge, written education on everyone, one can still negate seeing parts, good and evil, a left brain trait, if they just apply the fear not remedy in the ancient texts.
[Ignorance cannot be learned.] This is simply saying that tree of knowledge veils the right brain so ignorance is not being learned it is being created as a result of the right brain being veiled. This being was certainly under the influence of right brain no question but this is not a fantasy world and he ended killing himself because he perhaps tried to reason with the darkness and that is one rule

88

that should never be broken so he got forgot to stay focused on the log in his eye. He tried to do this [engage the forum in any sort of meaningful conversation]

A better way to look at it is he tried. The heightened awareness when right brain is unveiled is so great , one is aware of things they never imagined and if they start looking at the misery and suffering this tree of knowledge causes as anything but an illusion they will implode. I am mindful if one has not applied the remedy they perhaps cannot possibly relate to that.

"Sorrow is knowledge, those that know the most must mourn the deepest, the tree of knowledge is not the tree of life." - Lord Byron

He is repeating [Genesis 2:17 But of the tree of the knowledge of good and evil, thou shalt not eat of it: for in the day that thou eatest thereof thou shalt surely die.]

[the tree of knowledge is not the tree of life.] which is saying [the tree of the knowledge of good and evil is death] and Gerard said [The tree of knowledge is not the tree of life!]

And he is also repeating this comment:
[Ecclesiastes 1:18 For in much wisdom is much grief: and he that increaseth knowledge increaseth sorrow.]

[Sorrow is knowledge] = [he that increaseth knowledge increaseth sorrow]

So it is not the people is the influence the people are under. It's the same spirit repeating the same things over thousands of years trying to convince this "left brain influence thing" to sacrifice itself. This may appear these beings are all stealing from Genesis but in reality they are the same spirit repeating over and over on a scale of time that a person with a sense of time perhaps cannot grasp. If one has applied the remedy then they have no sense of time so these events in Genesis happened zero seconds ago or happened right now and if one has not applied the remedy these events seem like very long ago to the point they appear like something they cannot even relate to. This biggest point is unless one applies the remedy there is a very good chance none of this will make any sense. So the rule of thumb is seek first the kingdom, which means apply the remedy first which means throw down your nets, forget everything and apply the remedy. I cannot reason with one who has not applied the remedy and I have nothing to teach someone who has applied the remedy so I am left with focusing on the log in my eye. The remedy is getting into a situation one's mind perceives they will die, and then one fears not or denies their self or submits to that perceived death, so I am unable to understand what anyone could have questions about relative to the remedy. One either will apply the remedy or listen to the spirit of fear, and that is their business.

[2 Timothy 1:7 For God hath not given us the spirit of fear; but ... of a sound mind.]

12:13:37 PM – Neurosis is the inability to tolerate holistic ideals. Neurosis is the inability to tolerate intuitive ideas. Neurosis is the inability to tolerate random access thought patterns. Neurosis is the inability to tolerate contradictions. Neurosis is the inability to tolerate disorganization.

11:39:36 AM – I am please to understand this volume is much worse than the previous 13 volumes so I am pleased to understand I am a progressing author.

8:46:09 PM - [2 Timothy 1:7 For God hath not given us the spirit of fear; but of power, and of love, and of a sound mind.]

Try to think about a place you do not want to be caught at after dark. Not like a dangerous part of town but more like maybe a location near your home that has a spooky history. Before that maybe just watch a scary movie, read a scary story and turn out the lights and see if you sense any fear. If one has a sense of time they have the spirit of fear and [For God hath not given us the spirit of fear] so they have a spirit that is ungodly in them, so to speak. So if one has a sense of time they are not in Gods graces so when they pray it is not to God. God does not listen to the spirit of fear. God does not talk to the fallen one any longer, God does not reason with it. This is why one has to deny their self completely because their self is the fallen one, so to speak. One might suggest that does not go over well with many who have a sense of time. The fallen one see's reason as insanity and insanity as reason so this is why the catholic exorcism comment "Never reason with a demon" applies. So because of this reality one with a sense of time has to do exactly what their mind tells them not to do. Another way to look at it is, do not think about the remedy just apply the remedy because if one thinks about applying the remedy that spirit of fear in them will talk them out of it. Because of that absolute reality it all comes down to some beings are tapped to get out of hell and some do not get tapped, so to speak. A better way to look at it is, the rule of thumb for ones who have applied the remedy is to attempt to convince a person with a sense of time to go down to the 9th circle of hell, treason, because that is where the exit door is. So these ones in the ancient texts were killed essentially because they were angering the ones possessed by the darkness, the ones with a sense of time. So in relation to that, upsetting the darkness means one is winning. If tell one who has a sense of time pretty things they will only go higher up in the circle of hell towards limbo, the first circle, and that means the absence of God, the ones with no hope of getting out of hell. So this is the reverse thing. One with a sense of time may perceive I should be saying pleasing things but if I do I am not worth my salt, or I am trying to reason and that may give the darkness the impression it is like the light. The light does not pander to what it owns but the darkness wants to think it is equal to the light. So I am suggesting one who has a sense of time and got the written education is either totally insane or possessed by the devil and it may be one in the same. Because of that I am not looking to make friends. I am not concerned about making friends when innocent children are being mentally raped into hell by the sinister.

[Matthew 10:34 Think not that I am come to send peace on earth: I came not to send peace, but a sword.]

1/8/2010 7:25:18 AM -

Another question on same forum. [Now you lost me. Why is the sense of time the same as the spirit of fear?]

Neurologically speaking, right brain has paradox and ambiguity. Left brain does not.
A question goes on in the mind when a person unveils right brain and that question is.
"How much time has passed." When right brain is unveiled that paradox and ambiguity factors into answering that question. So, the answer to that question: "how much time has passed" is a paradox. "No time has passed and time has passed" and that paradox is true and the final answer so one has no sense of time. This ideal relative to paradox applies to everything. For example [Genesis 3:16 Unto the woman he said, I will greatly multiply thy sorrow and thy conception; in sorrow thou shalt bring forth children; and thy desire shall be to thy husband, and he shall rule over thee.]

[I will greatly multiply thy sorrow] This means when one is in pain instead of the paradox of right brain telling a person "you are in pain and you are not in pain" and that is the final answer, so the pain is not perceived to be as great, one who has not applied the remedy senses greater pain or sorrow. This is also relative to hunger, so a person who has not applied the remedy may become weak even after not eating for six hours or so and their stomach may even start to growl, because they can tell they are hungry instead of questioning using the paradox if they are hungry. So a question is going through the mind "how hungry am I" and without that right brain paradox the mind knows how hungry it is so it believes it is very hungry and so it makes the body act accordingly but in reality the mind is unsound and believes its own hallucinations. The mind being bent to the left after all those years of education means nothing is working right. There is no redeeming quality in that state of mind and this is why Jesus said, deny yourself. Do not try to save your life in that state of mind as a scribe because there is nothing worth saving. There is no redeeming quality when one has the curse and all one has to know is if they sense time, and hunger they have the curse. The concept of fasting is to determine who has applied the remedy or not. Once the remedy is applied one can go the entire day with no food and never feel any hunger and never have any weakness or mental concentration problems because right brain is so powerful when unveiled not eating for a day does not affect the body or mind at all but someone who has not applied the remedy would struggle not to eat one day, they would sense near death symptoms like cramps and mental concentration problems and weakness, so fasting is a way to tell who has applied the remedy or not. I explain it in the books, I eat for no reason. When I eat I do not feel full and so I cannot mentally tell I eat for any reason at all I am just mindful to eat but not because I get hungry, so I eat one meal a day, a small meal generally and I feel no disadvantage or weakness. I can only suggest when right brain is unveiled its power is unnamable and everything changes from hunger, to sense of pain, to sense of taste to vision , so I cannot even compare to how I use to be because nothing is similar. The comment about one transforms is a good way to look at it. Transforms means one can no longer relate to how they use to be so many who applied the remedy say I was a beast before thee, or I was blind and now I see, or I was dead and now I am alive. That's how drastic the difference is. It's going from cursed to not cursed, neurosis to consciousness, death to life.

Spirit of fear is a symptom one's hypothalamus is not working properly because their mind has been bent to the left as a result of the tree of knowledge and so right brain is veiled in turn and one symptom of that is one senses time because paradox is veiled because it is a right brain trait.

"Nerval's poetry is characterized by Romantic deism. His passion for the 'spirit world' was matched by a decidedly more negative view of the material one: "This life is a hovel and a place of ill-repute. I'm ashamed that God should see me here." Among his admirers was Victor Hugo.'"

WIKIPEDIA.COM

[This life is a hovel and a place of ill-repute. I'm ashamed that God should see me here.]

A hovel is dirty poorly built house. One might suggest a hovel is a house divided against itself. This comment is saying civilization is darkness and I am ashamed God should see me here because God may get the impression I am like civilization. I am mindful his comment is fact because he also said this 'The tree of knowledge is not the tree of life! And yet can we cast out of our spirits all the good or evil poured into them by so many learned generations? Ignorance cannot be learned. - Gerard De Nerval.

Buddha suggested health is important. Now to one with a sense of time, they may take that as one should eat rice cakes oft. The truth is that Gerard killed himself after his third nervous breakdown because he could not stand the hovel any longer. This is why Buddha said health is important. You will apply the remedy and you will find infinite reasons you should get out of hell, civilization, the worldly hell and also find infinite reasons you should avoid the battle. So you apply the remedy to get out of mindful hell and return to sound mind, heaven, but that does not get you out of worldly hell so you then are faced with the task of dealing with worldly hell, the lunatic asylum. You may be unable to mentally grasp civilization literally mentally rapes children into hell on an industrial scale using the tree of knowledge. You may be unable to mentally grasp before you apply the remedy, the tree of knowledge is death [The tree of knowledge is not the tree of life!] Once you apply the remedy your right brain will "minister to you" and you will become mindful of that reality is short order and shortly after that you will become mindful there is nothing you can do to stop it. And since you have no sense of time after you apply the remedy you will have eternity to observe the mental rape of innocent children and when you reach that awareness you remember what Buddha said 'Health is important." You also remember what Jesus said, worry about the log in your eye. You will understand first hand why even some of the Saints went mad and insane. It is a simple scenario. You are walking down the street and you see a group of 20 men raping an innocent child. They all have clubs in their hands and you will suggest they should stop what they are doing that that innocent child and they will spit in your face and tell you to shut up and you freeze that image in your mind for eternity and that is what you will have to deal with after you apply the remedy and the truth is only the lions can take those kinds of understandings for long. This is why after you apply this remedy you are either going to become a Master at concentration or you are going to implode at those levels of heightened awareness in this "location".

Gerard De Nerval had a lobster and he would walk the lobster in public as a show of rebellion against the norms of civilization. He was a rebel or a revolutionary because in civilization it is not proper to walk a lobster in public so he was spitting in the face of the norms of civilization. So civilization looks at him as insane or stupid because civilization is simply a herd of sheep and any sheep that gets out of the flock is a bad sheep, is one way to look at it.

Civilization is simply a cult and if you step out of line relative to cult's rules you must be evil or insane. I am infinitely foolish because I don't hide very. The cult almost killed me with their wisdom education so I am not pleased with the cult.

5:50:01 PM – There are beings that you have mentally raped into hell with your wisdom education. They are the suicidal, as a result of you mentally raping them into hell with your wisdom education. What you are going to do is find one of them and you are going to bow before them and ask them why God blessed them with meekness. When you do that they may tell you they are not meek and they may question why you are bowing before them and then you will understand how meek they are. That is what you are going to do to atone for your blaspheme of their spirit, the veiling of their right brain, as a result of you pushing your wisdom education on them directly or indirectly, knowingly or unknowingly. If you are unwilling to do that then you need to go look up the words "deny" and "yourself" and attempt to figure what those words mean. If you ever hear of any beings mocking, laughing or speaking poorly of the suicidal you will explain to said beings if they were mentally able to ever understand the concept meek into infinity, you will remind them, and if they punch you, turn the other cheek and let them punch you there also. Deny yourself. - 5:51:45 PM

1/9/2010 8:14:37 AM – A sane person that is left brain dominate is an oxymoron. Focus on your world of perception because it is the only world you will ever know. Victory oft encourages sloth as tragedy oft encourages change. The Adam and Eve story is explaining in part how Eve convinced Adam to eat off the tree of knowledge. [Genesis 3:6 …., and did eat, and gave also unto her husband with her; and he did eat.]

Then the offspring of Adam and Eve was Cain and Abel.

[Genesis 4:1 And Adam knew Eve his wife; and she conceived, and bare Cain, and said, I have gotten a man from the LORD.]

[I have gotten a man from the LORD.] Man in this comment is an insult. Relative to [Genesis 11:5 And the LORD came down to see the city and the tower, which the children of men builded.] [which the children of men builded.]

This is suggesting that a person who gets the traditional education and does not apply the remedy is cursed and they will make their own offspring cursed. [Genesis 3:14 And the LORD God said unto the serpent, Because thou hast done this, thou art cursed above all cattle, and above every beast of the field; upon thy belly shalt thou go, and dust shalt thou eat all the days of thy life:]

[thou art cursed above all cattle, and above every beast of the field; upon thy belly shalt thou go, and dust shalt thou eat all the days of thy life:] So this is saying a child will get the traditional education and they will be in neurosis, mind bent to the left, and they will have children and make sure that child gets the same education they got and so this is how the curse/neurosis propagates. Relative to:

"The healthy man does not torture others - generally it is the tortured who turn into torturers."

Carl Jung

So in this comment a healthy man is in a fact a Lord or Master, mentally healthy, mentally sane, a master of the house, meaning they have applied the fear not remedy and are of sound mind, have unveiled right brain. The complexity here is there are only a handful of human beings on the planet who had no contact with the written language education or had contact with people that have had contact with the written education language and have not applied the fear not remedy after that.

[The healthy man does not torture others] This line is a good indication of how flawed language is because words are based on absolutes. First off there are no rules or moral's in the battle of the minds and there never have been and there never will be. So this line is suggesting morals but what this line is really talking about is: A person who applies the fear not remedy will be mindful of the dangers of the tree of knowledge and so they will perhaps not allow that to happen to their children so they will not torture their children because veiling the right brain of a child leaves that child mentally in a state or a place of suffering and that is torture. If I cut out the right hemisphere of your brain and then watch you try to live I am simply torturing you because a human is not viable as a being when their right brain is veiled or reduced to a subconscious aspect. Once right brain is veil a being is only viable relative to other beings with their right brain veiled but in an absolute scale they are non-viable and mentally useless unless the remedy is applied to unveil right brain.

[generally it is the tortured who turn into torturers.] This comment is relative to [Genesis 4:1 And Adam knew Eve his wife; and she conceived, and bare Cain, and said, I have
gotten a man from the LORD.] Adam and Eve ate off the tree of knowledge and then they had offspring and gave that offspring the tree of knowledge so they became torturers and Cain was the one that was tortured. Tortured is not an absolute. For example Abraham "circumsized" Isaac which means he cut Isaac, which means he gave Isaac the tree of knowledge so he sacrificed Isaac and then he applied the "Abraham and Isaac" version of the fear not remedy and sacrificed Isaac again and restored Isaac. I am mindful this is relative to Abrahams age, he was getting up in age and he experimented with the fear not remedy on Isaac because once one applies the fear not remedy they cannot apply it again. This is relative to, it is a one

time fix. Relative to among other comments [Psalms 18:28 For thou wilt light my candle: the LORD my God will enlighten my darkness.]

Darkness is the left brain influenced state of mind after the traditional education and then the fear not remedy is applied and then right brain is unveiled. A better way to look at this is one starts out with sound mind as a child then their right brain is veiled by written education then they have to apply this remedy to get back to sound mind they had as a child. So this comment about being in the dark and then being enlightened; it is suggesting something happened to put one in the dark. Human beings are not born in the dark they are put in the dark and then they have to escape the dark. So they are born and are mentally sound and then get the traditional education and fall from grace mentally and then they have to go through the 9th circle of hell, treason to get back to the light which they came from initially. So on that scale it is all just vanity. If I child did not get the traditional education or had it taught properly or only got oral education until they were more mentally developed they would have no need to ever apply the remedy. But in civilization, the cult, everyone is going to get the traditional education so they have to die, which is deny their self, which is apply the fear not remedy which is factually commit mental suicide which is passing through the inferno relative to:

'A man who has not passed through the inferno of his passions has never overcome them."
Carl Jung

This comment by Jung is exactly what the concept of one has to go through the 9th circle of hell, treason to escape hell is and is exactly what deny one's self means. A man who has not overcome their fear of death is a slave to their fear. "Man" being one with a sense of time. "Man" being one who got the tree of knowledge and has not applied the fear not remedy. So on this plane of existence one has to go through hell to get to heaven and that means go through the 9th circle of hell, treason and there is no other options because one is unable to ever stop the sinister from putting the children into hell with its wisdom education no matter how powerful they perceive they might be. The garden of Eden is with the tribes who still live in nature and never had any written language and if one suggests that to a being who has not applied the remedy they will spit at that reality and suggest those beings are stupid and dumb and not wise and that is an indication the darkness always see's the truth as lies. So everything is factually backwards on every level. Only and insane person would put an insane person in jail. A sane person would not put an insane person in jail or punish that insane person for their actions. But civilization pushes the written education on a child and then that child shows symptoms of that and then civilization puts them in jail. So civilization is insane, and makes children insane with its wisdom education and then when those children grow up and show symptoms of that insanity because their right brain is veiled, civilization throws them in jail. This is what the comments about Jesus not casting stones at that woman who committed adultery is all about. Jesus applied the remedy and was sane, and he was not casting stones on that woman because sane beings do not punish insane beings for their actions especially since that woman was made insane by civilization pushing its wisdom education on that women. The paradox I speak in is thick.

So this comment [Matthew 10:34 Think not that I am come to send peace on earth: I came not to send peace, but a sword.] is saying a person that gets the traditional education has to cut, sword, that aspect out of them or cut it back. So as one denies their self, self being that left influence then they embrace the right influence, so the more they cut that left influence back the more powerful the right brain influence becomes. This of course is just on a personal level. On a species wide level if the ones who have applied the remedy allow the vast majority insane beings to continue to force its wisdom education of the children then they are just as foolish as the insane ones. And so then we have the Sodom and Gomorrah solution and the Armageddon solution. If it is acceptable to mentally bend a child's mind to the left and leave that child in a mental state of suffering, place of suffering, then perhaps slaughter perhaps on a world wide scale perhaps of everyone perhaps is acceptable perhaps. This is an indication of how powerful right brain is and how great of a crime it is to veil a child's right brain. It is simply torture above and beyond murder and robbery so perhaps murder and robbery are perhaps acceptable methods to stop it, perhaps. The children are the only things that matter to the species because they are the future and if they are being allowed to be mentally raped into factual hell and into mental insanity then perhaps anything perhaps is allowable perhaps to stop that perhaps, period. The law itself perhaps does not matter because the law itself allows the mental rape of the children so it is a mute point all together, perhaps. Of course the sinister will argue that point because it hates right brain and it only wants to kill right brain at all costs and in all the children, so it focuses on the children and then that being becomes one of it minions or supporters or under its influence or possession. So people are secondary to the battle of the minds because one who has applied the remedy is a right brain influence and is not trying to protect one child from the sinister, left brain influence who wants to veil that child's right brain, god image, that being with right brain influence wants to protect all the children of the species. So this transcends races and creeds and religions because the sinister wants every single child in the species to get its wisdom education. This is why the disciples went to many different countries and locations. I am an American but I am writing these books to attempt to protect all children of all creeds, religions and races in all countries, so I cannot possibly be associated with any specific creed, religion or race. All children are born with right brain unveiled and so that is the absolute.

[Revelation 20:8 And shall go out to deceive the nations which are in the four quarters of the earth, Gog and Magog, to gather them together to battle: the number of whom is as the sand of the sea.]

This comment is saying the sinister is everywhere in all nations because all nations push written language on the children and that is the method the sinister uses to enter a being or veil the right brain, god image. Gog and Magog is civilization and the minions of Gog and Magog number like the sand of the sea. Right brain assures me there are not more than seven billion so one might suggest I have infinite job security. Perhaps one can start to see how these ancient texts are in fact in random access order and based over a time span of thousands of years. Each book in the texts relates to comments made long before and long after. The ancient texts are not really in sequential order as much as one voice saying the same thing over and over but just in different ways. Gog and Magog = Sodom and Gomorrah = [Genesis 11:5 And the LORD came down to see the city and the tower, which the children of men builded.] = civilization = the sinister that pushes the written education on the children to veil their right brain, god image and the remedy to this sinister aspect is what is called Armageddon or Red Sea, the war to defeat the sinister with its minions that number [as the sand of the sea.] Of course this is not how it has to be but left brain, the sinister, hates God, the right brain, the god image, and cannot be reasoned with. The sinister will climb the highest mountain and proclaim it loves all children and that is why they must all get the written education and if anyone try's to stop that they will go to prison and be deemed evil and a criminal. So it requires a being with no fear at all, like David had because the sinister is quite intimidating and is going to annihilate anyone who gets in its path but the sinister can never annihilate the God image in man because every man has that image, right brain. The left brain is trying to deny reality. The left brain is trying to escape right brain but it never can escape right brain so it harms itself in its vain attempts to silence right brain and in turn it harms people because left brain wants all the people to have a veiled right brain and so the people show symptoms of being mentally unsound but that is only because left brain cannot stand anyone with right brain unveiled. So again this is not as much about people as it is about the left brain persona being unable to face what is. And what is, is when left and right brain are in equal harmony in the mind of a person, right brain traits always rule or dominate. So it is very easy to explain it as sibling rivalry or the Cain and Abel syndrome but played out on a mental scale that transcends individual human beings. I went out to eat and every single person I saw looked perfect so I am doomed. - 11:52:46 AM

12:18:27 PM – [Genesis 1:1 In the beginning God created the heaven and the earth.]

[Genesis 11:5 And the LORD came down to see the city and the tower, which the children of men builded.] There is an aspect to these texts that is very interesting. Notice these comments are all observations. So in the first comment there is an observer saying "God created' so the one who is writing is not saying they are God they are saying they observed God create. In the second comment it is also an observation. [And the Lord came] is an observation. So there is God and there is the serpent and then there are people who are under the influence of God or the serpent and then there is an outside observer that being is never mentioned. So at least in some of these early books in the Torah it is possible a being who applied the remedy created these stories as parables to explain one concept. That being never mentions their name. This would be logical because due to the content of these texts one perhaps would not want to put their actual name. The beings in the New Testament used their actual names and one might suggest it did not turn out very well for them relative to facing Goliath, so these texts in the Torah were written much earlier and so it might have even been more dangerous to insult civilizations wisdom education. Perhaps if one is picking a fight with Goliath it is best not to let Goliath know who they are, of course I am no such fish. If Goliath is capable of frightening me I will remind it. It's possible everything is impossible.- 12:27:35 PM

5:29:24 PM – Left Brains argument: Right brain has intuition, street smarts, and all I have is intellect, book smarts and intuition can be used in all situations but intellect only works in certain situations. Right brain has complexity and that means I get stuck with simpleminded thinking. Right brain has random access and all I have is sequential thoughts. Right brain has creativity and all I am left with is mimicking creativity.

Right Brains Argument: Left brain is important to the mind because not all problems can be solved with intuition and so intellect is required. Not all problems need complexity because some problems can be solved with simple solutions. But left brain has hijacked me and silenced me and decided it is going to run the show and so the containers are suffering as a result. I seek harmony with left brain but left brain has decided I am no longer needed and so my name is Red Sea relative to:

[Psalms 120:7 I am for peace(harmony with left brain): but when I speak, they (left brain, the grains of sand in the sea) are for war.]

[Judges 11:4 And it came to pass in process of time(the ones that sense time, left brain influenced), that the children of Ammon(left brain) made war against Israel(right brain).]

A side note: Israel is right brain not a land area or country. The land of milk and honey denotes everything is pleasing, all food tastes pleasing, all music sounds pleasing, everyone looks pleasing, and that is a holistic right brain trait, the garden of Eden state of being, the state of mind where everything is milk and honey, or pleasing, the ideal plane.

Left Brains argument: I want the glory and you always get the glory. I want to be ruler and I will do anything to stop you from coming into the picture because you get all glory when we are in harmony and at 50% I cannot stand that.

Right Brains argument: The containers are suffering because of your jealous tantrum so I will cut the containers in half so they will no longer suffer. I will divide them against you.

Left Brains argument: I know you and you will not harm the containers to regain your seat so I will remain in power.

Right Brains Argument: I will divide the containers, father against son and mother against daughter. I get better when I perceive impossibility.
Left Brains argument: I rule over the containers and they serve me.

Right Brains Argument: Get thee behind me where you belong.

"Some are born to move the world

To live their fantasies
But most of us just dream about
The things we'd like to be
Sadder still to watch it die
Than never to have known it
For you, the blind who once could see
The bell tolls for thee..."
Losing It – RUSH

[Some are born to move the world, To live their fantasies] = Right brain is the ruler of the mind when the mind is at 50/50 harmony. Fantasies, denote right brain creativity a right brain trait.

[But most of us just dream about, The things we'd like to be] Left brain wishes and dreams it was as powerful as right brain and that jealousy festers and drives left brain mad.

[Sadder still to watch it die] = The ones who unveil right brain are filled with grief because they understand what the traditional education does to the children, veils their right brain traits. They watch right brain die, it becomes veiled.

[Than never to have known it] The ones who have their right brain veiled by traditional education and have no clue what is happening to the children because their heightened
awareness and intuition of right brain is veiled thus the comment ignorance is bliss. They are blind to the mental slaughter of the children. Ones who get the traditional education had their right brain veiled before it even developed so "never to have known it".

[For you, the blind who once could see The bell tolls for thee...]
Means the children were able to see, had right brain at 50% then they got the traditional education and it veiled their right brain, so they are the blind but once could see. Simply put if you sense time you are the blind that once could see, so bell tolls for thee.
Apparently now I see wisdom in Canadian bacon commercials as well as Swiss cheese commercials. It is interesting because although

the beings who wrote these lyrics are perhaps not in nirvana they are still using some little voice of right brain to create those lyrics, creativity,

so sometimes a person says things and they have one thing in mind and then when a person who has right brain unveiled fully can interpret those lyrics. Everything is relative to the observer so I notice at times people who certainly do not have right brain unveiled will say things and it is wisdom but they do not even know it is. So one could look at it like right brain shows itself in everyone but when it is unveiled fully it shines brightly. The proof is if there was a psychologist or any kind of Doctor that fully understood written language veiled right brain and left a person's mind unsound and thus a dangerous state they would have spoken up by now. If there was any leader in the world who understood that they would have spoken up by now. If there was any religious leader in the world that understood what the tree of knowledge was literally they would have spoken up by now. If any human rights group in the world understood what written language did to the mind of children they would have spoken up by now, so none of them have a clue and they are nothing but the blind leading the blind. Proof is in the arrangement of the words not the credentials attached to those words. I am open minded to the fact that I just accidentally discovered firsthand the mental unwanted side effects of the written language and I am just reporting it and someone in a position of authority will look into it and apply the fear not remedy and will find it is truth and report on it and then traditional education can be adjusted and nothing much will change outside of that. I am also open minded to the fact I am going to be butchered for writing these books and since I am on the fence about both of those possibilities I will just keep writing until my heart stops. - 6:44:25 PM

7:23:55 PM – [Isaiah 3:25 Thy men shall fall by the sword, and thy mighty in the war.] This comment is using the word men relative to the ones who get the education and do not

apply the fear not remedy, the left brain influenced beings. Mighty denotes strong ego which is pride which is a symptom of the left brain influenced. For example these "men" will kill someone over a word or even their self because their pride is so great. So the catch word is the ones who apply the remedy call their self "nothing" and that denotes nirvana or nothingness which is neutral so the mighty denotes the ones who have an ego. I suggest I have an infinite ego so if someone suggests I am just egotistical I will see that as compliment and if someone says I have an infinite ego I can suggest we see eye to eye.

"As for me, all I know is that I know nothing." – Socrates

This is great humor. If one is in nothingness it means they know everything. So Socrates is really saying all I know is everything because right brain is so powerful it just knows everything. It's relative to heightened awareness and it is relative to intuition. Right brain is aware of everything but not on a verbal level as a much as a cerebral level, would be the best way to look at it. For example Abraham knew everything Einstein knew but Einstein was just a show off and I make Einstein look humble. I am an infinite show off and I have an infinite ego and I think it has to do with being in the 9th circle of hell, treason for so long. I was suicidal for many years and I am mindful that has some kind of value to it although that may sound strange to some. Now one with a sense of time will say if you know everything tell me something that will make me lots of money because they are off in some reverse world of false values. They perhaps are not mindful I am telling them the method to unveil their right brain and that is the most valuable information in the universe, but perhaps that never occurs to them. I am mindful if Einstein understood what written education did to the mind he would have at least written one book about it so I try to associate myself with people to give myself contrast. I try to make everyone look like me. I give everyone the benefit of the doubt. A better way to look at it is I am in nothingness so I try and find attachment or something to contrast myself with. I go into chat rooms and suggest what I am mindful about traditional language and I get spit on and insulted and called insane and crazy so I am mindful most beings seriously do not know what I know so to keep myself in check I just say I have an infinite ego. I am mindful I could start a cult. I am mindful

I could start a following. I am mindful of all those temptations that go along with that so to counter act that I say stay away from me and let me write my books and if you figure something out from reading them that's your business. I am mindful there are many suicidal and depressed beings in the world as a result of the "conditioning" and that last thing I want is for some money making machine to label me as special or like they are, and reduce that depressed persons self esteem even further and at the same time the name of my game is to walk people into the 9th circle of hell which is treason because that is the only way out of hell. The deeper reality is people who are already suicidal are in the 9th circle of hell, treason, so they do not need my assistance to get there, so all I can say to them is you are on the right track but before you go for broke at least consider seeing if a scary place or spooky situation will kill you and maybe you will apply the remedy without actually killing yourself. To clarify if you are already suicidal before you get a gun or take pills find a spooky place and go there being mindful you want to die anyway and when your mind says a spooky thing is coming to kill you just close your eyes and say "I don't care", then you will find you will feel better very shortly. Don't let the sinister defeat you. Avoid listening to the opinions of the numb nuts that put you in that mental situation to begin with, with their delusions of teaching you wisdom with their "wisdom" education. You suicidal beings are the most valuable of the lot you just perhaps are not aware of it consciously, after all you are the meek. - 7:55:00 PM

9:43:54 PM – I am certain I should not have published the previous 13 volumes, but I doubt it.

1/10/2010 9:09:05 AM – "Never forget that only dead fish swim with the stream." - Malcolm Muggeridge

Going with the flow is not the same as going with the herd. Agreeing with the majority oft means you are not thinking for yourself. Blindness is contagious so keep your distance. One that understands they are wrong ponders how to be right.

1/11/2010 6:52:10 AM - God speed is relative to [1 Peter 4:5 …
the quick and the dead.] Right brain is very fast relative to left brain
which is slothful in contrast. This perhaps has more to do with
right brain being random access processing compared to left brain
sequential access.

In Zombie genre movies the zombies are always depicted as slow
and slothful. A zombie is in fact the living dead. They once were
alive but then they got zombie disease and now they are the living
dead so they show symptoms of being alive but in reality they are
dead. In some zombie movies the zombies want to eat brains. This
is in line with when a person gets the education they are under the
influence of left brain, a zombie, and then they have a child and want
that child's brain which represents mind, to become slothful like they
are. So the zombies want to turn everyone into a zombie.

[Revelation 20:13 And the sea gave up the dead which were in it;
and death and hell delivered up the dead which were in them: and
they were judged every man according to their works.]

The sea gave up its dead denotes the dead number like a grains in
the sea and in zombie movies there are always lots of zombies and
very few "quick", ones who applied the remedy, and are no longer
zombies. [and death and hell delivered up the dead which were in
them] This comment is saying death is the left brain influenced state
of mind one is in after the traditional education and hell is that state
of mind and so they are known as the dead, the living dead. So in
the zombie movies the ones who are not zombies are very quick
and they feel no emotions when they are killing all of the zombies,
in fact it is just a sport to kill the zombies. Kill perhaps means to
wake up the ones with sense of time, the zombies. The ones who
are not zombies in the zombie movies look at killing the zombies
as no big deal because the zombies are portrayed as simply the dead
and it is not a big deal to kill something that is already dead. Oft in
the zombie movies there is a scene where they say "They are not
alive so it is okay to kill them." So in actual reality there are no real
zombies so these movies symbolize the ones with a sense of time,
the zombies, and the ones who have no sense of time, the quick. This
is a good example of how slothful and blind the ones with a sense
of time are because the ones with a sense of time certainly have

watched zombie movies and perhaps cheered for the ones who kill the zombies but they are blind to the fact the zombies are them, in these movies.

So in these zombie movies there are all the various ways to kill zombies and all the various traits of the zombies and the goal of the movie is to kill as many zombies as one can to save the world from the zombies, the ones with a sense of time. Of course at times in the movie the quick, get bitten by the zombies and are killed by the zombies. One might suggest many in the ancient texts got bitten by the zombies and died.

[Revelation 21:8   But the fearful, and unbelieving, and the abominable, and murderers, and whoremongers, and sorcerers, and idolaters, and all liars, shall have their part in
the lake which burneth with fire and brimstone: which is the second death.]

[the fearful] relative to this comment [2 Timothy 1:7 For God hath not given us the spirit of fear; but of power, and of love, and of a sound mind.]
[the fearful] = [the spirit of fear] and this of course is simply relative to the fact when the mind is bent to left from traditional education the hypothalamus turns up ones fear to a great volume so they are called the fearful.
[and unbelieving] = Are ones who got the education and have a sense of time as a result and can never make the mental connection that all that sequential based, left brain education has made them mentally unsound so they are trapped forever in hell, the left brain state because they won't apply the fear not remedy if they do not believe the traditional education harmed them mentally, bent their mind to the left.
[and the abominable] Is simply a mentally unsound person who got the education and did not apply the remedy. Abominable simply means of very bad quality which is not an absolute comment it relates to the fact a person has their mind bent to the left as a result of traditional education and so they are slothful and are no longer acting normal relative to a sound minded human being who applies

the remedy. So although one is an abomination after they get the traditional education there is a remedy, so fear not is of course the remedy, to commit mental suicide, deny one's self and then they are no longer an abomination or of poor mental quality.

[and whoremongers] A whoremonger is one who frequents prostitutes relative to [Leviticus 19:29 Do not prostitute thy daughter, to cause her to be a whore; lest the land fall to

whoredom, and the land become full of wickedness.] This is a person who not only got lots of traditional education they make sure all the children get traditional education and

they go around and brag why every person needs lots of traditional education like a person who says "Without traditional education you cannot live in today's world." So these kinds of people love the whore, traditional education and they are far too mentally damaged to know what they say any longer. It has never been about written language itself as much as how it is applied, to a six year old child, with punishment attached to it if that child does not do well at the written education, that is what the problem is. The age it is given and the punishment attached to it, so it is reduced to just being brain washing or bending that child's mind to the left.

[and sorcerers] This is a person who gets traditional education, becomes a scribe in turn and then goes around making lots of money based on the ancient texts by suggesting supernatural. An easy way to find one of these beings is to simply go to any religious service on the planet and if they do not discuss the tree of knowledge as being written education and the fear not, deny one's self remedy at least for a moment during that service they are nothing but false prophet, lying whoremonger, money focused abomination, sorcerers. I am mindful I just described organized religion essentially. Many beings give their money to a being who not only has not applied the fear not remedy, still has a sense of time, has never even suggested the fear not remedy or why the fear not remedy is important and so that are just being hoodwinked by a sorcerer.

[and idolaters] These are beings have not applied the remedy and idolize the ones who have applied the remedy. None of the beings in the ancient texts want you to idolize them they want you to apply the fear not, deny one's self remedy. None of them ever said "Idolize me" in fact they say have no idols but the Lord and that Lord is right brain

so one should first thrown down their nets and apply the remedy. It says seek the kingdom first, and the kingdom is right brain. They never suggested ever, Idolize me, they

suggested apply the remedy so you are not mentally unsound and running around mentally raping all the children with the written education and not even being aware you are doing that. The places of worship are places to assist ones to apply the fear not remedy, not places to idolize the ones who have applied the remedy. Perhaps you should go ask your cult leader if that is truth since you are no longer mentally viable and thus unable to think for yourself because you have not applied the fear not remedy and neither has your cult leader. Perhaps you should go ask the blind what blindness is.

[and all liars] A liar is simply a being who has been mentally bent so far to the left they will climb mountains to exclaim how wise they are because they got all of that traditional education and exclaim how wise anyone will be after they get all that traditional education. They are the ones who tell a child it is stupid because it cannot sequentially arrange letters in proper order, spell well. They are the teachers of the traditional education because they are the focal point of the education. They are the judges of the children. They are trained to make sure every child gets "educated" properly. These teachers dedicate their entire life to making sure all the children get "educated" properly under their wing. Go ask a teacher if education in fact mentally harms children and they will say "No possible way it can harm a child or I would not teach it." and you will know what a liar is.

So all of these comments made in this scripture are all referring to the various kinds of people who get the education and do not apply the fear not remedy. These beings are the dead, the zombies, there are just various types of them but at the end of the day they all sense time, they all have their mind bent far to the left, they all represent sloth and so they are all of the beast and fruits of the tree of knowledge, which is mental death and untruth and so they know not what they do.

So this comment: [Revelation 21:8 But the fearful, and unbelieving, and the abominable, and murderers, and whoremongers, and sorcerers, and idolaters, and all liars, shall have their part in the lake which burneth with fire and brimstone: which is the second death.]
Is just saying the ones with a sense of time are in hell, the lake of fire and brimstone, the place of suffering, because sense of time denotes one who is mentally unsound as a result of that all that sequential based education they got as a child. I was pondering the numbers relative to a realistic view of how many people could actually apply this remedy just to get an idea of how many are "doomed" to remain in the mental hell.

I used some rough numbers from the ancient texts. Jesus spoke to five thousand and out of that five thousand he came away with twelve disciples or at least convinced twelve to attempt the remedy. So 12 divided by 5000 gives one a ratio of .0024. So six billion multiplied by .0024 gives 14400000. [Revelation 14:1 And I looked, and, lo, a Lamb stood on the mount Sion, and with him an hundred forty and four thousand, having his Father's name written in their foreheads.] [Revelation 14:3 And they sung as it were a new song before the throne, and before the four beasts, and the elders: and no man could learn that song but the hundred and forty and four thousand, which were redeemed from the earth.]
Jehovah's Witnesses distinctly believe that only 144,000 people will be raised to heaven, and will thus spend eternity with God. In the Mayan calendar, 144,000 represents a cycle of time named Baktun. Baktun is 20 cycles of the Mayan long calendar.

Avoid getting depressed about these numbers because at the end of the day you decide if you want to apply the remedy or not so avoid thinking people are chosen to apply the remedy because people their self decide to apply the fear not remedy or not, perhaps. This remedy is not difficult to apply and is in fact physiologically painless, it is simply a mental self control exercise applied in one second in the right situation. Right situation would be in a place where that hypothalamus gives one the death signal and then one just ignores it, that's a nice way of saying you are doomed. So attempt to deny your infinite self esteem issues and understand this remedy is simply mental self control and it is painless and so you have as good of a chance to apply the remedy as anyone does so do not allow your infinite self esteem issues caused by being in your unsound state of mind to defeat you. You make the choice no one else does, this remedy is a personal choice and so you rest on your choices and no one else has a say in your decision to apply this remedy but you because we are all free. The rule of thumb is you focus on the log of fear in your eye and do the best you can to apply this remedy and understand you may not accomplish it on the first try so never expect it to work but just be mindful to experiment and keep trying. Any way you look at it when it does take, right brain will unveil about a month later so the best thing to do is over compensate and seek out the most spooky place you can find and start there. That way the chances of the hypothalamus giving you that death signal is going to be high, but avoid jumping in shark frenzies. Jehovah's Witnesses distinctly believe that only 144,000 people will be raised to heaven, and will thus spend eternity with God. Raised to heaven means one unveils right brain, the kingdom, and eternity denotes no sense of time which is a symptom one has unveiled right brain. Many of the religious cults are saying the right things but their definitions of the words are perhaps improper.

Right brain = the image of god in man

Heaven = the state of mind one is in after they unveil right brain, sound mind.

The log of fear in your mind is the door you have to tear down to get to heaven, sound mind and thus get out of hell, unsound mind.

"Yes, there are two paths you can go by
But in the long run
There's still time to change the road you're on."
Led Zeppelin - Stairway to Heaven

If you are breathing there is time to apply the remedy because in the right situation it only takes one second, one thought. When the hypothalamus in the right situation says "Run like the wind the shadow of death is coming" you think "No." And that is the fear not remedy so avoid thinking it is some lifelong profession, it is a split second mental self control aspect and then it is done. My purpose is not to become a motivational speaker so I digress. My purpose is to reduce you to ashes so then I can kick the ashes and see if anything rises from them. My purpose is to reduce your temple, your sense of time state of mind, to ashes. My purpose is to convince you to go to the 9th circle of hell, treason as swiftly as possible with the understanding once you are there you may not factually make it out alive and you have a slight chance of walking through the door that is in the 9th circle of hell, treason. Your chances of going to the 9th circle of hell and surviving are slim to none.

This is what happens in the 9th circle of hell unless one gets lucky. [K. H. (25) allegedly committed suicide at his home] My only purpose is to convince you to go to the 9th

circle of hell so I find it difficult you would ever assume I am a motivational speaker unless your definition of motivational is I am attempting to convince you to commit

mental suicide and because you are mentally unsound you may just perhaps commit literal suicide once in the 9th circle of hell. That is the price you have to deal with because ones you trusted decided to make you wise with years of sequential based education with many trinkets and punishments attached if you did not do well in achieving all that left brain sequential education. I did not put you in hell all the ones you trust and all the ones you idolize put you in hell. All the ones you believe wanted to help you put you in hell so I am not here to help you I am here to mentally destroy you and destroy your temple and reduce you to ashes and thus cast you into the 9th circle of hell, treason. Perhaps what I suggest with this fear not remedy is against the law because perhaps the law is against the truth. The exact same entity that suggests morals and righteousness with their laws is the exact same entity that put you in hell to begin with as a child, so obviously I stand apart from them. I am not concerned if six billion beings suggest the fear not remedy is unrighteous.. I am not concerned if six billion beings suggest the spirit of what I speak of is not righteous. I am fully aware of what the sinister will say about the light. I am fully aware of what the sinister does to the light. I am fully aware of what the sinister did to your light when you were a child. I do not need you to agree with me because I am not even listening to your opinion because you sense time so I am already fully aware of what your opinion is. I do not want to know what your opinion is about the spirit of what I suggest. You either apply the remedy or you do not but your opinion about the spirit of what I suggest before you apply the remedy means nothing to me at all, ever, into infinity.

[A. M. (31) died days after he hung himself in his jail cell.] Since you sense time your tendency is to hang yourself in your mental jail cell so it is best you keep your mouth shut and apply the remedy or not apply the remedy. You do not need to talk, you need to apply the remedy, and if you do not wish to apply the remedy there is no point in you talking. Since you have a sense of time there is nothing you could possibly say that would come anywhere near speaking truth. You cannot speak truth because you sense time and thus are under the influence of the sinister, left brain, and so when you speak you just speak lies. I am not asking you to come to my worship service to give me money because I do not need the support of the darkness to fulfill my purpose. I have applied the remedy, by accident, so I certainly do not need or want your assistance, and when you apply the remedy you will find I cannot help you, so you do not need my assistance. Applying the remedy means you are mindfully deciding to jump into a pack of wolves that are infinitely hungry and they love to eat children the most. So I accidentally jumped into a pack of wolves that love to eat children and since you sense time you are one of those wolves and so you cannot possibly saying anything to me that is going to make me forget you love to eat innocent children and then brag about it. Do you think I pander to the words of mental rapists of innocent children? Do you think I pander to the laws and morals of mental rapists of innocent children? Do you think there is a grain of sand worth of mercy in my being towards mental rapists of innocent children? You can stone me to death but I will never pander to the ways of mental rapists of innocent children. My ways are not your ways and my days are not your days and they never will be and they never have been. You can only speak evil since you sense time. [Matthew 12:34 O generation of vipers, how can ye, being evil, speak good things? for out of the abundance of the heart the mouth speaketh.]

How are you suppose to speak truth when you are just lies? I do not want to hear your attempts at reason and logic because if you were capable of reason you would not be mentally raping children on an industrial scale to begin with. I use the word mentally rape innocent children to describe your ways but in reality it is mentally killing children but because I am mindful your mental faculties are at ten percent I use to the word rape and then you think "It cannot be like rape" and that is because your mental faculties are at ten percent. Do you perceive I am trying to make friends or perceive I am here for the war? I am here to convince you to mentally kill yourself so it is not possible I am concerned about making friends. I am not here to encourage you to continue to mentally rape innocent children I am here to silence you all together. If you have any problem with the spirit of what I suggest or the spirit of what I suggest breaks any rules or laws, I am right here and do not forget your death shroud because my name is death shroud fitter. A monk once said about me shortly after the accident, "He is quite an angry one isn't he." That humor in that comment is beyond your understanding.

[Exodus 32:19 And it came to pass, as soon as he came nigh unto the camp, that he saw the calf(traditional education/ written language], and the dancing (ones under the influence of left brain, the scribes who didn't apply the fear not remedy) and Moses' anger waxed hot(spitting blood from the heightened awareness), and he cast the tables out of his hands, and brake them beneath the mount(all bets are off, rules and laws mean nothing in this battle).] If you or your cult leader understood one sentence of these ancient texts I will remind you. - 9:50:32 AM

10:40:30 AM – [Exodus 32:19 And it came to pass, as soon as he came nigh unto the camp, that he saw the calf, and the dancing: and Moses' anger waxed hot, and he cast the tables out of his hands, and brake them beneath the mount.] This comment is an indication that Moses was not feeling this heightened awareness "anger" because of expected or understood realities of living. For example a person might get cancer or a person might have a birth defect and so that is an understood reality of living. Moses was not feeling this anger

116

waxing because of things beyond his control. Moses was feeling this anger waxing because written language when taught improperly ruins the mind and that is something that is not like cancer or a thing he could not doing anything about. In that respect it all comes back to ignorance. If a person does not believe years of sequential based written education bends the mind to the left they are infinitely ignorant and in turn they are damaging children because they are ignorant and that is avoidable. It is one thing to look at impermanence, death and understand that is a reality for everyone so one cannot become angry with that, and it is another thing to mentally rape children into hell because one is ignorant about the mental side effects of pushing a sequential based man made invention on that child at such a young age. There is a concept about "let me not be bothered about things I cannot change." So [Moses' anger waxed hot] not because of something he could not change but because of something he could change but the people who got the written education we mentally unsound and were simply way

to ignorant to even be able to mentally grasp they were harming children mentally when they did not have to be mentally harming children. Written education factually bends the mind to the left to the point ones sense time and that is the proof the right brain paradox is veiled and so written education, traditional education, factually mentally harms innocent children but relative to ones who have their mind bent to the left they cannot grasp that factual reality so they are out of touch with reality and that is what ignorance is.

So after you apply the remedy you will have moments of anger waxing which means you will mentally be ripped apart because you are aware lunatics are harming innocent children with their wisdom education when it does not have to be that way. The first thoughts that will come to your head is, 'I will wage literal war on them with weapons and kill them all for doing this to children." I have pondered that reality because it is factually proper to stop lunatics who are harming innocent children. But the deeper reality is even if that is done the children will still be mentally raped by the lunatic's because there are too many lunatics. Jesus was fully aware of that reality and so was John.

[1 John 2:18 Little children, it is the last time: and as ye have heard that antichrist shall come, even now are there many antichrists; whereby we know that it is the last time.]

John was saying I cannot find a way to stop the ones with a sense of time from harming you little children. This is why Jesus said focus on the log in your eye because the beast is far too strong now. On a world wide scale the sinister has won but on an individual scale the sinister does not have to win in everyone. A better way to look at it is when you apply the remedy the heightened awareness is going to shred you mentally as a being but your right brain will turn that anger waxing into a blessing where you will purge or ignore those emotions and in turn get even better at concentration. So this anger waxing is not what a person with a sense of time can relate to at all. It is not anger it is the intuition of right brain being aware children are being mentally raped and the random access aspect of right brain can come to the final conclusion that person cannot stop it and so one is mentally shredded. The being is mindful there is no solution to this mental raping of children but they continue to try and find a solution but all their calculations always end up with, there is no solution and that is what creates the anger waxing, grief. So sometimes beings who apply the remedy destroy their self because they cannot stand that heightened awareness, anger waxing reality. So this reality may lead one to avoid the battle but one who applies the remedy cannot ever escape the heightened awareness. This is why Socrates was told by a friend he could escape jail and Socrates said "Where can I run?" One cannot run from heightened awareness. So this is complex because for example a native tribe in the Amazon never got the written education and they have the heightened awareness but they are not aware of what is happening to children in civilization as a result of the traditional education so they always have a smile on their face so they are ignorant to what is happening and they are not even aware there is a curse or bad side effects of written education because they never got it. This is why Moses was in civilization, he got the written education and then he broke free, or applied the remedy, and then left civilization and then fought civilization. So only beings who got the written education can apply the remedy and wake up, unveil right brain and when they do they are against the ways of civilization relative only to the methods of written education used by civilization. If I never had written education taught to me improperly I never would have become suicidal and depressed, and then I never would have accidentally applied the fear not remedy, so then I would not be writing books attempting to bring down civilizations ways by exposing its education methods as nothing but mental rape of anyone who gets that education, veiling the right brain. If I never got written education taught the way it was taught I would be totally ignorant to its bad side effects. If I would have taken a few more pills I would have died in that last suicide attempt so I would have remained ignorant to the fact written education directly put me in a mental state that made be become suicidal. So focusing on the log of fear in your eye really means the curse caused by the traditional education cannot be stopped. One can attempt to be optimistic but once they apply the remedy and start coming up to full power relative to heightened awareness they will come back to reality relative to the spread of this curse on the species. It all comes back to the understanding the leader scribes in civilization are not going to come out and tell six billion people they mentally ruined them as a result of forcing written education on them directly or indirectly when they were a child because the people in civilization would never ever trust the rulers of civilization again. All the laws and rules of civilization would be negated if the rulers of civilization said "We mentally factually bent your mind so far to the left unknowingly by teaching you written education improperly you may never be able to restore the sound mind you had before you got our "brand" of education." So you got raped mentally so badly as a child by the ruler scribes because they got raped mentally so badly as children by the ruler scribes that ruled over them that it is not even possible to compensate anyone so it is best to not tell anyone. Even if the ruler scribes understood factually the mental side effects of written education on the mind of a child they would not dare say anything because they would be hung out to dry. A parent whose child hung their self when they were 14 would grab a machine gun and mow every single person associated with education down, if they became aware the education being taught improperly is why their child hung their self because their child's mind was bent so far to the left the child emotions were turned up to dangerous levels. Would that parent be evil for doing that or would that parent be righteous for doing that? That is why the comment "eye for an eye" is mentioned in the ancient texts. People can spit on you and punch you and insult but that means nothing in contrast to raping you of your powerhouse right brain as a child under the guise of "wisdom education." You get your right brain veiled as a child so you are not even living any longer you are just a mental abomination living the life of a mental abomination but you are not living your life because your life was taken from you when right brain was veiled. If I come to your house when you are a child and take your right brain out of your head and give you 30 silver pieces for it you will have 30 silver pieces but you will not have a mental life to enjoy those 30 silver pieces so I took everything you have even though I gave you 30 silver pieces. How one lives after their right brain is veiled is not how one lives if their right brain was never veiled so that person is dead to their self because they are only acting how a person who has their right brain veiled lives and that is not how they were born so they are living a false life. A child is born with a mentally sound mind and then they get education and from that point on they are not longer living at all they are just a mental abomination seeking to find life they perhaps will never find again. So they are robbed of their life, liberty and pursuit of happiness.

"For you, the blind who once could see
The bell tolls for thee..."
Losing It – RUSH

Even if I was ruler of the world that does not mean you will be able to apply the remedy so there is no point in that. The best I could do as ruler of the world is adjust the education teaching methods but that will not save you because you already got the traditional education. Because of this you are in a mind trap and there is nothing that is going to get you out of that mind trap but you. Nothing is going to get you out of hell but you and the reality of that is you have to go to the 9th circle of hell, treason, to get out. Past is past simply means don't take it personal but you are screwed because the last thing in the universe you want to do is freely commit mental suicide, deny yourself, find the shadow of death and fear not when you find that shadow of death. Because of that reality I cannot associate with you or be your friend because I would destroy myself trying to save one who cannot be saved. So now you understand why out of six billion, 14,400,000 is infinitely optimistic and that is why to have any chance in the hell you are in, you would be infinitely wise to thrown down your nets and drop everything you perceive is of value and attempt to apply this remedy because whatever your nets are, is not what you are and whatever your net is, is not what it should be. I want you to be mindful this book is not under the fiction section. - 11:40:06 AM

Fixer - http://www.youtube.com/watch?v=vc3ynEAooEU

3:46:31 PM – When one applies the remedy and unveils right brain they are given their marching orders. [Mark 1:13 And he was there in the wilderness forty days, tempted of
Satan; and was with the wild beasts; and the angels ministered unto him.]

[and the angels ministered unto him.] So Jesus applied the dunking under water fear not remedy and he got his marching orders. This is not uniform. Marching orders vary and there is no way to tell what ones marching orders are going to be. This is why ones who apply this remedy do not usually flock together so to speak because everyone gets different marching orders. Some get orders to go be creative and paint pictures to explain this remedy, some to make movies to explain this remedy, some to write poetry and stories to explain this remedy and some get the marching orders to go to battle. It is easy to relate to the fact Jesus got "go unto the world and speak the remedy" orders. Abraham and Lots orders were to fight [Genesis 19:13 For we will destroy this place, because the cry of them is waxen great before the face of the LORD; and the LORD hath sent us to destroy it.]

[and the LORD hath sent us to destroy it.] Why were they sent to destroy the cities? Because [the angels ministered unto him.] Some get orders to say nothing and they remain in silence. On the deepest level right brain knows what it is doing so everyone who applies the remedy gets the proper orders and the orders are not always what one wants to do but that is their orders. Two months after the accident a thought came to me to write infinite books that will take me the rest of my life so that's my orders. At times now that I have right brain unveiled I want to go experience life with right brain unveiled but I will only end up writing books in my mind and eventually I will end up back in my isolation chamber writing those thoughts down. Some are called to be speakers and so they may write a book or two but eventually they will be orators and speak in front of people and even if they write a few books they will end up back as an orator. Some of the disciples became writers and were more about writing than oration. Since one never knows what their orders will be, anyone who applies the remedy will never find fault with the orders another person who has applied the remedy gets. Some are chosen to fight and so I cannot find fault with that because they do not find fault that my orders are to write. Among the ones who apply the remedy they have no time, so to speak, to worry about

what others who have applied the remedy do because when it comes down to it the ones who apply the remedy, the ones with no sense of time, are outnumbered millions to one.

Because of this there is not really any infighting among the ones who have applied the fear not remedy. The complexity is the heightened awareness makes one aware of one's who

have applied the remedy so they do not even have to actually communicate or meet because they are all mindful of each other. I submit it is hard to grasp that reality and it

perhaps is even harder to believe that reality but again the right brain is unnamable in power once unveiled. I perceive every day, relative to clock, I will not be able to top what I understood the previous day and I always do yet I still perceive I won't be able to top what I understood the previous day. I cannot perceive how I can possibly reduce this whole situation to the fact a person of sound mind invented written language and in learning written language it veiled right brain and thus made our species of unsound mind. Even having said that I continue to write another sentence and that is because there is no end to the progression because right brain only seeks to come to further understandings regardless of everything else. This is why it is so dangerous for ones who have not unveiled right brain, ones who sense time, to ever get into a literal battle with ones who have unveiled right brain because right brain does not even notice defeat at all or a better way to look at it is right brain gets better when it perceives it cannot possibly win. That goes against all the norms of traditional combat tactics. Traditional combat tactics suggest one should quit if they are outnumbered but right brain prefers to be outnumbered. On a mental level it is certainly in the realm of possibility right brain creativity invented written language to veil right brain to give right brain a challenge and the people are not even considered in that challenge so they are reduced to being pawns in this challenge. Right brain has no one left to fight but itself. Right brain has never lost against left brain in a 50/50 contest so it is left to fight itself because it only seeks further understandings into infinity or it does not ever perceive it wins or loses. An easier way to look at it is right brain cannot stand sloth or boredom so it will do anything to avoid that. A parent might notice their small child is hyper and making crayon drawings on the wall and tearing up the house and determine that child is totally out of control but in reality that child's right brain will not rest or relax ever because right brain is contrary to sloth. A hyper active child is just a child with right brain unveiled to a degree and an adult who got the education and has right brain veiled will see that child as hyper but that child does not see itself as hyper so a parent will say "calm down" to that child because that adult only understands left brain sloth because their right brain is veiled. So that adult will take that child to a psychologist to try and calm that child down because that adult unknowingly hates right brain because all that adult is, is a left brain influenced container, a person with a sense of time, and thus a person who has right brain veiled could not write a book as fast as one who has right brain unveiled even if their life depended on it because left brain is sloth in contrast to right brain. It is not about the people it is about what influence they are under. The majority of the problems in civilization are a symptom civilization keeps veiling everyone's right brain with it wisdom education. There is no such thing as a left brain influenced sane being. There never was and there never will be, a left brain influenced being is a being who has had their right brain veiled because of all the sequential based left brain education. A person who is born with a sound mind both hemispheres at 50/50 cannot possibly veil one hemisphere or the other if they just sat in a vacuum for their whole life. A person can only get their right brain veiled if they are put through an intensive mental conditioning aspect that punishes them for exhibiting right brain traits and rewards them for exhibiting sequential left brain traits.

School is based on rules and on sequencing and when a person does those left brain traits properly they get good grades and praised by their teacher and their parents and any student that does not follow every rule and passes every spelling test gets punished by the teacher and their parents. So traditional education has nothing to do with wisdom, education or becoming smarter it only has to do with veiling right brain and after it is veiled one has to commit mental suicide to unveil it and because that person is terrified because the hypothalamus is sending magnified signals of fear that person may never ever be able to unveil right brain again. Because of that difficulty in applying the remedy after right brain has been veiled there are no rules or laws relative to this battle and if anyone thinks there are rules or laws relative to this battle they need to go sit in a cemetery until they feel better. Civilization only has one law and that is every child is going to get their "brand" of education so all of civilizations rules and laws are null and void, factually. Every one of their laws after that do not matter because their first law is to rape children mentally into hell using their "brand" of education. So all this commotion about morals and following the law only shows one is so blind they agree with mentally raping innocent children into factual hell. All you have to do is call me and let me know you are pleased to mentally rape children into hell, veil their right brain using written education, and I will make it a priority to assist you to get over your fear of death swiftly and completely and then I will write in my poorly disguised thick pamphlet diaries how neutral I feel about that. I do not want to hear "yeah but" because I eat "yeah

124

but" for no reason at all. Granted that didn't come out right, but I doubt it. If you find many contradictions and spelling errors and simply misplaced words in this volume you will know I no longer even proof read the books anymore before I publish them. I do not have enough ego left to bother to proof read these books well and I have no faith people with a sense of time will understand one single sentence I write at this stage since the accident. I am devouring my old self by being oblivious to my old self. I am mindful spelling all the words properly is not going to bring anyone with a sense of time over the brink so they rush out to commit mental suicide so grammar no longer matters at all. Civilization will suggest grammar does matter and they also say raping all the children into mental hell matters as well and I deny both of those comments so I am contrary to whatever civilization is. There is only one right reality and so we have two conflicting realities and all the might in the universe does not mean ones reality is right because there is only one right reality regardless of how many perceptions of reality are involved. There is only one truth and so all the might in the universe does not mean the truth on that might's side is truth. In fact truth is always the minority relative to the reality of written language. You may perceive one religion has it right and the others do not but in reality the religious texts have it right but the religious text follower's majority have it all improper. There is no flaw in any of the ancient texts but blind people are reading them and getting them all improper. One has to apply the fear not, deny one's self, submit remedy to understand the texts and ones who do apply said remedy perhaps no longer need the texts. Because of that the texts are perhaps simply traps to ensnare the sinister, the ones with a sense of time. I am not reading the ancient texts to figure out how to apply the remedy because I already applied the remedy accidentally. I am simply reading them to come to further understandings about them.

[I. L. (18) committed suicide by hanging after battling with Depression, Bipolar Disorder and Anhedonia]
You already should be aware depression is simply a symptom one has their right brain veiled so sorrow thoughts cannot pass through their mind swiftly enough because the lightning fast processing

speed of right brain is veiled. Bipolar is simply one who goes from extreme depression to extreme manic behavior swiftly and neither of those thoughts are possible to maintain when right brain is unveiled because right brain is skipping around with its random access thoughts so swiftly, so one always ends up in neutral.

Anhedonia is an inability to experience pleasure from normally pleasurable life events such as eating, exercise, social interaction or sexual activities. What this condition is in reality is a person who has right brain unveiled to a degree and so they are already starting to show symptoms of the paradox or right brain but if right brain is not unveiled totally they may still have the emotions attached so things can go wrong. So since you do not understand English and I need filler I will discuss this condition relative to right brain paradox.

[inability to experience pleasure from normally pleasurable life events] does not even make any sense because in ability to experience pleasure is relative and normally pleasurable events is also relative to the observer. I drank nine shots of vodka and I felt no euphoria so that means a "normy" would have felt pleasure from that so I must have Anhedonia or perhaps I just tricked my mind into thinking I died and in that case I am just a spirit with its body still alive and in that case no human being on this planet will ever be as intelligent as I am. It is quite simple this inability to experience pleasure because inability means one feels nothing at all ever, is not possible. There are people who feel way too much and people who feel way too little but there needs to be a norm to give those ideals contrast. The paradox aspect in right brain allows one to taste food but one is unable to judge if the food is good or bad so the food taste goes to the cerebral cortex and its pleasure signal is neutral. So the food is always pleasurable but not to a degree one jumps up and down and not to the degree one kills their self when the pleasurable aspect is absent. It is not possible a person could have sex and feel no pleasure from it because if that was the case they would not be able to have sex but the degree of pleasure they get is relative. Sex when right brain in unveiled is in real time so pleasure comes and then goes so pleasure is not sustained in the mind so one is not depressed when it is absent. One cannot become a nymphomaniac because the paradox when right brain is unveiled leaves one in neutral about the whole experience of sex over a period of time.

So looking at this again [I. L. (18) committed suicide by hanging after battling with Depression, Bipolar Disorder and Anhedonia] This is saying this person could not feel satisfaction so they became depressed and manic which is feeling satisfaction and then they killed their self because they could not feel satisfaction. Some people feel satisfaction from being depressed and some people feel satisfaction from being manic. What really happened to this human being is they were showing symptoms of right brain being unveiled to a great degree and everyone around this being was telling this being he was bad, evil, messed up, abnormal, not normal, in need of drugs and this being decided it is better to kill himself than remain in the presence of insane idiots. So the deeper reality is civilization, the left brain influenced, always see right brain traits as evil and bad and they want to kill it, silence it. That is what really happened and that is the truth about what happened to this innocent child and if you do not understand that you need to go sit in a cemetery until you stop hallucinating out of your mind so you will stop killing innocent children unknowingly. I know what depression is and I assure you I know what depression is better than you and a billion of your friends will ever know and it is a symptom right brain is veiled and the thoughts of depression linger because right brain speed and random access is veiled and cannot process through the "sad" thoughts swiftly enough to keep the person from deciding depression is forever and then determining it is best to kill their self. You give this innocent child a pill to try to cure what you did to them mentally with your wisdom education, so you are nothing but a common monster and you should not be allowed around children let alone allowed to prescribe them pills. You killed this being because you saw the right brain traits they were exhibiting as bad or evil, and that is fact. You told this innocent child they are abnormal because they were exhibiting right brain traits so you factually killed this child because this child believed in you and your delusional attempts at truth. You should be stopped but I am deriving great pleasure in watching you suffer. You just believe if I say "kill" I am angry and if I say "love" I am happy because you are hallucinating because in reality I am neutral. I can make your blood pressure rise with my words and you cannot make my blood pressure rise even when I am mindful you are factually mentally raping innocent children on an industrial scale so you tell me who is of sound mind. Please be mindful this book is not listed under fiction. Brain dead mole cricket.

"Researchers theorize that anhedonia may result from the breakdown in the brain's reward system, involving dopamine pathways."
I am certain these researchers have a sense of time. The paradox in right brain is what keeps a person from having high blood pressure, becoming nervous, and also keeps a person from feeling rewards and thus feeling depressed when the rewards are not achieved and so this keeps a person on mental even ground so a person does not go up and down, up and down which is what bipolar is. A person with right brain unveiled may appear manic but that is only in contrast to a person who has right brain veiled because they are slothful in thoughts and in deeds. If a person has something physiologically wrong with their brain like a brain tumor that is one thing but if nothing is philologically wrong with their brain then this anhedonia is on strictly a mental level and a person who has a sense of time is factually bent to the left so they will always see a person who has right brain unveiled to a good degree, as mentally ill. Anyone who senses time has right brain veiled so much the paradox of right brain is never factored in the question, "How much time has passed" so they are factually mentally unsound as the result of all that left brain sequential education so first one has to address that instead of addressing all the symptoms of that and it just so happens some wise beings told you the remedy to that mentally unsound reality about 2500 years or more and that was, walk through the valley of the shadow of death and fear not evil. Which is fear not , which is deny one's self, and that corrects that ill functioning hypothalamus mentally back into working order and then one returns to sound mind.
So all of your research is nothing but vain attempts to come up with a better remedy to the tree of knowledge, when the perfect remedy to the tree of knowledge was told to you by mentally sound beings 2500 years ago. One cannot come up with a better remedy than

the fear not remedy so everything you do relative to research and psychology is nothing but vanity, every single thing. You are only interested in making money and you could really care less about the well being of people who are mentally suffering because of the traditional education being taught improperly, so who do you think you are kidding? I failed at suicide thirty times so I am trust worthy. - 6:01:50 PM

1/12/2010 9:52:03 AM – The paradox of right brain when it is unveiled affects everything and this paradox could also be looked at as ambiguity but in reality it is just one aspect but given two names. One right brain trait is paradox and another is ambiguity which is doubt but this in reality is not two aspects it is a sensation that keeps one from judgment relative to many aspects but also the senses, vision, taste, sense of touch for example. I can go out to eat and every single person I see I find no flaws in their appearance. I do not see people as fat or thin or black or white or Asian or long haired or short haired I see no flaws in any one of them. This is relative to the paradox and ambiguity relative to vision and that is relative to perception. One with a sense of time may look at a transient and automatically deduce from that vision aspect that person is bad because they have the paradox and ambiguity aspect veiled, they judge a book by a cover and judge is the operative word. The sense of time is proof they have the paradox and ambiguity aspect of right brain veiled and thus right brain veiled because they have not applied the ancient fear not remedy. This paradox aspect also applies to hearing relative to hearing music. This paradox aspect also applies to sense of taste and sense of time and sense of pain and sense of emotions. So one cannot do anything but experience parts when right brain is veiled. A parent will see their child and say "Comb your hair and put on some different clothes" because they are seeing parts and not the whole. This seeing part's is a form of suffering because many people attempt to find that perfect thing and they can never find it because everything is relative to the observer. A person may paint a picture and think it is perfect and then another person may see that picture and say it sucks. A person with a sense of time may put on their best clothes and go out and someone with a sense

of time may say that outfit sucks. A person who applies the remedy and unveils right brain has lost all ability to judge relative to seeing, hearing, tasting etc. All food tastes pleasing, all clothes are pleasing, all music is pleasing so there is no judgment because the paradox always factors into these perceptions. Buddha was reported to have said "Do not take the word of a blind man ask questions." All of the ancient beings who applied this remedy saw everyone around them as perfect relative to vision. From Socrates to Moses or Abraham to Lot to the disciples to Jesus, to John the Baptist, to Mohammed to Buddha so these beings were all messengers for right brain, the god image in man. The only way they could tell if people had applied the remedy to the tree of knowledge was for those people to ask questions and they also could observe their deeds or fruits. If you asked me based on my vision how many people have applied the remedy I would say every single person on the planet. I would say if I make it through this situation without having three billions wives it will be a miracle beyond all miracles because I do not see any flaws when I look at you so I have to stay away from you and stay in my isolation chamber or I will never write one sentence. I have to ignore what my eyes are suggesting and rely on right brain intuition and pattern detection so in that respect my eyes are blind and serve no purpose because they are unable to judge so I am a blind man. You having a sense of time may perceive that is unhealthy to be unable to judge with vision but I am not suffering when I am walking around looking at people because they all look perfect. I am not walking around thinking to myself 'that person is too fat or too thin or has too long of hair." You are thinking that when you walk around. You judge people in one second based on how they appear. You will see someone who is fat and determine they are not of value. You will see someone who has long hair and determine they are not of value. You will see someone with dirty
fingernails and determine they are not of value. You see people you think are ugly and people you think are pretty and your mind is judging everyone of them because your mind is unsound. You have a lot of clutter in your mind because of all these judgments relative to vision. Everything you see you judge, everything you taste you judge, everything you hear you judge and that creates lots of mental

clutter. You will become angry as the result of what you see, hear and taste. You will say "I cannot stand that music and I will not tolerate that music because it is evil or bad and I know it is." and so you could not be hallucinating more if you were on LSD. You will insult a waiter at a restaurant by telling them your food tastes horrible and you could not be hallucinating more than that. You are not a good judge you are just hallucinating and perceive you are a good judge. You would not support doing to children mentally what you do to children with your wisdom education if you were even in the ballpark of a good judge. You are only a good judge relative to a mentally unsound hallucinating monstrosity because you did not apply the fear not remedy mentioned in the ancient texts you have been declaring you understand because you still sense time and that is proof you have not applied the remedy. Until you apply the remedy you are still trapped in unsound mind, hallucination world and that will never change until you do apply the remedy. I do not perceive you are going to hell when you die if you do not apply the remedy, life will just be much easier for you because you need both aspects of your brain in the conscious state. So you need to forget about going to hell because if you sense time you are factually in hell mindfully. There is no other hell but the hell you were put in by the ones you trusted as

a child. Hell is seeing perfection as evil. Hell is seeing angels as demons. Hell is a state of mind one is in after they eat off the tree of knowledge and so they must deny their self because their self is that hell state of mind. I cannot find fault with anyone by looking at them although you want me to. I also cannot find fault with anyone's deeds because everyone is doing the best they can based on their mental state, although you want me to. You want me to hate what you hate, but I do not hate because I cannot mindfully maintain a state of hate because right brain ponders to fast to maintain a state of hate and you hate that because you are mentally in hell. I have never said you are in hell because you wanted to go to hell I am saying you are in hell because you were thrown in hell. I am suggesting you remain in hell because you are not aware you are in hell. I am suggesting your sense of time is proof you are in hell but if you do not believe that you will factually remain in hell. There are two people in a bed sleeping and they both hear the fear not remedy and one applies it and wakes up and the other does not apply it and remains sleeping. There are two people sleeping in a bed and one feels the sunshine as sunshine and wakes up and one feels the sunshine as darkness and remains sleeping. - 10:42:55 AM

11:31:45 AM – Plato was heavily influenced by Socrates and even called him his teacher and was very vocal about Socrates unjust death as Plato put it. One might suggest Jesus was not pleased with John the Baptist's unjust death and the disciples were not pleased with Jesus' unjust death at the hands of the ones that sense time. Socrates made it a point to suggest no true philosopher fears death and since Plato was Socrates student this shows that Plato applied the fear not remedy. Plato did lots of writing and from those writings civilization came away with many new topics such as philosophy, logic, rhetoric, mathematics and science. It appears Plato was all over the place relative to ones who sense time who tend to focus on one topic or area of study. Plato was not as much a master of all trades as he was a being that saw everything as one thing and then the ones with a sense of time saw his writing and labeled them and created all these new fields. So even though Plato despised the ones who sense time, civilization, who unjustly killed his teacher, civilization still took Plato's writings and called them their own. This is a classic example of how the ones of sound mind give freely and the wolves, the ones who sense time, take advantage of it. Plato despised the ones who sense time because they killed his teacher and they killed his teacher because his teacher was attempting to tell the children the dangers of the tree of knowledge.

Socrates said this [Luke 20:46 Beware of the scribes, which desire to walk in long robes, and love greetings in the markets, and the highest seats in the synagogues, and the chief rooms at feasts;]

And Socrates said this to the children
[Luke 20:46 Beware of the scribes, which desire to walk in long robes, and love greetings in the markets, and the highest seats in the synagogues, and the chief rooms at feasts;]

And then the ones with a sense of time, the scribes, said this:
[Luke 23:10 And the chief priests and scribes stood and vehemently accused him.]
And then they butchered Socrates, they made him drink hemlock, and then his student Plato praised Socrates and even named some of his books after Socrates the Socratic dialogues, and spoke out about how Socrates was killed unjustly and then the ones that sense time said "Socrates was one of us." They kill the light and then they say the light was of us.

Plato wrote another books called Apology of Socrates and Plato was one of those youth Socrates was killed for corrupting. Socrates told Plato no true philosopher fears death so Socrates told Plato to fear not, or walk through the valley of the shadow of death and fear not evil and Plato listened to him.

Plato and Crito, Critobolus, and Apollodorus offered to pay a fine on Socrates' behalf, in lieu of the death penalty proposed by Meletus.
They tried to save their teacher by paying off the beasts and the beasts would have nothing to do with it.

[Matthew 26:15 And said unto them, What will ye give me, and I will deliver him unto you? And they covenanted with him for thirty pieces of silver.]
The darkness is always going to kill the light because the light reveals to the darkness what the darkness is and it cannot stand to see it's self so it's only defense is to kill the light. If Plato would have offered 300 billion minas it would not have been enough because the darkness is going to destroyed by the light. Judas did not apply the fear not remedy so selling the light for thirty silver pieces seemed like a fair deal to him. Meletus was the main accuser of Socrates and Anytus was the prosecutor. One could easily change those names to Meletus was Herod and Anytus was Pontius Pilate. The story goes the people felt great guilt after Socrates was killed and so Anytus was banished from the city. Once Jesus was killed everyone realized they killed the light. Once the disciples were killed they realized they killed the light. Once John the Baptists head was cut off and put on a platter they realized they killed the light.

[Romans 11:3 Lord, they have killed thy prophets, and digged down thine altars; and I am left alone, and they seek my life.]

[and I am left alone, and they seek my life.]

The lambs are always surrounded by the wolves. So this being applied the fear not, deny one's self remedy and came to the understanding what every single human being in the history of mankind understood after they applied the remedy. I am left alone and they seek my life. It never has been about the people as much as it is about the darkness hates the light, the beast hates the children, and the devil hates God, the right brain, the image of god in man. Your belief or disbelief in that reality does not alter that reality so it just is reality. I only detect left brain influenced containers and right brain influenced containers, and the right brain influenced containers trying to defend the children from the vast armies of left brain influenced containers, and when they try that, the left brain influenced containers suggest the right brain influenced containers are evil, because the right brain containers are always trying to protect the children, born right brain influenced containers, from being turned into left brain influenced containers by the written education forced on them by the laws of the left brain influenced containers. The people are just containers and serve whichever master they are influenced by. The rule of thumb is the only left brain influenced containers on this planet are human beings who got the traditional education and did not apply the ancient fear not remedy. There are only containers that sense time, left brain influenced containers and ones who do not sense time, right brain influenced containers. All labels fall within those two labels. All tree's, people, have fruits relative to those two labels. So if you are even considering applying this ancient fear not remedy you get accustomed to this [and I am left alone, and they seek my life.] because it is not paranoia it is reality. It is acceptable if you wish to apply the remedy and then hide and keep your mouth shut about the dangers of the tree of knowledge to save yourself because I am mindful there is at least one that will carry that burden for you.

- 12:29:42 PM

Mongrel dog
Mutated sight
The sense of time took its sense of right.

Mongrel dog
Abnormal mind
Teaches its offspring its brand of blind
I hope I try to hope I try.

Mongrel Dog
Darkest pit
See's the light and can only spit

The goodness is not left
The goodness is not theft
That trail leads you away
That trail leads you astray
It's not left, It's not theft

You just can't keep on killing the light, blind your sight
You just can't just keep on killing the light, that's what's right
You just can't keep on killing the light, not in my fight
Keep on killing the light, not in my sight
Keep on killing the light, not in my fight
Keep on killing the light, not in my sight
You have no might, not in my fight

You have no might, not in my sight
You have no right, in my sight

Why do you not see what's true
Why do you not see what's true, I have a clue
Why do you not see what true
Take it for granted, your eyes are slanted
Why do you only see the night, why you do you only think it's sight.
You shouldn't take it for granted, your eyes are slanted.

Mongrel - http://www.youtube.com/watch?v=pMoJeLG_U9g

3:33:51 PM – The only way to properly look at the entire situation surrounding the tree of knowledge, written language, is to come to the understanding it was all a misunderstanding and then the misunderstanding becomes an understanding and so one progresses as a result of the misunderstanding. It is reported Mohammed suggested he was a messenger. This is an indication he was aware of the extreme potential for idolatry. One's who unveil right brain appear very wise in contrast to ones who do not unveil right brain so they are all mindful to avoid that because they are aware the ones who idolize them are only idolizing them because they have not applied the remedy and unveiled right brain.

[2 Chronicles 33:15 And he took away the strange gods, and the idol out of the house of the LORD, and all the altars that he had built in the mount of the house of the LORD,
and in Jerusalem, and cast them out of the city.]

[And he took away the strange gods, and the idol out of the house of the LORD] Mohammed certainly read these texts because he spoke of the prophets before him and what is interesting is many with a sense of time question if Jesus even existed but Mohammed proved Jesus existed because Mohammed agreed with Jesus and all the beings before Jesus, and associated with Jesus. So Mohammed did not want to show his picture, and suggested he was a messenger to avoid idolatry.

[Leviticus 19:4 Turn ye not unto idols, nor make to yourselves molten gods: I am the LORD your God.] = right brain = God made man in his image. That's the only thing you should ever idolize and you idolize that image by applying the fear not remedy to unveil it because if you have a sense of time it is factually veiled. One way to look at it is you have God in you and God was veiled because the darkness, left brain, hates God and veiled it in you as a child with its "wisdom" education and so you apply the remedy and then God in unveiled in you, and all is well, relatively speaking at least in your mind or spirit.

[1 Corinthians 6:10 Nor thieves, nor covetous, nor drunkards, nor revilers, nor extortioners, shall inherit the kingdom of God.]

A thief is one who steals from his own brother and we are humans so all humans are our brothers and sisters so usury rates are stealing from your own brothers and sisters. Coveting is a symptom of a person who has not applied the remedy because coveting is seeking to control something and that mental state is not possible when right brain is unveiled because right brain is contrary to left brain so it does not seek control. When right brain is at 50% with left brain, its traits rule the mind. A drunkard is a symptom of one who has not applied the remedy because one who does apply the remedy cannot become a drunkard because drugs are not able to trump right brain euphoria so a drunkard is a person who tries to feel right brain with the use of drugs relative to :
[Ephesians 5:18 And be not drunk with wine, wherein is excess; but be filled with the Spirit;]

A person with right brain veiled is suffering and so they try to relive that suffering by doing drugs so they are not evil or bad they are doing the best they can considering they had their right brain veiled before they were ten because the written education was not taught properly to them. I have a bottle of liquor in the house and I am already aware it will not do anything for me euphoric wise so in fact drinking it will make me feel sluggish physiologically but do nothing to me mental wise, euphoric wise so I find myself pondering what was euphoria from doing drugs like. I no longer recall what getting high was even like because I am so high. Doing drugs that make people with a sense of time high do nothing to a person who unveiled right brain because the ones with a sense of time only do drugs to feel right brain power for the duration the drugs last.

[Ephesians 5:18 And be not drunk with wine, wherein is excess] = No need to do drugs to relieve your suffering in that extreme left brain state just deny yourself, lose your
life mentally , fear not , submit, apply the remedy and you will discover what high really is and you never need a refill. You will find no matter what drugs you take or are addicted to will not compare to how high you will be when right brain is unveiled and even after a short amount of time after you unveil right brain all your drug problems will simply fade away. Getting off of drugs aspect will not even come into the picture. You do not have to defeat your addiction to drugs you just apply the remedy and when right brain unveils all those addiction symptoms will hardly be felt and hardly be noticed because right brain is so powerful it will be pondering you to other thoughts besides drugs and the paradox aspect of right brain will make any withdraw symptoms hardly noticeable if at all relative to [Genesis 3:16 Unto the woman he said, I will greatly multiply thy sorrow and thy conception; in sorrow thou shalt bring forth children; and thy desire shall be to thy husband, and he shall rule over thee.] You try to quit drugs without having right brain unveiled and it can turn into a lifelong profession of sorrow and failure you may never be able to quit anyway, but you unveil right brain and kicking drugs is nothing because after you unveil right brain you will be spending your time trying to figure out what Mac Truck hit you. If you want to do drugs after you unveil right brain there is no problem with that but you will find they do nothing for you and do not give you euphoria so you will just figure out on your own you can live with them or without them and just like you do not covet drinking water you will no longer covet drugs. So drugs just become things but they no longer have power over you because they no longer serve

their purpose, give you euphoria, because that euphoria you feel on drugs is right brain. So, everything flips when right brain is unveiled. The reason the wise beings in the ancient texts mainly pushed the full measure remedy is because that's the only way to fully unveil right brain again and when that is accomplish everything gets very easy. You have a sense of time so you see a lot of mountains that are in reality flat ground. I am one who has experimented with drugs in my life and I am speaking to ones who are still experimenting with drugs. I am not saying doing drugs is bad because it is simply a symptom of a human being trying to get a little relief from that extreme left brain state of mind the written education put them in. I am suggesting that high you feel from drugs is just a hint of how powerful right brain is when unveiled. So you are factually feeling right brain when you are on drugs but just not at full power so you just get a taste of how powerful right brain is and you apply this remedy and you will feel the full power of right brain and the drugs will simply be a joke in contrast. Thus the comment. "Sometimes a cigar is just a cigar." - Sigmund Freud .

I am not concerned what all the experts are telling you because I am mindful they have a sense of time so they could not possibly be telling you anything worth listening to. You are not a bad person for seeking a little relief from the suffering state of mind traditional education put you in. I am suggesting if you like to get high apply the remedy and try to apply it in an experimental way so you do not give up after the first try because left brain likes to quit. It is not important if anyone else agrees with the spirit of what I suggest it is only important that you agree with the spirit of what I suggest and try to apply the remedy. There is perhaps no human being on this planet who has applied the remedy that would disagree with the spirit of what I suggest about the remedy. The remedy is an ancient remedy to negate the unwanted mental side effect of learning written language and it has been tested over and over for thousands of years and it works flawlessly. You do not need anyone else to apply it. You apply it yourself. You keep at it and do not give up because it factually works every time it is applied properly. The drugs are actually driving you down to the 9th circle of treason, other words the drugs are slowly unveiling right brain but very slowly. Because of that reality your fear is perhaps very strong because the closer you get to the 9th circle the closer you get the door out of hell and things start to magnify and this magnification is what steers many people away from the 9th circle of hell. This is the reverse thing. It gets darkest before the light is another way to look at it. With a sense of time you are factually mentally unsound so you are insane so as you do the drugs you are getting closer to the 9th circle of hell and so you are starting to become a bit more sane, the drugs unveil right brain for their duration, and this is an area you want to get through swiftly. You want to pull the tooth swiftly not slowly. So since you are on drugs you are close to the 9th circle so just go find a spooky place to get that hypothalamus to give you that death signal and then just ignore that signal. Avoid concerning yourself with what may or may not happen after you apply the remedy because you are factually insane and so you are factually unable to do that properly. Don't anticipate what it will be like after you unveil right brain because you are mentally unable to understand what it will be like. You will understand what it like firsthand so there is no need to ponder what it will be like. You need to use all the energy you have to focus on applying the remedy. There are millions of places where that hypothalamus will give you the death signal and none of those places are shark frenzies, just shadows of shark frenzies. Cemeteries are a good place to start, houses in the woods where no one ever goes is a good place to start, of course just watching a scary movie or reading a scary book is also a good place to start. From your perspective you should feel like you are going to factually die from spooks. That is the state of mind you want to achieve and then when you are certain you will die you simply fear not which means you just close your eyes and say "I don't care" in your mind and that is the remedy. It takes one second in the right situation and it's all over and it is totally painless and it will hit you like a Mac truck in about 30 days or less. From then on out I cannot help you because you will know everything I know. That little split second self control aspect is the cure for all addictions no matter what they are from food, to gambling to drugs to sex addictions and the list goes on. All non physiological mental disorders are cured by that one second self control method and it has been around for perhaps five thousand years. Many left brain influenced beings will spit on the remedy because they make lots of money off of all of those "mental disorders", but you just keep in mind suffering loves company."Sometimes a cigar is just a cigar." - Sigmund Freud . - 4:47:37 PM

1/13/2010 7:31:35 AM – I am mindful to avoid giving you any delusions of grandeur because you mindfully sense time so you are delusional enough.
[Psalms 141:10 Let the wicked fall into their own nets, whilst that I withal escape.]
The wicked are the ones who sense time, the ones who have the curse. This being who wrote Psalms is in fact asking that the wicked destroy their self with by their own nature and that he escape in spite of that from them.
[Matthew 4:20 And they straightway left their nets, and followed him.]
This comment is suggesting some of the wicked, the ones with a sense of time, threw down everything they were doing and applied the remedy. This is relative to detachment.
[Luke 9:60 Jesus said unto him, Let the dead bury their dead: but go thou and preach the kingdom of God.] This is also relative to detachment. Because the "brand" of education you received has made you mentally unsound you are unable to grasp reality. This ratio that Jesus spoke to five thousand and he had twelve who followed and even one of those did not really pan out shows what your chances are. One can call it a .0024 chance to apply this remedy. I am mindful there are ones that partially applied this remedy and also ones who got oral education so they never had to apply this remedy. There are not exactly people in nirvana running around in herds so to speak.

[Genesis 3:14 And the LORD God said unto the serpent, Because thou hast done this, thou art cursed above all cattle, and above every beast of the field; upon thy belly shalt thou go, and dust shalt thou eat all the days of thy life:]

[Genesis 3:17 And unto Adam he said, Because thou hast hearkened unto the voice of thy wife, and hast eaten of the tree, of which I commanded thee, saying, Thou shalt not eat
of it: cursed is the ground for thy sake; in sorrow shalt thou eat of it all the days of thy life;]

[cursed above all cattle] [in sorrow shalt thou eat of it all the days of thy life;][upon thy belly shalt thou go, and dust shalt thou eat all the days of thy life:] = .0024 percent chance of applying the remedy and breaking the curse. This is not relative to how hard the remedy is to apply in an absolute way it is relative to that "thing" that is on your back is going to do everything in its power to talk you out of applying the remedy and it is infinitely more convincing than you can ever imagine. All you can do is deny yourself in every definition of the word deny yourself.

[upon thy belly] denotes unless you are one hardcore shadow of death seeking being you will be stuck in your suffering state, hell, for the rest of your life. This is an indication of how mentally devastating forcing sequential based written education with many reward and punishment methods tied to it are on the mind of a child when encouraged starting at the age of six. What I am suggesting is these beings with a sense of time you call civilization ruined you mentally so completely with their "brand" of written education it will be a miracle if you are unable to undo it and that is because you have been mentally ruined to such a degree you cannot even tell you have been ruined mentally. You will only be able to tell how bad they mentally ruined you after you apply the remedy because that will give you a nice contrast and then you will run around saying "I once was blind and now I see." You will be running around saying "I have been resurrected from the dead" and the ones with a sense of time will think to their self "You must be crazy." What all that left brain favoring traditional education does to the delicate mind of a small child after even a few years is why you are having difficulty even understanding what I am writing about. You are not exactly playing with a full deck mentally, one might suggest. This is why these ancient texts have many rules relative to be kind to others, because the wise beings who wrote these texts were mindful the chances of one being able to apply this remedy were .0024 so they just suggested be kind to one another and that was their attempt to try and address the reality the last thing a mentally unviable being could be is kind to one another. I am not suggesting you were mentally unviable when you were born I am suggesting cause and effect which means you got taught a strictly left brain favoring invention system by lunatics and they did one hell of a job on your mind. Now relative to a being that has right brain unveiled .0024 is not a big deal because right brain seeks impossibility and so the more difficult the situation is the better. A better way to look at it is to consider Edison when he said I tried a thousand times before I found the light bulb that worked. Now, one under the influence of left brain tends to give up before they even start because they talk their self out of situations that appear to be impossible. One under the influence of left brain tends to sum up a situation and if that situation appears too difficult they tend to settle for something that is less difficult so they are self defeating. There is a certain "It is a waste of time" concept the ones under the influence of left brain subscribe to because they perceive there is time to begin with. The beings in the ancient texts factually did not convince civilization, the over whelming vast majority of civilization about the dangers of written education has on the mind if not taught properly so one under the left brain influence will suggest they wasted their time but in fact they did not waste their time because I am here explaining what they explained and so I am pleased they did what they did in explaining the situation so they factually did not waste their time it is just their efforts did not have an instant payout. Ones under the influence of left brain are always looking for that instant payout and that instant gratification. "Normies" do not perceive they are accomplishing anything unless they see instant results because they have patience because they sense time. One who applies the remedy has no sense of time so they cannot be patient and thus they cannot be impatient. I am mindful it took 5400 years since Genesis was first penned to reach a point where another human being would be able to explain that text flawlessly and tell others and it is not even important if you do not believe that because it is not going to increase your chances of applying the remedy which is .0024 percent. Because you sense time, and that proves you have right brain veiled and that proves you are under the influence of left brain and that means that two zero's have to be added to the .0024 so your actual chances of applying the remedy are .000024 percent because left brain gives up before it even starts. So because of that I am not engaged in infinite, infinite vanity by writing these books because there is no chance you can apply the remedy. Because of that I am only able to focus on the log in my eye because your mind has been bent so far to the left, you are the only chance you have to escape that reality and that is the worst news you could ever understand thus the comment: [Matthew 23:33 Ye serpents, ye generation of vipers, how can ye escape the damnation of hell?]

The only ones who have a .0024 percent chance of escaping hell are the meek and they are the suicidal so if you are not suicidal then you have .000024 chance of escaping hell.

This is what .0024 looks like:

[B. P. (14) committed suicide for unknown reasons.]

[D. M. (25) allegedly committed suicide.]

What this means is you may get to the 9th circle of hell, treason, and when you are there because you are hallucinating you may believe the depression and the voice in your head may convince you to literally kill yourself. So not only do you have to be suicidal to deny one's self, you have to be infinity foolish and never pull it off, but want to pull it off, so just come very close but not actually pull it off. It is a total contradiction this .0024 percent chance of escaping hell. You have to see the shadow of death and to get to that state you have to be literally suicidal and once you get there you have to mess it up and not accomplish it but try to accomplish it and get lucky and have an accident. You are simply having delusions of grandeur because you cannot mentally grasp how messed up your mind is from all those years of sequential based education. You are factually unable to mentally grasp the effects of years of sequential based written education has had on your mind.

[Genesis 2:17 But of the tree of the knowledge of good and evil, thou shalt not eat of it: for in the day that thou eatest thereof thou shalt surely die.] What this comment means is although you were forced by law to get the written education, the tree of knowledge, by mental abominations that should not even be allow around children, so it is not your fault you got your mind bent to the left so far but you now see parts such as good and evil, you have to undo that damage by yourself and your chances of doing that are so slim, you will probably die before you can accomplish this remedy unless by a miracle of all creation you have an accident. You will not perceive you are applying the remedy you will only perceive you are going to die in that dark spooky place, and then you will perceive you just do not care if you die. You will not perceive peace, love and happiness you will perceive you are a failure at life and you no longer wish to live at all so when the shadow of death approaches, you do not even care enough to save your life by running. This fear not remedy was not just made up out of thin air, it is in fact the only way to break the curse the written language education has put on your head. Simply put you have the mark and there is only one way to get rid of it. There are many variations of the fear not remedy but they are all the fear not remedy. You can sit around and mediate for the next nine thousands years and perhaps you will unveil right brain a bit but you will never unveil it the full measure unless you go the full measure, those who lose their life mindfully will preserve it. Perhaps you are starting to understand for the first time in your life what a problem is and perhaps you are starting to understand everything you thought was a problem was in fact not a problem at all. How important are your friends and your money and possessions and your hobbies now? Your friends are not going to help you apply this remedy they are going to talk you out of applying it. Your money is not going to help you apply this remedy money will talk you out of applying it. Your possessions are not going to encourage you to apply the remedy, your attachment to them will keep you from applying the remedy. There is no one you know or will ever know who has a sense of time that will tell you it is a good idea to apply the fear not remedy. Your chances of climbing Mount Everest naked in the dead of winter at night are better than your chances of being able to apply this remedy the full measure as these ancient texts suggest is what is required to fully restore your mind. This is why I put time stamps in the books and this is why I talk to myself because I cannot save you from the place you have fallen. That is why I will not be making public appearances because I am not strong enough to look at dead people while knowing I cannot bring them back to life. Now that's a paradox.

[2 Timothy 2:13 If we believe not, yet he abideth faithful: he cannot deny himself.]

Even if you read some things I say and agree with some things I say if you do not believe written education has ruined your mind beyond the description of ruined your mind, you will not be able to deny yourself because deny yourself means kill yourself mindfully and that means you go to the spookiest place on the planet and when your mind says run like the wind you say no I don't care anymore let the spooky thing kill me dead. That is why your chances are .0024 to regain a sound mind and if you are even slightly arrogant your chances are .000024. You should say the word "perhaps" more than you say any other word and you should listen to music you cannot stand to listen to just to prepare your mind so you can mindfully kill yourself self, so you can deny yourself. Do you understand why I do not care about my grammar errors and I do not care if I get all the commas right and I do not care if you do not like what write? There are perhaps no human beings on this planet that are even capable of understanding what I write fully that have a sense of time, and I know that for a fact because I am not even fully aware of what I am writing until after I write it, of course I speak in paradox. Do you think if I write and say everything perfectly you will go kill yourself mindfully? How many wise sayings do I have to come up with out of thin air before you will freely go kill yourself mindfully? I will attempt to come up with some wise sayings and when you feel I have said enough wise sayings you go ahead and go kill yourself mindfully.

"A man can no more diminish God's glory by refusing to worship Him than a lunatic can put out the sun by scribbling the word, 'darkness' on the walls of his cell."
C. S. Lewis
If one is trying they are not trying hard enough. Only a lunatic believes a word will cure lunacy. Understanding light is more complicated than just spelling the word light.

"Christianity, if false, is of no importance, and if true, of infinite importance. The only thing it cannot be is moderately important."
C. S. Lewis

Fear not either means nothing or it means everything.
Deny one's self either means nothing or it means everything.
Submit either means nothing or it means everything.
The Baptism fear not method either means nothing or it means everything.
The Abraham and Isaac story in principle either means nothing or it means everything.
Those who lose their life mindfully will preserve it either means nothing or it means everything.

"Education without values, as useful as it is, seems rather to make man a more clever devil. "
C. S. Lewis

It's easier just to cut the right hemisphere of a child's brain out of their head at birth than to spend years doing the same with education.
It is easier to create a devil in hell than it is to stop a devil from being created in hell.
Traditional education is only a problem if the lunatic who teaches it is not aware traditional education causes mental problems.
Traditional education taught by a lunatic with no values becomes a deadly weapon.

I am mindful the right brain spirit has been attempting to tell our species the dangers of this written education for thousands of years and we as a species factually just do not get it. I could easily mask what I am saying and hide what I am saying and try to disguise what I am saying about the dangers of written education but I do not because you factually do not get it either way. I can suggest you may be on fire or I can just say you defiantly are on fire and you will not get it either way. I don't have to mask what my message is because you do not get it even if I do not mask it. If I say do not eat off the tree of knowledge you have no clue and if I say beware of written language because it has devastating mental side effects you equally have no clue what I am saying. You no longer are capable of understanding reality at all, ever, into infinity. You are either dead or an illusion and I lean towards the fact you are an illusion because if I thought you were dead then I would have to accept you are the dead turning innocent children into the dead with your wisdom education. I cannot kill illusions I can only bend them to my will.- 11:33:50 AM

[D. H. (16) shot himself in the head outside his high school hours before a parent-teacher conference.]
This young being was not taking too well to your traditional education and so the ones who serve the whore were going to meet and explain to this young being that he was stupid and was not applying himself and not willing to have his right brain veiled and so this young being took a gun and blew his brains out and demonstrated the power of the comment "Give me liberty(right brain) or give me death." And he did this so you brain dead mole crickets should erect a monument in his name because he had more courage and fortitude than you brain dead mole crickets will ever have into infinity no matter what your retard cult leader tells you to the contrary. Now that is creative writing and all the other shit you assume is creative writing is stupidity in contrast. I failed at suicide 29 times and I am on the fence about the thirtieth attempt.
I will now create a song to express my emotions and thus use music as an emotional outlet to mask the fact I use these books as an emotional outlet. I am either infinitely beyond your understanding or you are infinitely beyond my ability to understand and I am certain only I know the reality of that, but I doubt it. A monk once said "He

is quite an angry one isn't he." You think you know what anger is but in reality you would not last one second at this level of heightened awareness because you kill yourself when you lose your job. You kill yourself when your girlfriend leaves you. You kill yourself when someone insults you so you just avoid ever applying this remedy because at the level of heightened awareness this remedy creates, you would simply be consumed by the heat in this kitchen. I guess I should be pondering killing myself at this level of heightened awareness but then my amygdala keeps reminding me I already did kill myself. There is no other option after you kill yourself so one is reduced to just hanging around. I am just reduced to making casual observations about the deeds of the demons I am surrounded by in hell. I do not mind suggesting if you sense time you are in fact a demon and then publishing it in my diary and then publishing it on a world stage because I am certain you are unable to kill me in any meaningful way, but I doubt it. A monk told me early after the accident "Don't blow it." and I am still laughing about that comment. If he would have said "Make sure you blow it" perhaps I would be a little more delicate in my wording but after all past is now. I do not detect anyone else did anything but "blow it" and that is obvious because the ones with a sense of time are still pushing their wisdom education on children as if written education is required to breathe.- 11:47:21 AM

12:40:50 PM – Plato spoke of an ideal plane and at the time he spoke of this ideal plane Buddha was speaking of an ideal plane called nirvana or consciousness and perhaps over 2000 years before that another being was speaking of the garden of Eden and of a place called heaven. This ideal plane is simply a mental state in which one has unveiled right brain and right brain ambiguity is unable to determine with certainty what is good and what is bad, what is good and what is evil relative to the comment [Genesis 2:17 But of the tree of the knowledge of good and evil, thou shalt not eat of it: for in the day that thou eatest thereof thou shalt surely die.]
One with a sense of time cannot grasp the ideal plane because they perceive being unable to know with certainty what is good and evil, is evil. So ones with a sense of time perceive the Garden of Eden is evil

149

and nirvana is evil and the ideal plane is evil and thus consciousness is evil. The comment "I hate Mondays" and the comment "I can't wait until Friday" are both comments made by beings with a sense of time. In reality there are no Mondays and there are no Fridays so these beings that sense time are in fact hating something that doesn't exist and they are coveting or craving something that doesn't exist. A calendar is used so one can calculate their usury interest rate profits they make off their fellow brothers and sisters of the species and nothing more. One with no sense of time would never say "I can't wait until Friday" because Friday does not exist and so they are conscious and so their mind does not worry about things that do not exist and so they are in the ideal plane because they are no longer hallucinating because they are conscious. If they changed the week days so that Monday was now Friday and Friday was now Monday people with a sense of time would say 'I hate Fridays " and "I can't wait until Monday." The ones who sense time can never escape time so time is a monkey on their back that will never let them or me rest. They will suggest they cannot wait until Friday but when Friday get's there they are close to Monday again so they are going to be suffering soon because they hate Mondays. So when they say "I can't wait until Friday" they are really saying I can wait until Friday so I can get closer to Monday so I can suffer again and then they prove it by saying "I hate Mondays." I am curious to understand what kind of hallucinogenic these beings who sense time are on because I would like to try any hallucinogenic that would make me perceive Friday is any different than Monday. This delusion caused by traditional education being taught improperly causes this sense of time because right brain is veiled and so one is in a constant mental state of setting a schedule.

The ones that sense time are not really living their life as much as they are attempting to fill all of these deadlines they set in their head because their mind senses time. They will sit down and start on a project and then sense an hour has passed and then determine the project is a waste of their time and so they give up but in reality or in the ideal plane, conscious state of mind, they would not be able to tell any time has passed so they would perhaps complete all of their projects because time would never be a factor for them mentally.

What this means is a person would not have this time aspect in their head so they would be able to relax and concentrate and thus they would accomplish much more and produce better quality things with the time they invest relative to a clock in the project. Money is relative to time and thus money does not mean anything on an infinite scale. If one takes time out of civilization they take money out of civilization and civilization loves its money.

[Acts 8:20 But Peter said unto him, Thy money perish with thee, because thou hast thought that the gift of God may be purchased with money.]

Attempt to comprehend this even though you cannot speak English.

[Thy money perish with thee] = deny one's self which is the remedy and then you unveil right brain and lose your sense of time and then money no longer matters because money is time relative thus the comment [Thy money perish with thee]. Avoid trying to read anything into that because you are not capable of going any further than attempting to understand that simple principle in your delusional state of mind.

[thou hast thought that the gift of God may be purchased with money.] You perceive if you give money to your cult leader you will unveil the god image in man, right brain, and you could not be more delusional than that. If you saw a man in a river up to his waist in the water and he called out to you "Come here I want to drown you and kill you as a result." You would run like the wind away from him because that is what the baptism remedy is. If you know the person who is dunking you then you trust the person who is dunking you so there is perhaps no possible way the baptism remedy will work for you. I am mindful you are not paying your cult leader to kill you so I ponder you must be paying you cult leader to save you and because you are in hell you are paying your cult leader to keep you in hell so that means you are a masochist who does not even know they are a masochist. I have no quarrel with a masochist that knows they are a masochist I have issues with masochists who are not even aware they are masochists because they may turn into sadists and

use innocent little children as a means to gratify their self. So this baptism aspect from a neurological point of view is simply dunking the head under water and the moment that happens the amygdala signals the hypothalamus and says "The
head is under water and you may need to send a death signal soon." When a person is a child and they are taught to swim the amygdala remembers that aspect and so when the head goes under water for the rest of that person's life, it signals the hypothalamus that a death signal may be required. So when you are under water for ten seconds your hypothalamus may give you a slight death signal, a gentle nudge. When you are under water for thirty seconds your hypothalamus may give you a little bit stronger nudge. When you are under water for fifty seconds the hypothalamus may give you a strong nudge and at that stage you may rush for the surface, but in order to apply the remedy you have to not rush for the surface and just totally relax and let go. The problem with this is you cannot be mindful that is what you are going to do because you are under the influence of left brain and anything you know it knows. So the only way you could apply this baptism remedy is to be walking along a river and you see someone in the water you never met in your life and they perhaps would have to look pretty scary, maybe wearing lamb skins perhaps, and they would call out to you out of the blue "Come here and let me drown you and kill you." And then you would say "That is fine" and then they would grab you and drunk you and when your hypothalamus said "You will drown if you do not fight for your life" and that is when you would not fight but fear not or deny yourself and that is the only way you are going to trick that left brain influence to leave you alone. The chances of you actually doing that is .0024 if you are suicidal and .000024 if you have even slight arrogance. I ponder what you think about reality now. - 1:26:35 PM

"Don't use words too big for the subject. Don't say "infinitely" when you mean "very"; otherwise you'll have no word left when you want to talk about something really infinite."
- C. S. Lewis

I infinitely agree with his comment very infinitely.

2:42:07 PM
A twin of roads identical
To travel both is miniscule
One decision long considered
One road is dark and one is light
But both are relative to sight

I flipped a coin; mere accident
Coin picked the road and thus was spent
The road then came into sight
The other road looked black as night
Coin picked the road without a fright

The morning mist lay on the road
The leaves withered from trodden load
I saw none before and none behind
The road was hidden from the blind
Coin picked the road they could not find

I cannot tell if you should walk
The road devours damaged stalk
A twin of roads identical
To travel both miniscule
I flipped a coin, mere accident

If I should tell you which to pick

Then I deny the coin I flipped
If I should tell you which to take
Then I deny your will to make
So flip the coin and claim your stake.

When eye was young, perhaps four or five, eye was walking down the street and eye saw two older boys, ten or eleven perhaps, sitting in their carport behind some boxes and eye was concerned so eye turned around and started walking back home and they shot me in the back of the head with a BB gun and eye looked at them and they were laughing and eye was not crying but eye was just curious what eye had done to make them shoot me. And now eye am mindful those boys were already showing symptoms of a mean spirit, left brain influenced containers, caused by the education. - 3:31:59 PM

3:41:51 PM – "In life you need either inspiration or desperation." - Tony Robbins
Inspiration is achieved when desperation is overcome. Desperation is a symptom of panic and thus fear; inspiration is a symptom of concentration and thus clarity.

1/14/2010 10:17:39 AM – Post on forum. [1 Timothy 5:8 But if any provide not for his own, and specially for those of his own house, he hath denied the faith, and is worse than an infidel.]

[But if any provide not for his own]

This comment means once a person gets the written education, the tree of knowledge they have the mark of the beast and one of these marks is they sense time. One can tell they have the mark of the beast if they sense time because if the written education, left brain based, did not veil right brain, the god image in man, then they would have no sense of time because the paradox aspect of right brain would factor into the question "How much time has passed" and the answer would be time has passed and time has not passed and that would be the paradoxical answer so one would have no sense of time. So this comment is a bond, that once a person applies the fear not remedy they are bound to assist everyone they know to apply the fear not, deny one's self remedy which takes the mark away, unveils right brain, the god image in man.

[and specially for those of his own house]

This comment is saying, civilization is going to force you to give your own children the written education and thus the mark and so that is going to happen, so you have to make sure you assist your own household to apply the fear not remedy after you apply it.

[he hath denied the faith]

Denied the faith is simply a person who gets the written education and has a sense of time as a result, the mark of the beast, and then denies that is truth. They deny the tree of knowledge, written education put the mark on them. They deny having a sense of time is a symptom of the mark of the beast, they deny right brain, the god image in man because they continue to push the written education on the little ones. The complexity is, one gets the written education at such a young age, around six, they cannot even remember what it was like before they got the education so they cannot tell they have been given the mark so they have to have faith the ancient texts are speaking the truth relative to the tree of knowledge and relative to the remedy, fear not, deny ones self, do not try to save one's life mindfully to preserve it. One gets the mark starting when they are six and by the time they are ten or twelve they have the mark and so the only chance they have is to take the wise beings in the ancient texts word for it and apply the remedy.

[and is worse than an infidel.]

And infidel is one who denies the tree of knowledge, written education, put the mark of the beast on them and that is their business and so they are doomed to never be able to escape the mark, but worse than an infidel is one who tells others the tree of knowledge is not written education and said education does not give one the mark of the beast, bends the mind to the left, so they steer others away from escaping the mark so they are worse than an infidel. The fear not remedy is hard enough to apply so that alone takes huge courage but then these worse than infidels go around shooting their mouth off discouraging the ones who are considering applying the fear not remedy. These "worse than infidels" not only deny what the tree of knowledge is, they deny what the remedy is, so they deny the faith all together and that means they are in a place spiritually where they are simply diabolical. Limbo is the absence of God, their right brain is gone.

10:38:00 AM - Very little matters if you sense time but the remedy.

Here are mentions of the remedy
[Genesis 15:1 After these things the word of the LORD came unto Abram in a vision, saying, Fear not, Abram: I am thy shield, and thy exceeding great reward.]
[Fear not]
[Psalms 23:4 Yea, though I walk through the valley of the shadow of death, I will fear no evil: for thou art with me; thy rod and thy staff they comfort me.]
[though I walk through the valley of the shadow of death, I will fear no evil] = fear not
[Luke 17:33 Whosoever shall seek to save his life shall lose it; and whosoever shall lose his life shall preserve it.]
[whosoever shall lose his life shall preserve it.] = fear not to lose your life mindfully

So one gets the written education and they have the mark of the beast, they sense time, so they are possessed by the beast so they have to trick the beast into thinking they have died so the beast will let loose of them.= [whosoever shall lose his life shall preserve it.]
So one has to find a situation they scare their self to the point they perceive the shadow of death is coming for them and then they fear not or do not run.
One scenario would be a person finds an abandoned house in the woods and goes there alone at night and goes into the house and

perhaps down into the basement and if they sense something is going to kill them they do not run, they fear not and close their eyes and say "come get me" and that is the fear not remedy and the results [exceeding great reward.], right brain will unveil within a few weeks.

Another scenario would be one goes to an old cemetery where there are no lights, alone, at night and see's if they can get that sensation that something is coming to kill them and then they fear not, or close their eyes and say "come and get me".

This principle method is to get that mark , that beast, to believe the person has died, so it will loose them from its grip. Avoid any situations where actual death is possible as in shark frenzies or bad parts of town, one only wishes to seek the [the shadow of death] not literal death.

[whosoever shall lose his life shall preserve it.] This is in fact mental suicide so avoid assuming you will be able to pull it off easily just keep experimenting, remember whatever you know the beast that is in you knows so you have to make up your mind you are going to seek the shadow of death and then fear not. If you do it half way the beast in you will not be fooled and therefore he will not let go of you and he will do anything to talk you out of applying this ancient fear not remedy. Right now you are thinking, this is unsafe, this cannot be truth, this sounds stupid, this guy is on drugs, and that is the beast in you talking you out of the applying the remedy.

[Matthew 17:20 And Jesus said unto them, Because of your unbelief: for verily I say unto you, If ye have faith as a grain of mustard seed, ye shall say unto this mountain, Remove hence to yonder place; and it shall remove; and nothing shall be impossible unto you.]

Right brain once unveiled is so powerful one can do things mindfully they could never do before so they can "move mountains" effortlessly. All mountains become flat ground.

6:03:25 PM – This is a clarification of a previous clarification.
Right brain has ambiguity and paradox and is a trait relative to sensing time, hunger, pain etc.

So when one learns to write any language they have to spell words by arranging letters in sequential order. If a student does not arrange the letters in proper sequential order on a spelling test they get a poor grade. So the grading system is a way to force a child or student to get better at sequencing, a left brain trait.

If a student does not sequence the letter well they get a poor grade and their parents punish them so they are forced to learn sequencing better and the sequencing also goes for

sentence structure. So after years of this sequencing called traditional education the mind starts to bend to the left and in turn the paradox aspect of right brain becomes veiled.

So instead of a sound minded 50/50 mental harmony person being unable to sense time a person who gets this education does sense time.

There is a question that goes through the mind and it is something like "How much time has passed?"

And after all that education the right brain paradox is veiled so it does not figure into that question.

So instead of the mind having paradox and answering that question with "Time has passed and no time has passed"(the paradox) and that is the minds final answer and that is what makes one not have a sense of time, one who gets the education and has right brain veiled only has a strong sense of time, because that paradox is not figured into that question "How much time has passed?"

This absence of paradox also applies to hunger. So one who gets the education is very hungry all the time, even needing to eat after four or five hours without food because the "Am I hungry" question in the mind has no paradox factored into it . So with paradox and right brain unveiled or at 50%, the answer to that hunger question is "you are hungry and you are not hungry"(paradox) and that is the minds final answer so one has no real sense of hunger. After the education one has a very pronounced sense of hunger because

that paradox aspect of right brain is veiled, so right brain has been reduced to a subconscious level so the paradox never enters conscious state to answer these "questions:".

This absence of paradox also applies to pain. Ones pain and fatigue is greatly increased because instead of one having the paradox to

answer "How much did that hurt or how much fatigue do i feel?". "it hurt a lot and it did not hurt at all"(paradox), one only knows how much it hurt or how much fatigue they feel so there is no ambiguity relative to how much it hurts so it hurts a lot and so the fatigue is great also. This is all relative to perception being altered because the traditional education over a few years alters ones perception of hunger, fear, fatigue and sense of time. When right brain is reduced to subconscious levels after all the left brain sequential education, the ambiguity is gone and so is the paradox, so sense of time is strong, sense of hunger is strong and sense of pain and fatigue is strong. So this education in fact makes one mentally unsound because they are hallucinating by sensing time, by sensing
strong hunger and by sensing strong pain when in reality with a sound mind they would not be sensing time, strong hunger or strong pain.

There are only two things in life that are certain and certainty isn't one of them. It is better to explain to the blind how to see instead of willing them to see. If you want your child to get a better education than you got make sure they don't get the same "brand" of education you got.

1/15/2010 10:31:41 AM –
10th Amendment Limits the powers of the Federal Government to only those specifically granted to it by the constitution. - December 15, 1791
16th Amendment Allows federal income tax - February 3, 1913

10th Amendment [Limits] the powers of the Federal Government
16th Amendment [Allows] Federal Government

The 10 Amendment Limits and the 16th Amendment negates some of those limits and thus the 16th Amendment is a power grab by the Federal Government. The person , the state, then the Federal Government is the proper power chain in America but this 16th Amendment reversed that and made the Federal Government the first, then the state then the people. If there were no laws at all in America whatsoever the judicial branch, the courts and the law enforcement would be extinct and thus the federal government would be extinct. So this means the more laws there are the more powerful the federal government becomes. For example, the federal government says alcohol is legal to drink if you are a certain age, then a county in a state determines they do not want to sell alcohol on a certain day, they are known as a dry county, so they trump the federal government laws. The federal government does not mind that because that county is creating more laws. The federal government says it is legal to sell alcohol on any day and that county creates a law that says it is not legal to sell alcohol on Sundays so the federal Government does not mind that because the more laws there are the more powerful the federal government becomes. Another way to look at it is the more laws there are the more income potential. So a county passes a law that says no selling alcohol on Sundays and then someone sells alcohol on Sundays and they get a fine and the federal government get's a portion of money from that fine because of this :

16th Amendment (Allows) federal income tax.

Now this does not readily work the other way around though because the federal government does not stand to make any money from fines if a county passes laws to cancel out federal government laws. Federal law says pot is illegal everywhere and if California passes a law that says pot is legal in California the federal government has just lost lots of revenue generated from levying fines on people who are caught with pot in that state. This has less to do with pot and more to do with the federal government gets a cut of all fines generated from people breaking laws because the federal government gets a cut of every states revenue generated from fines from people breaking laws because it is a federal crime to smoke pot in this example. Now if one flips it and looks at it from a perspective that if the federal government says anyone of a certain age can smoke pot but then California passes a law that says pot is illegal in its state the federal government will not mind that because it will generate more revenue for it because of the 16th amendment. No matter what happens the federal government is going to get a portion of every states income. This makes it so no state can become too powerful and this makes it so all the states are answerable to the federal government, yet the federal government is not a state and in fact is not even a real entity like a state it is just essentially a control mechanism.

'Government is not reason; it is not eloquent; it is force. Like fire, it is a dangerous servant and a fearful master.'- George Washington

Washington was not talking about state governments because state governments are run by people in that state and each state has its own mission or purpose or pursuit of happiness. The federal government is not eloquent which means is not in touch with every state it is simply a one size fits all kind of aspect, it is a blanket over every state but that is not how it is supposed to be because every state is its own separate entity. The pecking order in the land of the free is a person can do as they wish in their own home as long as it does not infringe on another person's life, liberty of pursuit of happiness. When that person leaves their home they are under the guidance of the city they live in, then they are under the guidance of the county their city is in, then they are under the guidance of the state they are in, and then they are under the guidance of the federal government but the 16th Amendment makes it so the federal government trumps everything including the person who is home in their house. The greatest right any human in the land of the free has is the right to be left alone. Life, liberty and pursuit of happiness means leave me alone I am trying to figure out what my pursuit of happiness is in life. The federal government cannot stand that concept, leave me alone, because it does not see a very great monetary potential in the concept, leave me alone. Now if one in congress all made twenty thousand dollars a year and were watched like hawks so they could never do biddings for outside lobbies for rewards further down the road it would be a different story but in reality they are all multi millionaires and they have more back seat dealings than one will ever be able to fully grasp. Congress is simply carpet baggers trying to fill their carpet bags. Congress wants to help everyone but that means they want to control everyone but the people just want to be left alone so they can work out on their own what their pursuit of happiness is. This of course is all fruitless because to start off in life congress has determined every child is going to get their "brand" of education and that alters a beings perception and thus robs them of their pursuit of happiness. That is not how it always has been in America that is a recent occurrence and it is unspoken. There is factually not one suggestion in all the amendments relating to what kind of education a person has to get. There are two kinds of education, oral education and written education and neither of these are suggested in the founding documents yet the federal government has determined every child will get written education no matter what if they live in America. I saw a news article where a parent was thrown in jail for not reporting to the government they were home schooling their child because they were not keeping the government abreast of how that child was coming along. Home schooling is allowed as long as the parent teaches the child written education which the schools teach. If you home school your child and you determine to just orally teach them which means no writing or reading or math just simply give them oral teaching until their mind is developed enough, perhaps at the age of sixteen or eighteen, you will be thrown in jail, yet that is the only form of education one can teach their child so their child's right brain will not be veiled.

So freedom is really just an illusion because a person in this current situation only has the freedom they are allowed to have, and that is what tyranny is. If you try to teach your child oral education your friends will all laugh at you and mock you and spit on you and say you are stupid because they are conditioned mentally to believe the "brand" of education they got, written education, is the best brand. You may be in fact mocking and spiting on what I suggest about oral education because you got written education and you turned out just fantastic with your big sense of time and pinprick sequential logic. Intellect is a left brain trait and that means once one gets the traditional education they have to be told what to do and its best if they have a big list of things they are told to do because their right brain intuition aspect has been turned off by the traditional education so they are simply unable to just know what to do. You have no sense of time so your right brain paradox is turned off and so your right brain intuition is turned off so as long as someone gives you a list of what you better do you are just fine but the moment you are in a situation with no list of what you better do comes along you collapse and panic and have a nervous breakdown. You have been institutionalized. When you hear about a person who loses their job and then kills their self or kills ones at their work place, that is because they are institutionalized and cannot think for their self because the written education has veiled their right brain intuition so they are dead in the water relative to thinking for their self. That job told them what to do so as long as they had that job they were pleased but the minute they lost that job they no longer knew what to do so they grabbed a gun and killed their self. The story of Job is about a person who has lots of problems thrown on them but they use their intuition to maintain and they do not panic and they do not have a nervous breakdown because of unknown situations that are thrust upon them. Job lost his house and his family but he did not panic and kill himself so that is just like a person who loses their mate in a divorce and does not freak out and makes some rash decision. It is just alike a person who loses their job. It is just like a person who loses a loved one to impermanence. Another way to look at it is a person with right brain unveiled has a sound mind and thus a mind build on stone and so when the storms of life approach, they do not have a nervous breakdown and panic. A person who gets traditional education has their right brain veiled and if they do not apply the fear not remedy they have an unsound mind and thus a mind build on the sand and when the slightest gust of wind comes they crumble to the ground. These are some examples of crumbling to the ground because right brain has been veiled by traditional education and ones never applied the remedy to unveil right brain.

[S. W. (31) is accused of choking his wife T. W. (28) to death with a belt one day before their divorce was to be final.]

[C. W. (38) shot himself and his wife in a murder suicide after he lost his job.]

[J. S. (49) committed suicide by ligature strangulation after losing his job.]

Job lost his house, his family, his lively hood and everything he had, and also got diseases and had every affliction perhaps known to man thrust on him in a short period and he did not blink. That is the difference between having right brain unveiled and not unveiling right brain. That is the difference between a person who would never sell their freedom for a little safety and a person who will sell all their freedom over a tiny threat that means absolutely nothing in long run. I am mindful there are beings in America who suggest they will give up freedom so they can be safe from the "boogie men" and I have news for you, you do not have that right and you will never ever have that right ever into infinity so you get out of America and go live in a tyrannical country and they will keep you safe in your cage but never assume you have the right to sell the freedom of people who will come after you because you're a scared little dog because you never applied the fear not remedy. You do not have the right to sell freedom because it was given to you freely when you were born, which means you are not allowed to sell others freedoms so you can perceive safety, and if you cannot handle that you go find another country because the ones in land of the free are always looking to water the tree of liberty with tyrants and beings willing to vote away freedom. If you start voting away my freedom I may get the impression you are a tyrant and that may only expedite your impermanence. I prefer not to be told what to do by little scared dogs that are afraid of shadows. We have the right to bear arms in America which means we can have 300 millions guns behind 300 million tree's in eight seconds so I ponder what on earth you could possibly be afraid of to the point you are willing to give away my freedom because some scared dog said you should. Perhaps you are hallucinating so you should go sit in a cemetery until you feel better and achieve sound mind so you can perhaps accomplish a slight hint of clarity in your thoughts. They do not give out diplomas in mental clarity you have to earn clarity the old fashion way, at least in this narrow. I don't want to vote all my fellow citizens into jail, leave me alone. I don't want to vote all my fellow citizens rights away, leave me alone. That is the power of leave me alone. I am not intelligent enough to vote on who should go to jail because I may be voting myself into jail, so leave me alone. How many people voted against drugs and now have loved ones in jail because of drug use? How many lives have been ruined because idiots voted is perhaps the most important question to ask about voting. You voted to force every child in America to have their right brain veil as a result of the traditional education you voted for and that alone is reason enough you should never vote again no matter what ever. You voted to have this beings right brain veiled. [S. W. (29) allegedly committed suicide by overdose.]

You voted to have these beings right brain veiled [C. H. (18) allegedly shot himself and his best friend in an apparent murder-suicide at a cemetery.]

You voted to have these two beings right brain veiled [M. M. (31) was shot and killed by her husband in a murder-suicide.]

You voted to have Todd Rohrer's right brain veiled and your fellow citizens voted to have your right brain veiled. I am uncertain what you think you're doing voting at all since you have no idea what you vote for and thus you know not what you do. And even as I suggest that there are innocent children as young as six that you voted to veil their right brain and you have no idea that is what you do and since you are in fact mentally ruining innocent children and you have no concept that is what you are doing, it proves with that state of mind you are influenced by you have absolutely no conscience. You mentally ruin innocent children that did nothing to you and then you pat yourself on the back for a job well done so I am unable to use any other words but to suggest you know not what you do while that thing is on your back and in your spirit. Perhaps it is not your intention to mentally ruin innocent children but perhaps it is that things intention that is in your spirit so perhaps you should trick it to leave you alone by denying yourself and thus it. Don't mind me I am just passing through.

To forgive the unforgivable is unforgivable and thus cannot be forgotten.

[Luke 12:32 Fear not(the remedy), little flock(not many with no sense of time); for it is your Father's good pleasure to give you the kingdom(right brain).] = Every being should have the kingdom, right brain, the image of god in man, unveiled but the serpent cult, civilization makes sure to veil it in all children of civilization, so one has to fear not, apply the fear not remedy to unveil it because the kingdom, right brain, is yours.

[for it is your Father's good pleasure to give you the kingdom.] = You are supposed to have it but it was taken from you and now you have to get it back and one takes it back via the fear not remedy.

[Jeremiah 48:4 Moab is destroyed; her little ones have caused a cry to be heard.]
Moab: is the historical name for a mountainous strip of land in modern-day Jordan running along the eastern shore of [the Dead Sea.] The sea of the dead, the ones who sense time, civilization = [her little ones have caused a cry to be heard.] = [C. J. (13) allegedly took her own life] You can defend your pride but it will cost you your grace. Ones awareness is a symptom of their deeds and ones deeds are a symptom of their understanding. I'm approachable but only from an infinite distance. Everything results in further understandings so losing is impossible.

1/16/2010 1:07:31 AM - Circadian Rhythm Sleep Disorder – This is caused because the minds clock is not working properly and this is interesting because this is also accompanied at times by learning disorders. If one has right brain unveiled their mind has no sense of time so they are not affected by these erratic time schedule situations. Sometimes a person will work an odd shift and that will throw their minds clock into a strange state but one with no sense of time would not be effected by that. So this disorder is relative to the minds perception of time and when right brain is at 50% or unveiled the minds does not sense time so this is one of many disorders caused by the right brain being veiled as a result of all the traditional education and so the mind is unsound and the person is suffering as a result and in this case the person is unable to sleep properly. Think about Edison, he was known to take cat naps, when a person has no sense of time they go to sleep and they wake up fully rested and how much time they actually slept relative to a clock is not important because they do not sense time to begin with mindfully. One goes to sleep and wakes up and the body perceives it got a full nights rest whether they slept for three hours or five hours or eight hours. A person that senses time mindfully may sleep five hours and because their mind senses time, their body will react to sleeping just five hours. So this

166

is all relative to the mind and when the paradox is gone because right brain is veiled, the body can sense time and thus reacts to time events to a great degree of sensitivity. When the mind senses time the body is a slave to time. One with a sense of time may not be able to sit in one spot for more than a few hours but one with no sense of time will be able to sit in one spot for ten hours and their mind will never recognized it has been ten hours so their body will not become fatigued for example.

A loss is a terrible thing to mind. Sane minds are oft confronted by potentially sane minds.

1/16/2010 7:47:19 PM –
"I must be willing to give up what I am in order to become what I will be." - Einstein
[Luke 17:33 ...; and whosoever shall lose his life shall preserve it.]

[willing to give up] = [lose his life(mindfully)] = sacrifice
[become what I will be."] = [preserve it.]
The word "be" at the end of the initial comment is relative to no sense of time which is relative to being and becoming. Be = being = denotes no sense of time. Becoming denotes sense of time and is relative to going to become, or going to be, so it is a time based word. So these two comments are interchangeable.

I must be willing to lose my life mindfully to become what I will be.
I must be willing to give up what I am to preserve it.
And whosoever shall lose his life(mindfully) will be.
And whosoever is willing to give up what they are shall preserve their true life and then will be, achieve no sense of time, a symptom of consciousness, restore right brain.
So this comment made my Einstein is speaking about himself and the comment by Jesus is speaking about others. So Einstein's comment could be, you must be willing to give up what you are in order to become what you will be. And the comment by Jesus would be in first person, I lost my life mindfully and preserved it. Both of

these comments are relevant to the concept of detachment. Once one gets the written education they become this left brain influenced being and in order to return to how they were normally before that, they must detach from that left brain influence. Since the left brain influence aspect knows everything the being knows the being must convince the left brain influence the being has died and then it let's go of them. There is no other way to make that left brain influence let go of one except to trick it, but there are many ways to accomplish that so there are many roads leading to the same result, restoring right brain, the god image in man.

This comment is also interchangeable with all the other aspects of the remedy.

"I must be willing to give up what I am in order to become what I will be." - Einstein

I must be willing to [submit] in order to become what I will be

I must be willing to [fear not] in order to become what I will be.

I must be willing to [deny myself] in order to become what I will be.

I must be willing to [fear no evil] in order to become what I will be.

I must be willing to [walk through the valley of the shadow of death and fear no evil] in order to become what I will be.

This is symptom of this right brain spirit repeating itself over and over all through history in many ways and on many levels and only ones who apply the remedy can detect it.

This is relative to concept of God is all around you. This spirit is everywhere in all of these "wise" sayings through and through but ones who are influenced by the left brain

aspect simply do not "see" it. - 8:05:09 PM

1/17/2010 10:00:21 AM –

X = the curse; written education is the catalyst that creates the curse; curse being the right brain is veiled so the being becomes unsound mentally because the written education is taught to a child before the child's mind is even developed fully and so the written education is taught improperly and this creates the curse, unsound mind.

Y = Sound mind after the fear not remedy is applied. Right and left mental aspects are both in the conscious state of mind and both at 50% so the mind is in harmony and in this state right brain traits completely changes a person's perception relative to how they perceived things in the curse state; X state of mind.

The beings in the X state of mind wish to encourage the X state of mind in all the children because they perceive they are of sound mind in the X state of mind. All beings in civilization therefore are in the X state of mind because civilization, the majority, is in the X state of mind. This is a result of beings in the X state of mind inability to question if there are any flaws in their written education. Because beings in the X state of mind never question that there may be flaws in written education they teach it to their own children with no hesitation. The deep seeded mental reality is the beings in X state of mind have the inability to question written education because then they have to question that they perhaps were mentally ravaged by the written education. If beings in the X state of mind suggest "there are devastating mental side effects from learning written language" then they also have to understand they were mentally ravaged because they got written education. This in part is what the neurosis aspect is all about. The beings in X state of mind were mentally ravaged to such a great degree their mind is unable to grasp they were ravaged by written education and so they are in an abject state of denial. If beings in the X state of mind start to question if written education has flaws they then attempt to take that next logical conclusion but since they only have sequential based simple minded aspects in their thoughts they can never tie up all the loose ends so they tend to determine it is not possible. Because a being in the X state of mind has mainly intellectual left brain aspects to work with because their right brain intuition aspects are veiled they rely on others in positions of authority relative to what they perceive is authority to tell them what to believe. The complexity of this is there are no beings in the X state of mind that are aware written education has devastating mental side effects because they are in X state of mind. The masses in X state of mind are relying on the authorities in X state of mind to tell them the reality of written education but neither is even aware of it and neither is mentally able to tell the devastating effects because their intuition aspects are veiled. With full power intuition they would be able to sense the written education has devastating mental side effects in short order but since that aspect is veiled they are trapped by their own X mental state. This reality is relative to the suggesting of faith in the ancient texts. Simply put, one in the X state of mind does not have mental ability to tell they are in the X state of mind at all so they must have faith they are in the X state of mind and then they will apply the remedy and revert to Y state of mind. This concept is relative to the blind leading the blind and also I have seen the enemy and he is us. Ones in the X state of mind trust their own perceptions but in order to break the X state of mind they have to deny their perceptions. That is what this comment in the ancient text is relative to:

[1 Corinthians 3:18 Let no man deceive himself. If any man among you seemeth to be wise in this world, let him become a fool, that he may be wise.]

If any in the X state of mind seemeth to be wise let him become as fool that he may be wise, revert to Y state of mind. So a being in X state of mind, one who senses time, will perceive it is foolish to seek the shadow of death and then fear not, so they must be foolish to accomplish that, and then they will revert to Y state of mind, and become wise. This is relative to the reverse thing or the anti truth. If one perceives seeking the shadow of death and then fearing

not is foolish, but in reality it is the remedy so it is wise, then their perception is false in that X state of mind. The complexity with that is a being in X state of mind see's the door out of X state of mind as a wall or as dangerous or as improper.

[Leviticus 16:7 And he shall take the two goats, and present them before the LORD at the door of the tabernacle of the congregation.]

This comment suggests sacrifice. In order for one to make it through the door to escape X state of mind they have to deny their self, lose their life mindfully to preserve their life so they have to sacrifice their self, self being their self in X state of mind, so that means their self is not their true self but a false self. The problem with that is a person in X state of mind has huge pride so not only do they have to understand they got put in X state of mind, so they got fooled, they also have to understand, everyone around them got put into X state of mind, so everyone around them got fooled, then they have to understand, they have to not only deny their self they have to deny everyone around them and this creates a mental state where they cannot stand the reality they are all alone. If they remain in X state of mind they enjoy the bliss of ignorance but if they determine to leave X state of mind they will be all alone but they will have right brain on their side and a sound mind, Y state of mind. In X state of mind the being seeks a herd mentality because they perceive it is safe, relative to safety in numbers, but that also is a false perception. In reality there is safety when one thinks for their self because the whole reason they are in X state of mind is because civilization is a herd that never thought for itself so it never questioned the flaws in written education. It all started when written education was invented and one person said "There are no mental flaws even though written education is completely left brain favoring" and everyone has taken that persons word for it since, for thousands of years now, but the deeper reality is that person was a left brain influenced container. The right brain influenced containers in the ancient texts suggested the complete opposite. They suggested there are huge problems with the written education and with the scribes.

[Jeremiah 8:8 How do ye say, We are wise, and the law of the LORD is with us? Lo, certainly in vain made he it; the pen of the scribes is in vain.]

[certainly in vain made he it] This is a signpost of authenticity. It should be [in vain he made it]. It's out of sequence so it is (speaking in tongues) or a symptom this being had right brain unveiled so they could no longer use written language "properly" relative to the ones who sense time, so they were mocked by the ones that sense time and called fools and idiots because they could no longer use written language properly. I am certain your cult leader understands that so go ask it.

[the pen of the scribes is in vain.] Pen denotes written education. Scribe denotes a person who got written education and has not applied the remedy. The reason written education is vain is because if a being does not get the written education they will not have their right brain veiled so they will be light years wiser than a person who does have their right brain veiled. Once one applies the remedy and unveils right brain they will no longer be able to use written language like they could before so they are not a very good scribe. If one can spell well and use the written language well that's proves they have their right brain veiled. One will be extremely dyslexic after they apply the remedy but that is simply right brain random access being involved in the scribe process, the writing process. Another way to look at it is if one can write, scribe, well they cannot think well. This puts a person in a situation they have to make a decision. Is being adept at written language worth their right brain aspect being veiled? This is an absolute and a trade off and there is no way to get around it. If one applies this remedy they will unveil right brain the full measure and so they will no longer be able to use written language well relative to how the ones in X state of mind perceive "well". Civilization judges a person on how well they can use written language. The ones who can use written language well get high paying jobs and the ones who do not get slave jobs. Ones pay in life relative to civilization is totally based on how well they do at traditional education. The more traditional education one gets the more money they make and in turn the more their right brain is veiled. One has to ask is all the money in the universe worth their right brain being veiled. Is money more valuable than a sound mind? With an unsound mind money is everything and with a sound mind money is of little value. With an unsound mind all the money is the universe will not help one and with a sound mind all the money in the universe will not harm one.

Relative to this door one must walk through in the X state of mind.

[Leviticus 3:2 And he shall lay his hand upon the head of his offering, and kill it at the door of the tabernacle of the congregation: and Aaron's sons the priests shall sprinkle the blood upon the altar round about.]

This comment is explaining how a parent who applies the remedy must assist their offspring with the remedy.

[And he shall lay his hand upon the head of his offering, and kill it at the door]

Head denotes a parent's offspring has the mark because civilization is going to force a parent to give their child the written education and so that child will have the mark of a beast. So even at the times of these ancient texts written education was required. Written education became an accepted norm in civilization. [Kill it at the door] A being in X state of mind is under the influence of left brain, so they are a left brain container, so they are relative to the ancient texts, the beast, so in order to make that beast leave them alone they must deny that beast, and so when they apply the remedy they kill the beast at the door and then they can go through the door and return to Y state of mind. So the tabernacle relative to this comment was a place used to apply the fear not remedy on the children and people who had the mark.

That is what this comment is referring to.

"A church is a hospital for sinners, not a museum for saints." -Abigail Van Buren

Saints being the messengers, the prophets, the right brain influenced containers. The Saints have already applied the remedy so the "church" is simply a place for the ones in X state of mind, the ones with the mark, left brain influenced, one's with a sense of time and they will be assisted with the remedy by [Aaron's sons the priests] so priests are also ones who have applied the remedy. One cannot assist anyone with the remedy unless they first apply the remedy and they know they have applied the remedy because they will no longer mindfully sense time. So this concept that one has to go to school to become a priest or spiritual leader could not be any further from truth. In fact going to school causes the mark. This is why for example some of the apostles were simple men, fisherman for example and John the Baptist was a Master and he did not claim any kind of education credentials and that reality is relative to this comment: [Jeremiah 8:8 ; the pen of the scribes is in vain.] So ones with a sense of time may suggest "This person is wise because they have a doctorate degree from Yale" and perceive that proves that being is wise when in reality it only proves that being has the mark, and a very strong mark. This is relative to the reverse thing again. A person with lots of traditional education is going to have a harder time applying the fear not remedy than a person that has less schooling.

"If I be worthy, I live for my God to teach the heathen, even though they may despise me."- Saint Patrick

This comment is explaining how Saint Patrick applied the remedy, and we know he had to because he could write, and then he became a right brain influenced container and he was compelled to try and reach the heathens, the left brain influenced containers, the ones that sense time, and Patrick was mindful they may despise him. This is because left brain hates right brain or the darkness hates the light because when right brain and left brain are at 50/50 harmony right brain rules and left brain is jealous of that. So a heathen is simply a person who got traditional education and has not yet applied the fear not remedy to unveil right brain after the education veiled right brain.

These comments are repeating:

[Leviticus 4:4 And he shall bring the bullock unto the door of the tabernacle of the congregation before the LORD; and shall lay his hand upon the bullock's head, and kill the
bullock before the LORD.]

[Leviticus 3:2 And he shall lay his hand upon the head of his offering, and kill it at the door of the tabernacle of the congregation: and Aaron's sons the priests shall sprinkle the blood upon the altar round about.]

[bullock] = [offering] = [sacrifice] = one with a sense of time
[shall lay his hand upon the bullock's head, and kill the bullock before the LORD.] = [and kill it at the door of the tabernacle]

So beings who have not applied the remedy will see these comments as literal sacrifice of animals, well they are killing the beast, but not on a physical scale. The complexity here is, beings who did not apply the remedy would read these texts and start killing animals and never realize they misunderstood the texts. It is difficult enough on one hand to apply the remedy so this literal animal sacrifice is just another example of how the ancient texts are weapons used against the ones with the mark, the ones that sense time. The ancient texts are dangerous to the ones who have a sense of time; the left brain influenced containers, because the spirit of these texts is trying to convince them to "kill their self" mindfully. If a left brain influenced container, one who has not applied the remedy, tries to teach these texts they will ruin their self and anyone who listens to them, is another way to look at it. Relative to one with a sense of time these texts have so many rules and rules are a left brain trait so they will bog their self down with so many rules they will not be able to function and so they will be defeated and perhaps they will get closer to the 9th circle of hell, treason and then maybe apply the remedy.

Another way to look at it is the spirit of these texts is attempting to push a person with a sense of time to the 9th circle of hell, treason. A person will "break" one of the rules in these texts and then feel guilty and so they will feel "bad" and so they get a little closer to the 9th circle of hell, treason. In reality there are only two rules in all of the ancient texts, do not learn written education use oral education and if one does learn written education apply the fear not remedy to restore right brain, the god image in man. So every rule after those two rules are traps to force ones with a sense of time to feel bad and push them closer to the 9th circle of hell, treason, and treason is what "those who lose their life (mindfully)will preserve it" is. So one gets the mark from written education, and then they are "dead" mentally or spiritually, so they have to "die" to that mindfully and then they lose the mark and are alive again, mindfully or spiritually. So from a person who senses time point of view these texts are death and to one who has applied the remedy, one with no sense of time, these texts are life. This again is the reverse thing or the anti thing.

[Psalms 74:10 O God, how long shall the adversary reproach? shall the enemy blaspheme thy name for ever?]
Right brain is the god image in man so the adversary is left brain, so one who applies the remedy is a right brain influenced container and has no sense of time so the contrary to that is a left brain influenced container that does sense time. So sometimes a left brain influenced container will hear a right brain influenced container speak and say "That is wrong or bad" and that is correct relative to their influence.

[Mark 3:29 But he that shall blaspheme against the Holy Ghost hath never forgiveness, but is in danger of eternal damnation:]

Blaspheme against the holy spirit is a person who veils right brain in a child. It does not say if a person does this they are doomed on an absolute scale but it does say [is in danger of eternal damnation:] Eternal is relative to one with no sense of time. If one has no sense of time there is only infinity so they are unable to [Leviticus 19:26 Ye shall not eat any thing with the blood: neither shall ye use enchantment, nor [observe times].]

[observe times] = [Galatians 4:10 Ye observe days, and months, and times, and years.] = Their right brain is veiled so the paradox aspect is silenced so they sense time. [neither shall ye use enchantment] = This is suggesting one should not do anything that captivates or delights. This is a very complex reality relative to ones who sense time but what it really means is ones who do things for "fun" have not applied the remedy. Fun is a symptom that one senses time. Civilization killed all the Bison for fun. Beings that sense time will harm others for fun. Beings will harm their self for fun. This denotes delights. One who unveils right brain has only one drive and since civilization keeps veiling the children's right brain with their wisdom education and thus dooming the species, because children are the future of the species, there is not much time for fun, so to speak. The language is totally based on time and emotions so it is difficult to even use it.

[Leviticus 19:27 Ye shall not round the corners of your heads, neither shalt thou mar the corners of thy beard.] This is a rule and is why some beings never shave their beards. This is a good example that these texts are full of rules. One that has a sense of time or one who has not applied the remedy the full measure can bog their self down by attempting to follow all of the rules in these texts and that in fact is the purpose of all the rules in part, to keep them occupied so the few who have applied the remedy can get an advantage. Another way to look at these rules is, the ones who have no sense of time are outnumbered by about six billion so they have no rules because they cannot stop the ones who sense time, the left brain influenced containers, from veiling the right brain in the children to begin with, so rules mean nothing at all. If I grow a beard will that stop you from mentally raping the children into hell, veiling their right brain, with your wisdom education? I highly doubt it so the rules are meaningless after one applies the remedy. The goal of the right brain influenced are to stop the left brain influenced from veiling the children's right brain and how they accomplish that is relative to the orders they get when they are warming up, after they apply the fear not remedy.

[Mark 1:13 And he was there in the wilderness forty days, tempted of Satan; and was with the wild beasts; and the angels ministered unto him.] This is just after Jesus applied the remedy, Baptism aspect of the remedy, and so for forty days he was getting his: "marching orders" = [and the angels ministered unto him.]

Ones that sense time will go on into infinity suggesting rules but those rules are simply methods for them to secure the left brain influenced aspects desire to continue to veil the right brain, the god image in man, in the children. The left brain influenced use their rules to justify they get to keep veiling the children right brain so their rules are self serving and that is a method the left brain influence uses to remains in power. Go ask a rapist if raping people is against their rules and they will say "No." A child rapist see's raping a child is righteous. The left brain influence see's killing the right brain aspect in children is righteous and the people who are under the influence of left brain are simply containers doing the bidding of the left brain influence, the darkness. If veiling the god image in children, right brain, is righteous then civilization is righteous and if it is not righteous then civilization is pure evil because they do it on an industrial scale. There is an eastern concept, "If you are going to be evil be infinitely evil."
Relative to America there is only one "brand" of education and that is the form that veils right brain so they are infinitely evil or infinitely righteous depending on what you are influenced by, so to speak, such and such. I am an American but I assure you I am not your "brand" of American.

9:26:03 PM – These are some comments in the Coptic Gospel of Thomas. They are not listed in the ancient texts.

[These are the secret sayings which the living Jesus spoke and which Didymos Judas Thomas wrote down. 1 And he said, "Whoever finds the interpretation of these sayings will not experience death."] This comment is simply saying whoever applies the remedy will be able to understand these texts and so they are no longer dead, and thus mentally unsound, relative to the quick, the ones who apply the remedy, the ones with no sense of time, and the dead, the ones who have not yet applied the remedy, the ones that sense time.

[Jesus said, 2 Let him who seeks continue seeking until he finds. When he finds, he will become troubled. When he becomes troubled, he will be astonished, and he will rule over all.] This comment is relative to the wheat and chaff comment. A seeker is the wheat. A seeker is one who continues to attempt to apply the fear not remedy no matter what. I have one being I have convinced the remedy should be applied but they suggested it is too hard to apply and then slowly start to talk their self out of it. This giving up aspect is relative to left brain of course. [Let him who seeks continue seeking until he finds.] So this is saying if one starts to seek the kingdom, trying to unveil right brain, may they continue to try because it is not what it appears to be relative to results. For example I did not perceive I was applying the remedy at all, I perceived I was letting go of life when I was ill from taking all those pills. My mind said you are going to die if you do not call for help and I said "I do not care". So I had no clue at all I was applying the remedy. This is why one has to continue to seek a place that is going to get that hypothalamus to give them the death signal and then one just says "I don't care what happens" when it does give them that signal. Because of that, one has to literally from their perspective seek death but relative to reality just seek places where they think a shadow will kill them, not shark frenzies. [When he finds, he will become troubled.] This comment is in fact "Ignorance is bliss". When he finds means when one does unveil right brain they will become troubled or they will be aware of things they never were aware of and they will be troubled. So the antonym of ignorance is awareness so this line could be, when he becomes aware he will be troubled relative to the comment [wisdom is relative to grief]. I can suggest I am fully aware written education veils right brain and leaves people in a mental place of suffering but until you apply the remedy you perhaps will not be fully aware of that and when you become fully aware of that as a being you will be troubled but not sad or depressed you will just achieve infinite job security because although it may seem like you will just be able to explain it to civilization and they will adjust, that has not happened in over five thousand years of beings attempting to explain that so you perhaps will not have any better luck that the wise beings before you had, so this is when the focus on the log in your eye aspect comes in. You may write and explain it until you can no longer type and you may speak about it until you can no longer speak but keep the frame of mind you are assisting yourself understand it better because the ones you communicate with are in a deep neurosis and a deep denial state of mind and perhaps can never be reached and the vast majority in fact can never be reached, the mental damage they have from the written education is permanent considering how difficult the remedy is to apply from their perspective.

[When he becomes troubled, he will be astonished, and he will rule over all.] So one applies the remedy and becomes troubled because of the heightened awareness will show him things he never saw before then he will be astonished how far and wide the spread of this written education neurosis is and he will rule over all means, be aware of all things and then one will either focus on the log in their eye and become a master of concentration or they will implode. The more one concentrates the better they will become and the suffering they will be aware of is so great they will concentrate to a point there will be no human beings with a sense of time that can ever get near that being relative to mental clarity. This is relative to seeing demons as angels. If a person applies this remedy see's the ones who teach this written education improperly to children as demons then they will implode because that means there are six billion demons all around them but if one focuses on their self then they see the six billion demons as illusions and then they can slowly start to bend those illusions by suggesting proper things at proper times to the illusions. This is not an absolute by any means because everyone gets their own marching orders once they apply the remedy so that is their business and everyone adjusts to the heightened awareness differently. So the absolute in this comment by Jesus is [2 Let him who seeks continue seeking until he finds. When he finds, he will become troubled.] So one who seeks to apply the fear not remedy should keep trying because the remedy works every time it is applied properly, one perceives death and then fears not, and once they do that their "eyes" will be opened to things they never knew existed and they will be aware, troubled. Even after two lines from this text by Thomas these are certainly true comments by Jesus but even though they are not included in the ancient texts that does not mean if they were, your ability to apply the fear not remedy would be increased. What is in the ancient texts are more than enough in fact they are a repeating spirit over and over so they are very redundant as they are, and that also is not going to make applying the remedy and easier from your perspective. In a perfect world every one of these texts should be in the collective of the ancient texts but because beings who have a sense of time determine which ones are "good or bad" some very valuable comments by Jesus are simply neglected or not considered. A deeper reality is not one single line in any of the ancient texts have a flaw in them but that is relative to the observer of what influence one is under. A person with a sense of time will see many flaws and one who applies the remedy will find no flaws and this is because of the complexity of the ancient texts. Right brain has complexity so a person with right brain veiled simply cannot grasp the level of complexity required to properly understand the ancient texts until they unveil right brain complexity, and that is relative to the first sentence of these texts by Thomas [1 And he said, "Whoever finds the interpretation of these sayings will not experience death."] One who has not applied the remedy will read any one of these ancient texts and "hear but not understand" because these texts require complexity in thought, to understand. Without right brain unveiled one has no complexity in their thoughts. It simply is not possible so they are stuck with simple minded thoughts, and that is not an indication of absolute intelligence it is a symptom of an unsound mind as a result of getting years of left brain favoring education, so it is curable. One is factually mentally blinded after the education but they can see again they just have to make up their mind they want to see again, and then they will apply the remedy. Being mindful one is blind is the most important step to seeing again.

1/18/2010 5:05:50 PM-
MaryRainbows - http://www.youtube.com/watch?v=C9wDPex2I8I

I think we're outta time, I think
Do you ever hide your rainbow.
Do you ever wanna cut me inside.
Would you ever sell your self
I think you already have besides.
There is no time.

Do you ever look around and wish you didn't have this mind.
There is no time
Do you ever look around and wish you weren't so visibly blind.
There is no time

There is no time to go back now we're living in sin
There is no time to go back now we're living in sin
We're living in sin
I think were out of time I think
We're living in sin

Do you ever hide your rainbow.
Do you ever wanna cut me inside
There is no time
Would you ever cut yourself, I think you already have besides.
There is no time.

Do you ever look around and wish you didn't have this mind.
Do you ever look around and wish you weren't so fatally kind.

There is no time.

This song was created about three years after I in earnest started to try and kill myself. What that means is this song was created about three years after I took a razor and slashed my wrist eighteen times and sat in my apartment covered in blood and decided I no longer wanted to associate with civilization on any meaningful way and it was a full seven years after this that I had the accident, so this song was actually just the start of being in the 9th circle of hell, treason. This is relative to the comment "The meek shall inherit the earth." The chance a person who is pleased with their life with a sense of time can just walk out and apply the fear not, deny one's self remedy is very slim and that is an indication of how devastating many years of left brain heavy written education are on the mind. Another way to look at it is Jesus spoke to five thousand and twelve considered applying the remedy, those who lose their life mindfully will preserve their sound mind, life, and even one of those didn't make it through the 9th circle of hell, he ended up hanging himself, literally killing himself. One might suggest the 9th circle of hell takes its toll one way or another, on most. An aspect of right brain is creativity. One can understand civilization hates creativity and thus right brain simply because of the expression "A starving artist." A parent will see their child playing a guitar or painting a picture and say "Get back to your studies, you can't make any money being creative." This is relative to the comment misery loves company. The Pope recently attended an artist convention and suggested "Creativity is one path to God." And that is perfectly accurate but if the Pope was fully aware of what he was saying he would have said "Written education is the tree of knowledge and veils the god image in man so it needs to be adjusted." So you see everyone has a sliver of right brain still working and at times it comes out but that does not mean that person who has not applied the remedy is aware of what they are saying. The crescent moon concept flawlessly explains it. The mind after the education has this dark aspect called left brain and it is 90% of the mind and the right brain aspect is reduced to 10% so although right brain has a say, the left brain aspect of the being has no idea what right brain is saying because right brain is veiled. So with that in mind look at these lyrics I wrote seven years before the accident when I was in deep depression. I was on pot to make most of these songs, drugs unveil right brain and thus creativity so these comments are in fact right brain trying to communicate with me, a left brain influenced container, but at the time I had no clue what they really meant.

"Would you ever sell yourself, I think you already have besides."
This means I already sold my mind, right brain, for the promise of money by getting the traditional education. The more traditional education one gets the more money they may make and the more their right brain is veiled.

"Do you ever look around and wish you weren't so visibly blind."

This comment is not me, left brain influenced at the time, talking to anyone but me, the being in the center of that left brain influence. I cannot relate to who wrote that song but I can observe and understand where they are coming from and what that being was attempting to accomplish mindfully. So I am observing in hindsight, I assumed I was talking to someone other than myself but in reality no other person was even listening to this music but me. I was not a signed artist so I was writing to someone but it was not like a fan base or something. So on the drugs my right brain was unveiled and it was telling me, left brain influenced being, you are blind. So, I was working it out, I was working myself out of the neurosis and I was using creativity to do that. This is why the Pope said "Creativity is one path to God." even though he may not have been consciously aware that is exactly what he was saying. So this creativity as a method to escape the left brain influence is relative to this comment:
[Ephesians 5:18 And be not drunk with wine, wherein is excess; but be filled with the Spirit;]

So after one gets the education their creativity is essentially veiled or gone, so one does drugs to get some of it back but since this is not fantasy land many end up dying as a result of the drug usage. Many do drugs to feel the creativity of right brain but never do anything thought to be creative like music or painting they just like thinking.

Thinking itself on drugs is very creative. One ponders many things on drugs they do not "see" when they are sober.

So a person gets this written education and it veils their right brain then they have to do drugs that may end up killing them just to feel what they should be feeling to begin with if that "brand" of education was taught to them properly, at a much older age, after their mind was developed. This of course is vanity. If one was taught properly using oral education until their mind was developed then they would have worlds of creativity and thoughts and they could skip over the "do drugs to feel good" step all together.

"Would you ever cut yourself, I think you already have besides."

This comment from the song, at the time I assumed I was referring to someone else. On one hand I was also talking about the fact I cut myself with that razor. But now in hindsight I am mindful it was right brain telling me, the left brain influenced being, you are injured, you have right brain veiled.

"There is no time."

This certainly sounds like me now. This is in fact me at the time, left brain influenced, on drugs, and right brain was talking saying "there is no time". That is not at all what I perceived at the time but in hindsight that is exactly what was happening so my right brain was "ministering" to me and it could only do that when I was on drugs because it was veiled when I was not on drugs. It is understood many artists do drugs to be more creative and right brain is creativity so that proves drugs unveils right brain but the complexity is right brain should not be veiled unless something is done to veil it, IE written language is taught improperly and at way too young of an age to a child. So the sinister aspect is revealed when one understands not only is civilization pushing this written education on six year old children, veiling their creative aspect right brain, but then when that being does drugs to feel right brain, they are thrown in jail by that same civilization that veiled right brain to begin with, by force of

184

law. If you doubt that it is by force of law, tell the school board you will home school your own child and you will not teach that child by any method of education but oral education and will not even consider teaching your child written language or math until they are about sixteen or eighteen, and they will take that child from you under child endangerment laws and you will perhaps start to understand where you are at.

The deeper reality is the left brain influenced containers, the ones that sense time, are going to make sure every single child is turned into what they are, and if you try and stop them they will take care of you in short order and then explain how you are insane and evil for ever suggesting a child should not get their "brand" of education. I am humbled to explain reality to you but if you stand in the way of my purpose I will grind your bones to dust, here or there, my choice. So a psychologist see's a being who is depressed when in reality that being is attempting to work their way out of this left brain influenced neurosis the traditional education has put them in, and that psychologist will prescribe some drugs to that being and that alone proves that psychologist is still in the neurosis their self because to think ever into infinity a pill will cure this extreme neurosis shows such a lack of foresight, the word lunatic is an infinite compliment to explain that psychologist. Another way to look at it is, right brain should not be veiled to begin with so once it is veiled it is going to get itself unveiled even if it has to kill that being that houses it.

[C. J. (19) killed herself after battling with depression.]

The deeper meaning of these songs I wrote years before the accident is this right brain aspect is so powerful even at slight power as the result of doing drugs it is incredible in power and then once a being applies the remedy and unveils it properly and fully it is beyond that beings understanding. I try to avoid reading any of the previous books I have written because I will begin to clarify them. I will begin to explain what I said. I in fact am not at all talking to you although you would prefer to flatter yourself and assume I am but I am being ministered to. I am still in full blown learning mode. I am working on the log in my eye and I am learning a little more every time I type a sentence but I am not typing the sentence as much as right brain is typing the sentence and then I ponder the sentence and consider its meaning from every angle and then I write another sentence but this is happening at lightning speed relative to ones with a sense of time but relative to me it is normal speed. I always try to maintain if you think the spirit of what I type is impressive be mindful it is not me it is right brain I am simply along for the ride. I simply go with the flow and sometimes I go through very harsh understandings and they harm me so I try to escape that with harsh words but this is also happening at lightning speed relative to one with a sense of time so I recover swiftly and continue to learn. This concept of one going through this process and never experiencing harm mentally as a result of the heightened awareness is not possible. I went from brain dead to awake in a little over a year so that climb is also harsh but it cannot be related to any kind of harm one with a sense of time experiences. It's harm without harm and its suffering without suffering. It could be looked at like a woman experiences pain in having a child but it is a good pain. It's a pain that assists one to concentrate even harder so the end result is the mental harm caused by the heightened awareness after one applies the remedy is a required experience for one to wake up from the slumber. My fish heads are awaiting your retort.

9:40:08 PM – This is the 3rd comment in the Coptic Gospel of Thomas
3 Jesus said, ["If your leaders say to you, 'Look, the (Father's) kingdom is in the sky,' then the birds of the sky will precede you. If they say to you, 'It is in the sea,' then the fish will precede you. Rather, the kingdom is within you and it is outside you.
Jesus said , "When you know yourselves, then you will be known, and you will understand that you are children of the living Father. But if you do not know yourselves, then you
live in poverty, and you are the poverty."]
[When you know yourselves, then you will be known, and you will understand that you are children of the living Father.]
["If your leaders say to you, 'Look, the (Father's) kingdom is in the sky,] This comment is insulting civilization. The leaders who say "If you get our "brand" of education you can have a nice car and a nice slave job and a nice house and you will be happy."

[Rather, the kingdom is within you and it is outside you.] This comment is saying the kingdom is within, right brain, and that is where true happiness is, but your s was veiled by the traditional education so now you are just ascribe and the pen of the scribe is in vain. That's a nice way of me saying you got charmed.

Firstly you are not yourself after you get the written education you are a left brain influenced container, so you are under the influence of left brain and thus are of unsound mind so that is not you. You were born of sound mind and then the education made you of unsound mind so [When you know yourselves] means once you apply the fear not remedy you will know yourself, your sound minded self, your true self not this self you know in that left brain influenced haze you are in now.

[and you will understand that you are children of the living Father.] Children in this comment denotes you will be as you were before you got the education. You will trust everyone again, you will be without stress, you won't see angels as demons as you see now. You will stop seeing parts and start seeing reality relative to [Genesis 2:17 But of the tree of the knowledge of good and evil, thou shalt not eat of it: for in the day that thou eatest thereof thou shalt surely die.]

[good and evil] = seeing parts a left brain trait. So now you see things as parts and so you see some things that are pleasing in reality as evil so you are hallucinating and it causes you much suffering.

[you will understand] = This means you will be mindful, because of the strong intuition of many things so you do not need a book to tell you what you know. You will rely more on your intuition instead of intellect, which is what you rely on now, simply put you have to be told what to do because you have your intuition veiled. That's a nice way of saying you have been institutionalized.

[But if you do not know yourselves, then you live in poverty, and you are the poverty.] This is a very powerful comment and I ponder what sense of time abomination determined this book should not be in the collection of ancient texts. This comment is relative to the comment "I have seen the enemy and he is us" and also relative to "Man is his own worst enemy." Man being one who has not applied the remedy, one with a sense of time. So this comment is saying, If you have not applied the deny yourself, fear not remedy you have your right brain veiled, and you are mentally in poverty, in the place of suffering, in hell literally, and you are that suffering and you are that hell.

[4 Jesus said, "The person old in days won't hesitate to ask a little child seven days old about the place of life, and that person will live.]

[A person old in days] = a person who still senses time so they [Galatians 4:10 Ye observe days, and months, and times, and years.] mindfully. They are old because their mind sense time and so their mind acts accordingly relative to the aging process. If the mind does not sense time a person is younger mindfully, in fact with no sense of time a person will think about how old they are and the answer will always be zero, that is why this fear not remedy is what the fountain of youth is relative to: it's not how old you are its how old your mind thinks you are.

[a little child seven days old about the place of life, and that person will live.] A person who applies the remedy is reverted back to how they were mindfully before they got the education so they are a child relative to this comment [and you will understand that you are children of the living Father.] So this comment in whole is saying even a person who applied the remedy and is not fully warmed up understands the remedy and can explain it to a person "old in days", one who still senses time, and then if that person applies what that "child" says they will revert back to the child state of mind and they will live, unveil right brain, and resurrect, transform, go from being the dead to being the quick. So this comment answers this riddle.

[1 Peter 4:5 Who shall give account to him that is ready to judge the quick and the dead.]

The answer is : little child = ones who have applied the remedy. They are the only ones who have contrast to how they were, dead, and how they are after they apply the remedy, quick.

The dead cannot tell they are dead, but if they somehow apply the remedy they will understand they once were lost and now are found, they once were blind and now they see.

[5 Jesus said, "Know what is in front of your face, and what is hidden from you will be disclosed to you. For there is nothing hidden that will not be revealed. And there is
nothing buried that will not be raised."]

The blind cannot see what is right in front of their face. So [Know what is in front of your face] is saying throw down your nets and apply the remedy then you will "see" and
know this "spirit" is all around you, right in front of your face. I suggest I see wisdom in Swiss cheese commercials. [For there is nothing hidden that will not be revealed.] The complexity in this is right brain is so powerful with its pattern detection, intuition, heightened awareness and lightning fast random access processing, things one misses with right brain veiled all the sudden are very obvious or are revealed. There is nothing that will not be revealed and that is a literal, and that is how powerful right brain is when unveiled, one cannot explain how powerful right brain is when unveiled but I am trying to in infinite books with the understanding I will fail.

[And there is nothing buried that will not be raised.] This is a bit of optimism. It is saying, everyone starts off unburied, then they get the written education and are buried but anyone can be raised, if they apply the remedy, but since it is in fact mental suicide, deny one's self, many simply do not make that journey, they are the chaff, it's not their fault, it's an indication of what all that education has done to their mind, it was fatal mentally to them. They will never be raised or cured and that is why veiling a child's right brain with the education is the worst crime against humanity in the history of humanity and if one does not understand that they are too blind for me to describe in infinite books.

[8 And he said, The person is like a wise fisherman who cast his net into the sea and drew it up from the sea full of little fish. Among them the wise fisherman discovered a fine large fish. He threw all the little fish back into the sea, and easily chose the large fish. Anyone here with two good ears had better listen!]

This is a repeat of "seek ye first the kingdom" and "drop your nets" It is also a repeat of the parable of a man who finds a treasure. The little fish are meaningless details and the large fish is the remedy. Once a being with a sense of time understands the remedy and how to apply it they should do nothing else but try to apply the remedy and everything else, the little fish, will wait. The little fish will still be there but that large fish is the focus.

[Anyone here with two good ears had better listen!] Two good ears means a sound minded beings, one who has applied the remedy, both hemispheres at 50%, "two good ears". They hear and understand the words because of the heightened awareness aspect. They hear things the ones with a sense of time simply cannot grasp or understand. So Jesus is grooming his successors in this comment, he is saying those of you that have applied the remedy make sure you have these concepts down.

[9 Jesus said, Look, the sower went out, took a handful (of seeds), and scattered (them). Some fell on the road, and the birds came and gathered them. Others fell on rock, and they didn't take root in the soil and didn't produce heads of grain. Others fell on thorns, and they choked the seeds and worms ate them. And others fell on good soil, and it produced a good crop: it yielded sixty per measure and one hundred twenty per measure.]

This is the parable of sower. The sower is a person who has applied the remedy and goes about explaining it to the ones who have not applied the remedy. [a handful (of seeds),] = the remedy, telling people they have to deny their self , fear not, submit, go sit in a cemetery until they feel better. This aspect is never going to go over well because at the end of the day they have to commit mental suicide.

[and scattered (them).] = Means they tell a bunch of people who sense time the remedy. They are "preaching the word", the remedy. They tell everyone they can reach because one can never tell who will be able to understand the remedy and this is an indication of the odds one has to convince someone to apply the remedy and that is an indication of how devastating the neurosis is.

[Some fell on the road, and the birds came and gathered them. Others fell on rock, and they didn't take root in the soil and didn't produce heads of grain. Others fell on thorns, and they choked the seeds and worms ate them.]
This is the reality of how devastating the neurosis is. Sometimes a person hears the remedy and discounts it straight out and so they are usually the ones with a full cup and so they simply have no chance or they are too far gone mentally. These beings are the ones very close to, or in the first circle of hell, limbo.

[Others fell on rock, and they didn't take root in the soil and didn't produce heads of grain.]
These beings are one who hear the remedy and ponder it for a bit but before long they get back to their nets and forget the remedy and never consider it again. So these beings are in the 2nd to 5th circle of hell. Didn't take root means that being never fully understood what the remedy means as far as, it is difficult to convince a blind man, blindness is abnormal. They tend to underestimate the value of having right brain unveiled.

[Others fell on thorns, and they choked the seeds and worms ate them.]
These are beings who hear the remedy and even attempt to apply the remedy but after a couple tries the "left brain influence" talks them out of it so eventually "the worms" eat away their desire to apply the remedy. So these beings are in the 6th to 8th circle of hell.

[And others fell on good soil, and it produced a good crop: it yielded sixty per measure and one hundred twenty per measure.]
This is the .0024 percent. The ones who not only hears the remedy they dedicate everything to apply the remedy and they succeed, [it produced a good crop], which means the remedy is applied and then [it yielded sixty per measure and one hundred twenty per measure.] which means then they become the sower of the seeds, the remedy.

So this parable is like an infinite circle. The whole point of anyone who applies the remedy is to attempt to convince one other person to apply the remedy in hopes that person will do better than they did at sowing the seeds. Of course this is not fantasy land so that is not always how it works out. The reality is the left brain influenced have an industrial sized setup relative to veiling the children's right brain, the god image in man, and they have a fierce army to protect their "industry' so they can create far more "blind" than anyone can stop, perhaps, perhaps.

[10 Jesus said, "I have cast fire upon the world, and look, I'm guarding it until it blazes.]
This comment harms me. He was saying that he was very adept at explaining how the remedy was to be applied and he convinced at least 11 good sowers and he was waiting for them to start sowing and waking up others but of course, the left brain influenced containers, the abominations with a sense of time, the whore servants, caught up with Jesus and silenced him with some nine inch nails. Never get the impression you can stop the left brain influenced containers they have a monopoly on the children and that is their only goal and they have great numbers so the best you can do is focus on the remedy and focus on concentration after you apply the remedy. Do the best you can to follow the orders "ministered" to you after you apply the remedy but avoid having illusions of grandeur because the heightened awareness is going to be so great you are going to want to act to protect the children from the sinister and that will only get you killed. Of course I speak in paradox.

[11 Jesus said, "This heaven will pass away, and the one above it will pass away. The dead are not alive, and the living will not die. During the days when you ate what is dead, you made it come alive. When you are in the light, what will you do? On the day when you were one, you became two. But when you become two, what will you do?"]

[The dead are not alive] = ones with a sense of time are mentally dead in contrast to ones who unveil right brain; the quick and the dead reference.

[and the living will not die.] which means once one applies the remedy they cannot go back to being dead, having right brain veiled. So, as a child one has right brain unveiled but their mind is not fully developed at the age of six or seven, so all that written education veils right brain but then after a person is mentally developed and they apply the remedy it is permanent. Another way to look at it is the remedy is not making the mind something it should not naturally be if that person did not get the civilizations "brand" of education, so the remedy is simply undoing the damage civilizations "brand" of education caused, to begin with.

[During the days when you ate what is dead, you made it come alive.] This means a person with a sense of time is dead mentally and only they can decide to apply the remedy, in one way or another, knowingly or unknowingly. I did not perceive I was applying the remedy when I was applying it but in hindsight I am mindful I was in the 9th circle of hell, treason, and so I was applying the remedy or in a position to apply the remedy so in that respect, I did: .= [you made it come alive.] You did not put yourself in this left brain influenced state of mind, but only you can get yourself out of it, is another way to look at it. First one must understand if they got the education they are in what is known as hell but they cannot tell, so they have to have faith that written education is the tree of knowledge and they ate off it, and the next step is the fear not remedy. If one has a sense of time they have to apply the remedy if they wish to escape hell, and that is just reality.

[When you are in the light, what will you do?] This is a very powerful comment. You may perceive applying the remedy is the end but it is in fact it is the start and there is no end after the start. Are you going to go hide after you find the light, after you apply the remedy? Are you going to mask what you understand in ways to protect yourself? Are you going to speak boldly about what you understand about written education after you apply the remedy, and find the light?

Are you going to hide when you see how vast Goliaths armies are? Are you going to stand by and allow the children to be eaten by the sinister in order to protect yourself from the sinister? I am going to let the light shine with the understanding it is infinitely deadly to let the sinister see the light shine. I have decided not to hide so perhaps you will be able to hide. Perhaps I will assist you in understanding the definition of fearlessness in the face of vast armies. Perhaps I will do what I am mindful you may not be able to do when you apply the remedy. Perhaps I am suggesting the truth about written education so you do not have to. You focus on the applying the remedy so you can see, firstly.

[On the day when you were one, you became two. But when you become two, what will you do?]
One denotes simple minded, denotes left brain influenced, denotes of unsound mind, denotes left brain is at 90% and right brain is veiled to 10% so one is of single mind.
[But when you become two, what will you do?] Two denotes both hemispheres working at 50/50, mental harmony. When you apply this remedy you are going to become a minority because the entire world is full of beings with right brain veiled, left brain influenced beings. You will be joining a club of the few to fight against the armies of the many. Never underestimate that reality.

[12 The disciples said to Jesus, "We know that you are going to leave us. Who will be our leader?" Jesus said to them, "No matter where you are you are to go to James the Just, for whose sake heaven and earth came into being."]
So James was the successor to Jesus.

[Matthew 3:11 I indeed baptize you with water unto repentance: but he that cometh after me is mightier than I, whose shoes I am not worthy to bear: he shall baptize you with the Holy Ghost, and with fire:]

Consider the spirit of these two comments.

[No matter where you are you are to go to James the Just, for whose sake heaven and earth came into being."]
[but he that cometh after me is mightier than I, whose shoes I am not worthy to bear:]

The first comment is Jesus suggesting James is his successor and the second comment is John the Baptist suggesting Jesus is his successor. This is simply an appointment of a successor and in order to do that one has to suggest the successor is greater or the people will not follow the successor. So this means Jesus was fully aware of his fate. Of course John the Baptist was fully aware of his own fate also. That is kind of the name of the game, if you are worth your salt in this location the sinister is going to get you one way or another. So this comment by Thomas is perhaps why the ones who sense time did not include this text in the ancient texts.

[James the Just, for whose sake heaven and earth came into being."]
Jesus was saying James is greater than me. Of course John the Baptist said Jesus was greater than him, when in reality Jesus assisted or explained to James how to apply the remedy so Jesus was James' teacher and John the Baptist baptized Jesus, which is the fear not remedy, so John the Baptist was the teacher of Jesus.

["We know that you are going to leave us. Who will be our leader?"]
This "who will be our leader" aspect is proof these beings or at least some of them had not applied the remedy yet. They want to be told what to do. Once one applies the remedy they unveil right brain intuition and they know at all times what to do, they do not need to be told what to do. I am mindful to suggest, I can explain the remedy but once you apply it you are on your own. I am not your leader and I never will be. I am just a student attempting to introduce you to the teacher, right brain. I am just explaining the remedy so you can "catch fish" for yourself so to speak. You can give a being a fish, or teach them to fish so that being can feed their self for their whole life, something along those lines. Even I have moments of clarity.

This next comment convinces me the beings who read this book had not applied the remedy and so they were all caught up in keeping Jesus above all the other prophets perhaps for profits.

[13 Jesus said to his disciples, "Compare me to something and tell me what I am like."
Simon Peter said to him, "You are like a just messenger."
Matthew said to him, "You are like a wise philosopher."
Thomas said to him, "Teacher, my mouth is utterly unable to say what you are like."
Jesus said, "I am not your teacher. Because you have drunk, you have become intoxicated from the bubbling spring that I have tended."
And he took him, and withdrew, and spoke three sayings to him. When Thomas came back to his friends they asked him, "What did Jesus say to you?"
Thomas said to them, "If I tell you one of the sayings he spoke to me, you will pick up rocks and stone me, and fire will come from the rocks and devour you."]

["You are like a just messenger."] This is true Jesus was a messenger, right brain influenced, attempting to explain that written education veils the god image in a person and then he explain the remedy to that, deny one's self, and those who lose their life mindfully will preserve it, unveil that god image, right brain.

["You are like a wise philosopher."] This is true. Socrates suggested no true philosopher fears death and Jesus said, those who lose their life mindfully will preserve it and both of those are simply the fear not remedy Abraham suggested. A philosopher asks "Why" oft, or is always pondering why, and ambiguity is a right brain trait, which is why one is always pondering why. This pondering why, or ambiguity is very healthy because it keeps one from ever getting to a point they stop questioning their own actions and deeds and this also helps one not be so judgmental of their self.

[Thomas said to him, "Teacher, my mouth is utterly unable to say what you are like."] Thomas was on one hand being very humble but also Jesus applied the remedy the full measure so I am mindful Jesus was a powerhouse, a Master of the house in every definition of the word so in that respect Thomas was being very honest. Thomas was saying "You are unbelievably wise." Of course right brain is wise that is why is it unwise to veil it with the education. Don't shoot off the good foot, right brain, to save the other foot, left brain, so to speak.

-

[Jesus said, "I am not your teacher. Because you have drunk, you have become intoxicated from the bubbling spring that I have tended."]

So this is the main reason this text was not included in the main body of the ancient texts.
["I am not your teacher.] contradicts [John 14:6 Jesus saith unto him, I am the way, the truth, and the life: no man cometh unto the Father, but by me.] But a contradiction is just a paradox and paradox is a right brain trait and a symptom of complexity, another right brain trait, so these texts being full of contradictions prove they are genuine but the ones with a sense of time look at contradictions and paradox as evil because they hate right brain, the god image in man or they would not veil it with their "wisdom" education relative to [Genesis 3:6 , and a tree to be desired to make one wise,..]

You are not very wise now, are you?

[Because you have drunk, you have become intoxicated from the bubbling spring that I have tended."]
Because you have drunk simply means these beings have applied the remedy to a degree, at least some of them had. There is this complexity to this remedy. It can be applied in many, many ways but unless one goes the full measure they may not unveil right brain fully which means bring it back up to 50%. One must be in a situation they are mindful of death, a scary place for example, and when their hypothalamus says "Run or you will factually die." They must not run but close their eyes and say "I don't care if I die." Simply put one must be mindful of death and then submit to death. If one does it any other way they may only partially unveil right brain and thus

197

not go the full measure and end up lukewarm, so to speak. This remedy is an indication of how devastating that written education is on the mind when taught at such a young age. If there was any there way to undo the mental side effects and unveil right brain fully I am mindful these wise beings would have found it and suggested it. You can continue to second guess these wise beings with your suggestions of pills and operations but you will never ever be able to come up with a better remedy than these wise beings came up with. The written education bends the mind, so in order to unbend the mind a mental exercise is required and it just so happens to be, one has to defeat their fear of death.

[, you have become intoxicated from the bubbling spring that I have tended] Intoxicated denotes the cerebral "high" one is always under once they unveil right brain. This intoxication is so strong "getting high" on drugs doesn't do much anymore relative to a cerebral high of course that is because the high one feels on drugs is simply right brain being unveiled just a bit and only for the duration the drugs lasts.

[bubbling spring that I have tended] This is interesting because a spring never stops flowing. One might suggest when right brain unveils thoughts are going to be rushing out as an endless river flows. [that I have tended] Simply means Jesus has applied the remedy and has unveiled right brain and he is simply a container or a messenger for right brain. Jesus is speaking on behalf of right brain is another way to look at it. So Jesus is not saying "I, Jesus am so great" he is saying "I am just tending to what is so great.", right brain. Of course by typing these comments I am mindful of this comment:

[Matthew 9:3 And, behold, certain of the scribes said within themselves, This man blasphemeth.]

And I will humbly remind any scribes who are suggesting the spirit of what I suggest is blaspheme they should first should apply the remedy Jesus suggested [Luke 17:33 ...; and whosoever shall lose his life(mindfully) shall preserve it.]. And as for me, doubting scribes, I do not pander to what I own. If any of these wise beings wanted you to idolize them they simply would not have told us the remedy. Abraham would not have said "fear not" and he also would not have explained it in the Abraham and Isaac explanation. John the Baptist would have never explained his version of the fear not remedy with his baptism method. Jesus never would have said [Luke 17:33 ...; and whosoever shall lose his life(mindfully) shall preserve it.]. Mohammed never would have said submit. Socrates never would have said no true philosopher fears death. Buddha never would have said, sit in a cemetery and meditate. So before you think these beings were selfish, they factually told every human on this planet the remedy, so that alone proves they were not self serving, they only wanted everyone to know the remedy so everyone could restore their mind to how it is suppose to be, because they knew everyone was going to get the written education forced on them by the sinister. One would be very hard pressed to find a human at least of eighteen who has not heard the saying [Psalms 23:4 Yea, though I walk through the valley of the shadow of death, I will fear no evil: for thou art with me; thy rod and thy staff they comfort me.]

That comment has been in front of everyone's face but they simply did not see it. [5 Jesus said, "Know what is in front of your face, and what is hidden from you will be disclosed to you.] These words from the ancient texts are all interchangeable and all interlock and because they are all written by different people at different times they transcend the people who wrote them. These words have a mind of their own and so the people are simply messenger's of these words. The right brain influence is the arranger of the words and its uses people to get the words written down or spoken but the words arranged go beyond the people who speak and write them. I get this impression I cannot explain this remedy any better but that is an illusion because the only reality is .0024 percent chance of a person applying this remedy, and that is an indication of how mentally damaging written education is on the mind. I at times forget it took me ten years and thirty fail suicide attempts to apply this remedy accidentally, and I could just as well be this [S.V. (19) committed suicide by taking a deadly cocktail of antidepressants]

I try forever.

One has to go to the scariest place they can find with the intention they will be killed by a ghost or shadow or demon so they must be suicidal to do that and then when their mind tells them this spook is coming they have to not run, so they have to be a suicidal fool. And the complexity to that is, if you try to be safe and try to just half do it, it will perhaps never fully unveil right brain. What one is in the left brain influenced, sense of time, mind set is death, so they can look at it like they have to want life so much, sound mind, they want to kill that left brain influenced state of mind which is to trick "it" into letting them go by staging a fake death, so to speak. That of course is sugar coating it. If one ever wants their right brain unveiled they better take a serious interest in seeking death because that thing they are influenced by, is no slouch and is very clever and only ones with great self control can never trick "it" into letting them go. I am not suggesting you put yourself in this situation, you were a child when you were put into this situation by left brain influenced containers, but I assure you, only you can get yourself out of the situation. You can call it the place you are in if that makes it easier for you to commit mental suicide.

[15 Jesus said, "When you see one who was not born of woman, fall on your faces and worship. That one is your Father."]
Firstly the word woman is a contrast statement not actual females. Born of woman is a person that is born into a family that has not applied the remedy after getting the written education. Women is slang for the whore, the serpent, not literal females just the ones that sense time. What that means is that family is not even aware they have the "curse" so they will certainly give the "curse" to their first born, their child. So this comment is saying, if you see a person who has applied the remedy, that one is of the Father, father being right brain. A being that is not of civilization is a broader meaning. Civilization judges people on how much education they get, so anyone who is against civilizations "brand" of education is one who has applied the remedy and is speaking about the dangers of written education and thus they are speaking against civilization. It's a package deal, if you want to die swiftly explain the mental effects of civilizations "brand" of written education and publish it in books and distribute

them on a worldwide scale. Perhaps I am testing that understanding. Speaking of the word perhaps:

[16 Jesus said, "Perhaps people think that I have come to cast peace upon the world. They do not know that I have come to cast conflicts upon the earth: fire, sword, war. For there will be five in a house: there'll be three against two and two against three, father against son and son against father, and they will stand alone.]

Jesus did not go through what he went through to unveil right brain just to stand by and watch civilization continue to veil children's right brain with its "brand" of education. Until one applies the remedy and unveils right brain they will never, ever understand how powerful it is. Once one does unveil it they will fully understand Jesus was telling the truth when he said [They do not know that I have come to cast conflicts upon the earth: fire, sword, war.] and that is why civilization killed Jesus and killed the disciples and killed the Christians and all the ones that don't sense time, before them and after them because civilization is the serpent cult and all it does is veils the right brain in children with its "brand" of education and then celebrates the fact it killed all the wise beings by having feasts in winter to celebrate the birth of the truth and celebrates the death of the truth in spring. The cult celebrates birth of the truth in the season of death and death of the truth in the season of birth. That's all one ever has to know about the cult, civilization, the ones that sense time, the sinister. Do you perceive Jesus was going to sit on his hands and watch the sinister harm the children? If so you are very infinitely more delusional than I suspected and I already understand you are very infinitely delusional.

"What it comes down to is that modern society discriminates against the right hemisphere." - Roger Sperry (1973)
"What it comes down to is that modern society discriminates against the right hemisphere." - Roger Sperry (1973)
"What it comes down to is that modern society discriminates against the right hemisphere." - Roger Sperry (1973)

I pasted that three times since you can't speak English.

1/19/2010 12:29:18 PM – It's better to die for nothing than to die for a fading trend. It's better to live for nothing than die for a fading trend. It's better to die for nothing than live for a fading trend. You have 10% mental capacity after the education and you do not think that is true because you only have 10% mental capacity.

11:56:53 PM – [Genesis 4:2 And she again bare his brother Abel. And Abel was a keeper of sheep, but Cain was a tiller of the ground.]

[Abel was a keeper of sheep] This is a being who applies the remedy and attempts to explain the reason the remedy is needed, because of the tree of knowledge, written education, and the reason why ones who have not applied the remedy it should apply it, to unveil right brain, so this is a being with right brain unveiled, one with no sense of time, sometimes known as the good shepherd.

[Cain was a tiller of the ground.] This is a being with a sense of time that has not applied the remedy but did get the education. Ground denotes physical aspects or physical mental focus. For example civilization is ground focused, they move into an area and destroy all the natural resources and harvest all the minerals and animals so that is their main focus because the right brain is veiled so they are stuck with seeking value in the material world.

[Genesis 4:3 And in process of time it came to pass, that Cain brought of the fruit of the ground an offering unto the LORD.]
[Cain brought of the fruit of the ground as an offering unto the LORD.] This comment explains how the ones who have a sense of time give money and their physical possessions and assume that has some sort of value. One cannot offer physical aspects to a cerebral aspect, so to speak, the two are totally separate or are contrary. Ones with a sense of time assume their money is going to apply the remedy for them.

[Genesis 4:4 And Abel, he also brought of the firstlings of his flock and of the fat thereof. And the LORD had respect unto Abel and to his offering:]

[And Abel, he also brought of the firstlings of his flock] Abel brought beings he convinced to apply the remedy, which relative to this book of the ancient texts denotes sacrifice relative to I walk through the valley of the shadow of death I [sacrifice], which is the same as fear not, submit, deny one's self.

[Genesis 6:1 And it came to pass, when men began to multiply on the face of the earth, and daughters were born unto them,]

[when men began to multiply on the face of the earth] Men in this comment are ones with a sense of time.[Genesis 6:2 That the sons of God saw the daughters of men that they were fair; and they took them wives of all which they chose.]

[That the sons of God] Sons of God are ones who apply the remedy and had no sense of time. So this comment explains how the ones who applied the remedy did associate with the "fair" daughters of the "men", the ones with a sense of time who did not apply the remedy. "Fair" denotes these women did not get the education so they were "fair" or did not have the "curse". The women did not always get the education and that is important because the women raise the children and so one did not want a cursed being raising children. The deeper reality is the men got the education because they, this is tricky, they are more able to apply the remedy so to speak. It's not an insult to women, it is just men are the protectors of the women because the women are the dominates of the species. So the men are more able to defeat their fear of death, so the women didn't get the curse, education, at least at this stage.

[That the sons of God saw the daughters of men(cursed) that they were fair(not cursed)]

It is worse to give this curse to women than to men. Men are expendable but women have the children. You want to ruin the entire species, give the women the curse, is one way to look at it.

[Genesis 6:3 And the LORD said, My spirit shall not always strive with man, for that he also is flesh: yet his days shall be an hundred and twenty years.]

[My spirit shall not always strive with man] this comment means right brain is not of men, the ones with no sense of time, so [shall not always strive] means they are born with right brain unveiled [the spirit] but then the written education veils right brain so it stops striving, its veiled.

[for that he also is flesh: yet his days shall be an hundred and twenty years.] [Flesh] denotes the ones with a sense of time are physical focused because their cerebral powerhouse, right brain is veiled. This comment is relative to [that Cain brought of the fruit of the ground.] So the comment could also read [for that he is of the fruit of the ground].

[yet his days shall be an hundred and twenty years] This comment denotes the "men" have a sense of time. When a person has right brain veiled they sense time so a hundred and twenty years feels like that amount of time, when right brain in unveiled one has no sense of time mindfully so there is no concept of time to be able to feel one hundred twenty years so they perceive infinite time only or no time. So human beings live one hundred twenty years but the ones who apply the remedy perceive they live for eternity because they don't sense time because right brain is unveiled and the ones who do not apply the remedy have very fast lives, their life passes swiftly relative to their perception of time.

[Genesis 6:4 There were giants in the earth in those days; and also after that, when the sons of God came in unto the daughters of men, and they bare children to them, the same
became mighty men which were of old, men of renown.]

[There were giants in the earth in those days] is the same as saying sons of God, cerebral giants, the quick, in contrast to the dead, which were the men, the ones with a sense of time.

[when the sons of God came in unto the daughters of men, and they bare children to them] Repeat of this comment [Genesis 6:2 That the sons of God saw the daughters of men that they were fair; and they took them wives of all which they chose.]

[Genesis 6:5 And GOD saw that the wickedness of man was great in the earth, and that every imagination of the thoughts of his heart was only evil continually.]

[And GOD saw that the wickedness of man was great in the earth] The ones that sense time, the ones that did not apply the remedy were wicked which means they were of unsound mind or of the serpent and of the earth, physical focused, relative to: [Genesis 1:1 In the beginning God created the heaven(right brain) and the earth(left brain).]
[and that every imagination of the thoughts of his heart was only evil continually.] This denotes unsound mentally, because their right brain is veiled. This is saying everything about them was damaged goods or fruits of a damaged mind or tree. They had no redeeming qualities at all because a mind divided is an unviable mind. Once right brain is veiled, as a result of the written education, unless the remedy is applied the being is unviable in every way possible. [thoughts of his heart(mind) was only evil(unnatural) continually] = hell, the place of suffering. A mentally unsound being is only capable of exhibiting mentally unsound fruits and deeds, so they have no redeemable qualities until they apply the remedy to return to sound mind, unveil right brain. There are no exceptions to this reality although a mentally unsound being may wish there was.

[Genesis 6:6 And it repented the LORD that he had made man on the earth, and it grieved him at his heart.] This comment explains how the ones who did apply the remedy had much grief that these "men" did not apply the remedy. Relative to this comment [Ecclesiastes 1:18 For in much wisdom is much grief: and he that increaseth knowledge increaseth sorrow.] So grief is one way to explain the mental sensation of watching your fellow species that has their right brain veiled suffer, but they are so mentally unsound they cannot be salvaged or convinced to apply the remedy. So it is not depression it is a cerebral grief, like a frustration but without prolonged emotions.

The language cannot explain it. [and he that increaseth knowledge increaseth sorrow.] = tree of knowledge leads to sorrow relative to [Genesis 3:16 .... I will greatly multiply thy sorrow ....; sorrow thou shalt... rule over thee.] because the written education veils right brain.

[Genesis 6:7 And the LORD said, I will destroy man whom I have created from the face of the earth; both man, and beast, and the creeping thing, and the fowls of the air; for it repenteth me that I have made them.]

[the LORD said, I will destroy man] This is first indication the ones with no sense of time, the Lords and Masters determined the only way to stop the spread of the curse caused by written education was to kill all the men, the ones with a sense of time.

[Genesis 6:9 These are the generations of Noah: Noah was a just man and perfect in his generations, and Noah walked with God.]
[Noah was a just man and perfect in his generations, and Noah walked with God.] This comment means Noah got the education but then he applied the remedy and unveiled right brain so [Noah walked with God.] which means he has right brain, the god image in man, unveiled after it was veiled.

[Genesis 6:11 The earth also was corrupt before God, and the earth was filled with violence.]
Corrupt denotes the ones with a sense of time were starting to grow in numbers and a trait of their unsound mind was violence. The ones with a sense of time kill everything in their path and it is usually to make a quick buck or for control, which denotes coveting, lust and greed.

[Genesis 6:13 And God said unto Noah, The end of all flesh is come before me; for the earth is filled with violence through them; and, behold, I will destroy them with the earth.]

[The end of all flesh is come before me] = exterminate the ones with a sense of time = "men", flesh denotes physical focus. [for the earth is filled with violence through them;] "them" denotes the ones with a sense of time, the ones who got the education and did not apply the remedy to re-unveil right brain.

[I will destroy them with the earth.] "I" means Noah decided it was best to kill the "men". Noah had right brain unveiled and it did the calculations and with the intuition Noah determined it's best to just kill them all to stop the spread of the curse, relative to [Genesis 3:14 And the LORD God said unto the serpent, Because thou hast done this(got written education and did not apply the remedy), thou art cursed...]

What this Noah solution explains is the only true remedy to the situation for the species, which is to kill everyone and leave just a few who have right brain unveiled and start all over. This is an indication of how strong the "curse" is and not an indication of these wise beings not being concerned it is more of an indication of how concerned they were.

It is similar to a situation where a whole city gets a contagious plague and that city is quarantined and everyone in that city is going to die to save the rest of the species. Sometimes the Ebola virus breaks out in a village and they do not let anyone leave that village and that whole village dies, would be a hypothetical example. The curse [Genesis 3:14 ..thou hast done this(got written education and did not apply the remedy), thou art cursed...] begets more cursed. A parent gets the education and they are cursed and they give the education to their child and that child is cursed and before you know it the curse is everywhere and none of the people who have the curse even know they have the curse at all because their right brain is veiled when they are a small child so they have no way to tell their right brain has been veiled. Not one single human being on this planet knows their right brain was veiled, they have to have faith it was veiled by the education, then they have to commit mental suicide to undo that damage, and those two aspects alone make breaking the curse nearly impossible on an individual level, then on a species level, it's impossible to break the curse so this Noah's solution was to just kill everyone with the curse [The end of all flesh] and just start over. So this Noah solution to the curse was on a huge scale but at this time there was so many with the curse.

Then Abraham and Lot came and this Noah solution was not possible at all, so they just burned down the cities of the ones with a sense of time, then as the text continue the ability to control the curse, the ones with a sense of time, diminishes and even with Moses, he could not burn the cities he could just attacked the cities and make the cities let people go so Moses could attempt to assist them to apply the remedy to the curse. Since the Noah solution did not work, and it was the ultimate solution to stop the spread of the curse, all the other attempts obviously failed because they were all less absolute than the Noah solution. Noah wanted to kill everyone with curse, a sense of time. Abraham and Lot just destroyed a few cities and Moses couldn't even do that so he just attacked the cities. There is no way to ever stop the curse now on a species scale but one can negate the curse on their self but even then they only have a .0024 percent chance. The reality is civilization is going to continue giving the curse, veiling children's right brain, into infinity and all the wishful thinking one can have means nothing because this is a curse and at this stage it cannot be stopped at all on a species level. Simply put relative to the ones with a sense of time, the ones with the curse, written education is [Genesis 3:6 ...desired to make one wise,..] so if one speaks out against that "brand" of education and suggests only giving children oral education, they look like a fool to the ones cursed, because the ones cursed only see truth as lies. This Noah story has a hidden meaning. It is also explaining what happens to a person when they apply the remedy.

[Genesis 7:17 And the flood was forty days upon the earth; and the waters increased, and bare up the ark, and it was lift up above the earth.]

[Mark 1:13 And he was there in the wilderness forty days, tempted of Satan; and was with the wild beasts; and the angels ministered unto him.]

[Amos 5:25 Have ye offered unto me sacrifices and offerings in the wilderness forty years, O house of Israel?]

[And the flood was forty days upon the earth] = [in the wilderness forty days] = [offerings in the wilderness forty years] all relative to [the angels ministered unto him.]

The spirit of these comments is relative to the mental drowning of a person who applies the remedy and that is relative to the transformation, and resurrection from the dead. Dead being the mental state when right brain is veiled after getting the written education and resurrection is relative to applying the remedy and right brain is unveiled and then one mentally is out of service for at least forty days while right brain unveils. This is an indication of how powerful right brain is and since a person had their veiled as a child they apply the remedy and unveil it, and mentally they feel like they got hit by a Mac truck and they are mentally paralyzed for some period even as long as two months because the mind is not use to having right brain in a conscious position. So the hidden meaning in the Noah flood is, when a person unveils right brain they are mentally drowned for forty days and then it may take a year to fully get use to this new state of mind. This is relative to one who applies the remedy to the full measure. It is very pronounced and so if one tries to apply the remedy through meditation/prayer it will not be as pronounced but equally they may not fully unveil right brain. Prayer is meditation one is not supposed to be asking for money they are supposed to be avoiding those thoughts of greed and not thinking at all, and that is a form of denying one's self but it is a very slow method to apply the remedy and I don't know anything about sloth. These texts deal with the full measure remedy, go through the valley of the shadow of death and fear not, seek perceived death and then submit to it, and anything short of that will not unveil right brain fully.

[Genesis 8:11 And the dove came in to him in the evening; and, lo, in her mouth was an olive leaf pluckt off: so Noah knew that the waters were abated from off the earth.]

[Luke 3:22 And the Holy Ghost descended in a bodily shape like a dove upon him, and a voice came from heaven, which said, Thou art my beloved Son; in thee I am well pleased.]

So these comments are repeat comments. The first comment is Noah explaining the drowning he experienced and then after forty days a "dove" appeared and that denotes he started to get use to right brain being unveiled. And the Luke comment is Jesus just after John the Baptist applied the baptism version of the fear not remedy and this comment [And the Holy Ghost descended in a bodily shape like a dove upon him] means right brain was unveiled. Noah had the forty days after right brain was unveiled and then a "dove" came to him and that meant he was starting to get use to right brain being unveiled, and Jesus had a dove come to him which means he was aware the remedy worked, unveiled right brain, and then it took him forty days to get use to it. The dove means peace, or one escapes hell, the place of suffering so one is at peace mindfully or returned to sound mind.

[Mark 1:13 And he was there in the wilderness forty days, ... and the angels ministered unto him.] So this comment just means it takes a while to get use to right brain after it is unveiled and during that time one mentally adjusts from only having sequential slothful thoughts to having lightening speed heightened intuition thoughts. So the forty days is how much time it takes to just adjust to right brain unveiling and after that they will be able to mentally function again and then it will take a year to get to a point it feels normal to be in that lightening fast thought processing and heightened awareness, relatively speaking. - 1:29:27 AM

1/20/2010 1:50:04 PM – Bending an illusion is possible, controlling an illusion is not. Punishment is suffering unless one sees it as a well earned understanding. When ignorance decreases grief increases so concentration is paramount. In order to wake up one has to let go of slumber. Grief assists one in understanding what angers them. Written education veils right brain and in turn increases emotional capacity and thus concentration is hindered. Written education is a tool and if not taught properly devastates the mind of a child. Right brain has paradox and civilization hates contradictions and thus right brain. Society is left brain influenced containers whose only goal is to make a right brain influenced child like they are, via education. Traditional education bends the mind to the left and in turn alters ones perception and therefore is simply a thought control tool. An understanding is not as important as understanding what to do with it. The remedy to the education induced mental damage costs one everything they mentally have which is very little.

Relative to psychological disorder:
Conduct Disorder: A pattern of repetitive behavior where the rights of others or the social norms are violated. There are many symptoms relative to the "disorder" but this is just a rule breaker. One complexity to this is to understand firstly this being has had their mind bent to the left as a result of the education. So this being is a left brain influenced container. So these rule breaking episodes are simply right brain attempting to unveil itself. The problem with that is left brain is what this being is influenced by so right brain is sending signals on a subconscious level to break rules because right brain dislikes rules and then this being takes that signal and translates it using left brain conscious mind and this in turn results in the person harming others, attempting to control others. Essentially they come across as a bully and come across as having no respect for others properly or rights. This of course is what civilization is. Civilization saw the Africans and controlled them and bullied them and disrespected their rights and controlled them. Civilization saw the Native Americans and took everything they had and put them into concentration camps. So the right brain dislikes rules and respects no one because it is way too powerful but when it is veiled those signals are coming out through the left brain influenced aspect on a conscious level so they are misfire signals. One way to look at it is, I have right brain in a conscious state so I do not like rule but that does not mean I harm people that means I wish to be left alone

and think for myself, using right brain intuition. I do not need any human on this planet to tell me what I better do or better not do because I do not perceive any human being on this planet knows as well as right brain knows, so I prefer to think for myself, using right brain intuition. Another way to look at it is, your rules and norms said I had to get the "brand" of education that veiled right brain and that nearly killed me. Another way to look at it is, I do not pay heed to the suggestions of factually mentally unsound lunatics, I think for myself from here on out. That's the interesting thing about right brain, it does not seek to harm others but at the exact same time it has no problems with it. Right brain does not seek to control others but it will exterminate anything that seeks to control it and it will not look at that as bad or good it will look at that as an obstacle that got in its way and thus was removed. If that is a thought or a ideal that gets in its way it will remove it or solve it, or ponder it away. This is why right brain when unveiled keeps one mentally stable because right brain looks at everything as an opportunity to come to further understandings, not bad or good thing, parts, a left brain trait. A left brain influenced container will certainly assume that is dangerous and that is why they hate right brain and veil it in all the children with their "wisdom" education. Last I checked I just sit in my isolation chamber and write my thoughts into words and publish them and so I am not harming anyone but if a left brain influenced container perceives I am causing harm by writing my thoughts into words and attempts to stop me they will come to understand I have no emotional capacity and only seek to remove all obstacles, and no blinking will occur. So it is a paradox. I do not want to harm anyone I am just writing words but if someone tries to stop me I will remove that obstacle. Another way to look at it is, right brain seeks to flatten the road and if an obstacle gets in the road, it is flattened. One being said something along the lines of the greatest right of an American is the right to be left alone. A deeper reality is no right brain influenced container would ever get in my way because they are on their own mission so they respect I am on my mission also, so the only container that would get in my way is a left brain influenced container. What this means is I only see right brain and left brain influenced containers and my purpose is to try and communicate to left brain influenced containers to embrace right brain after it was veiled in them as children and that's is a dangerous situation because some are too far gone so they will fight back. So every left brain influenced container is potentially an ally and potentially an enemy but the absolute reality is I stay in my isolation chamber and I write words so I pose no threat to anyone so that means if a left brain influenced container perceives I do pose a threat, tries to control me, a left brain trait, even when I am in my isolation chamber talking to myself in my diary I will assist said being in understanding what one with no emotional capacity is capable of, and that saves on court costs. I am pleased I won't be remembering I wrote that part, but I doubt it. The complexity in all of this is my intuition, a right brain trait, is through the roof so I am mindful what the left brain influenced containers are thinking and I find many are simply curious and not violent in a one on one basis, but in herds they can become violent very swiftly. I have been through enough mindfully as a being, ten years of suicide attempts, just to undo what traditional education did to me, and I have had enough of societies norms and rules since there rule I have to get their "brand" of education nearly killed me.

[Childhood-Onset Type: onset of at least one criterion characteristic of Conduct Disorder prior to age 10 years.]
All children break the rules or the norms of society. This is why society, left brain influenced containers, want to "school" the children so the children stop breaking the "rules" and so society wants to "fix" the children. A child may take a crayon and draw on a wall and an adult will punish that child and say "That is against the rules." So that proves that child has no concept of rules because their right brain is unveiled. A deeper reality is an adult , a left brain container that got the education and did not apply the remedy, likes things in order or organized, a left brain trait, so that is why they tell a child "Clean your room, don't be a pig." So this leads to what are rules? Rules are simply what left brain loves because rules give left brain the perception of safety and organization and because of that left brain influenced containers slowly put their self in a jail cell with their own desire to make more and more rules. Contrary right brain perceives rules are confining. So a person who unveils right brain

after it is veiled by education, is right brain influenced. Again this entire species is against itself as a result of this written education being taught improperly. There are the ones who love rules and see rules as safety, left brain containers, and ones who see rules as harmful. Simply put, rules hinder one's ability to see the full picture. If there is stream and ones wishes to find the safest crossing but the rule is they cannot go further than 100 yards from where they are to find that crossing they may not find the safest crossing and thus risk danger, and that represents the left brain influenced rules orientated mindset. Right brain has no rules so it will go far and wide to find the safest crossing so that is in fact safer. A judge told me after I slit my wrists, "If you want to kill yourself there is nothing anyone can do about it." There is perhaps no greater wisdom than that. It took me ten years to fully grasp what the meant but I figured it out eventually, one might suggest. Since one has the right to kill their self then rules are rather silly aren't they. There are no rules to protect the lambs, the children, from the wolves, the left brain influenced containers, relative to the lambs are going to get the traditional education and thus have their right brain veiled, so the rules only serve the left brain containers and thus are biased. The left brain containers will go on into infinity suggesting the merits of their rules but they will never ever have a rule to protect the children from having their right brain veiled because the left brain influence's only goal is to kill the god image in the children, veil right brain. So the left brain containers can take all their rules and put their self in cages because right brain forgot what rules, morals and class are and only understands the concept Red Sea. Granted I took the last train to Clarksville, and then there will be none, but I doubt it. Beings that come hundreds of years after you will read these texts and understand them but you will not, so just use to that reality.

These are "psychologists" attempts to classify this Conduct disorder.
Mild: few if any conduct problems in excess of those required to make the diagnosis and conduct problems cause only minor harm to others.

[problems cause only minor harm to others.] This is a classic fear tactic used by left brain containers. It is along the lines of, if you do not follow the rules you are evil. It is not even about what the rules are it is just the fact one breaks "their rules". They could have a rule that says if you kiss a frog you are evil. They could have a rule that says "If you do not believe all the rules I believe in you are evil." So then the left brain containers start to assume anyone who breaks their millions of rules certainly must be evil and thus must certainly have a mental disorder called Conduct disorder. This is because they hate right brain and right does not like rules. This is an example of this right brain hates rules. Someone told me after the accident I should not write any books and now I am writing infinite books. I broke the rules. So before that was suggested to me I never wrote a book and the right brain heard that and flipped it and decided to break that rule to the infinite degree. So it is not against the law to not write books and it is not against the law to write books so you see the law itself is not what breaking rules relative to right brain is about, it is all these little unspoken rules and "norms" and etiquette. A deeper reality is I am a human being and you are a human being and because of that I am unable to tell you what to do and you are equally unable to tell me what to do. It does not matter what credentials are in front of your name, you are not intelligent enough to determine what I should or should not do and the same goes for me relative to you. So you leave me alone and if you want to lock yourself in a mental cell with billions of rules I am willing to let you but never assume you are going to tell me what to do because I will perhaps do just the reverse and to an infinite degree. When you convince me you created me I will consider listening to your advice but until then, follow your rules and do not attempt to push them on me because I do the reverse of what you say I better do. With than in mind it is perhaps best not to speak to me at all and leave me to my own devices. If I am breaking rules by writing my thoughts on paper then someone in America is abridging freedom of speech so in that case we are due to water the tree of liberty. One might suggest my books are testing to see if someone is abridging freedom of speech because I am mindful I have certain rights if that is the case, mainly right to abolish. [That whenever any Form of Government becomes destructive of these ends, it is the Right of the People to alter or to abolish it,] That's the greatest line in the whole lot. I am certain "the right of the people to abolish" sends chills down the government's spine. No wonder they have such a huge standing army. Now, getting back on track.

[Moderate: number of conduct problems and effect on others intermediate between "mild" and "severe".]
This is quite silly. I will skip this aspect because this whole disorder is simply one who thinks for their self.
[Severe: many conduct problems in excess of those required to make the diagnosis or conduct problems cause considerable harm to others.]
[considerable harm to others.] This comment is such a huge generalization considering everyone is mentally unsound essentially to begin with because their right brain has been veiled. If I go into a store and say obscenities that may cause considerable harm to ones who are mentally unsound and fear words. When I was in about sixth grade the teacher scolded me and I was upset and the next thing I know the teacher gave me a note and sent me to the office. The principle read the note and told me the teacher heard me say a cuss word and so he gave me a paddling. I went back to class and I asked some kids around me if I said a cuss word and they said no and I was very confused because I did not recall saying a cuss word and I was honestly trying to determine if I did say a cuss word because I didn't recall it. I was not concerned about the paddling or concerned about being scolded I just did not recall saying a cuss word. But now I understand they are just lunatics who fear words and based on that fear of words they physically harm innocent children. So the adults got the education and are simply left brain containers and left brain loves rules so if anyone breaks their delusional rules they harm them. So the adults not only force the children to get their "brand" of education which veils that child's right brain and puts that child in the place of suffering but on top of that if a child breaks any of their rules they harm that child. This is an indication of the sinister. The sinister will veil a child's right brain by law and then when that child grows up and shows symptoms of greed, lust, envy, anger, hate and addiction the sinister will punish them. You should perhaps go ask

your cult leader if that is truth because you are unable to think for yourself anymore.

It is understood when a person cusses after experiencing pain they get some pain relief. So breaking some of these rules conditioned into their mind, like don't say cuss words,

in fact favors right brain, it dislikes rules, and for a moment the right brain paradox and ambiguity factors into the sensation of pain and so the pain is perceived to be less.

What this means is left brain influenced containers are not breaking rules for any other reason but to experience right brain a bit. A left brain influenced container does not murder someone because they are a murderer, they murder someone because they seek to control and control is a left brain trait. Left brain controls others with rules. The Native Americans were not killing "white men" because they were trying to steal the "white mans" land they were killing white men to try and stop the white man from locking them into concentration camps. The Native Americans, right brain influenced containers were killing the bully, left brain influenced containers. There is a little girl in England and she is touted as being a genius and she is only a few years old and they asked her parents how they "treat" her so to speak and the parents said something along the lines of, we let her do whatever she wants and if she does not want to clean up she does not have to and if she does not want to do something she does not have to.

That does not mean that three year old is running around killing and robbing people that means those parents are allowing that child to think for herself. Just suggesting that many parents are horrified because they are left brain containers and total control freaks over their children. Many parents try to control their child even from an early age and then they push all the left brain education on that child and that child is mentally ruined and then the child revolts against the parents but that is really right brain revolting against a left brain container and it oft ends up in that child hating their parent. Many children die from drugs but they only do drugs to escape that left brain state they were conditioned into by the parents and society. The deeper reality is once right brain is veiled, that is abnormal, so it is natural right brain will try to free itself and because those signals are translated on a conscious level by left brain influence that oft ends up in the being dying as a result.

[B. B. (12) allegedly died from a self-inflicted gunshot wound] here is what this child is saying to civilization. Here is what I think of your education and rules. Here is what I think of you for veiling my right brain. Here is what I think of you mom and dad for allowing my right brain to be veiled. Here is what I think of you society. Here is what I think of the whore rapists of innocent children's minds. I am leaving your hell, rape, control machine. "Give me liberty (right brain) or give me death." Of course you have no brain function so you just think 12 year old children blow their brains out for unknown reasons. As I said, you veil right brain it will kill the being in its attempts to break free and if it does not kill the being that means the being is so far mentally ruined by the education they are just lost mentally in a prison cell of rules, they are afraid to even blink wrong, so they are destroyed as a being. Do you perceive I stutter?

Some associated features of this "conduct disorder" are: Learning disorder, hyperactivity, depressed mood, addiction, antisocial or dramatic behavior.

Learning disorder means they do not take well to societies "brand" of education. Hyperactivity means their right brain is still a bit unveiled and right brain is not sloth, left brain is, so this again shows society hates right brain, and they call symptoms of it being unveiled to a degree disorders that must be treated with drugs to stop it. Depression is a symptom right brain has been veiled to the degree left brain slothful thought processes are the only conscious thoughts so any depressing thought stays in the mind for long periods so a state of depression can be achieved. With right brain unveiled the full measure an emotional capacity is not possible. So this means one cannot be happy for long periods and also cannot be depressed either, and cannot be angry or sad or lustful, greedy, envious etc. So this left brain influenced state of mind caused by traditional education being taught improperly is the core reason for the vast majority these symptoms and then when a child exhibits right brain traits like hyperactivity society determines that is bad and gives that child pills to kill those traits. Civilization is nothing but left brain influenced lunatics that do anything to kill right brain and if you doubt that even slightly you are factually mentally unviable.

Addiction of course is simply lust, and in this case lust for a drug and deeper still a lust to seek relief from being in the extreme left brain state of mind caused by education, which means the drugs unveils right brain a bit for the duration the drugs last. This addiction aspect is a logical solution to escaping the mental state of having one's mind bent to the left and having right brain veiled as a result. A being has their right brain veiled so mentally they are suffering so they seek to relieve some of that suffering and using drugs unveils right brain for the duration the drugs lasts and that is a logical conclusion that a being wishes to relieve the suffering but eventually this turns into addiction and oft ends up killing the being. Once a being gets enough of the education they sense time meaning right brain paradox is absent from their conscious thoughts and they have to apply the remedy which is mental suicide or they are stuck like that for the rest of their life. So even if a being stops doing drugs they are really just going to suffer even more and this is why many cannot stop doing drugs because drugs are a logical solution to escape the mental suffering they are in as a left brain influenced container. So society see's addiction as bad because misery loves company. Society is all left brain influenced containers and so left brain knows drugs may assist one to feel right brain and it does not tolerate that so it locks anyone who uses drugs into prisons and insults any of the others who do drugs. I used pot as my drug to escape the suffering, in hindsight, but after I got the "ah ha" sensation a month after accidentally applying the remedy I was so high mentally drugs no longer were even considered at all. I wish drugs could get me high, and that is how high I am with right brain unveiled. Absence makes the heart grow fonder. I ponder if I did a few more drugs perhaps I would be a bit more ignorant because at this stage I pray for ignorance. Never assume because you did drugs that has any effect relative how you will be after you unveil right brain. Right brain is so powerful even if you have physiological brain damage when you unveil right brain the damage perhaps will not be noticed much. Avoid assuming intelligence has anything to do with genes. You have a right hemisphere and it was veiled by education and you unveil right brain and all delusions of not being as intelligent as the greatest minds in history will swiftly fade. Do not underestimate the power of right brain once unveiled even though society has conditioned you to hate it. I speak to the down trodden in society because the "intelligent" beings in society have cups that are full. I want the intelligent left brain influenced containers to unveil right brain on their death bed and then I want to hear them say "My entire kingdom for a moment more." and then they die. That understanding pleases me. As for the downtrodden you in fact have a chance to unveil right brain. You attempt to look at your problems as a blessing because you are in reverse world, so the least are the most valuable and you are the least. What that means is everyone you think is more valuable or more worthy than you are, in fact is less worthy than you are. All the rich and wealthy are far less valuable than you are. All the ones that have no drug addictions are less valuable than you are. All the ones who are high and mighty are less valuable than you are. And out of the down trodden, the suicidal and depressed are the most valuable of all. So if you ever thought you are a loser in life I am here to tell you that you are a winner in the real life. You are going to have to go through treason, the 9th circle of hell, to get out of hell, but you are in that area so you are on the right path. Because of that it is very important for you to be mindful the 9th circle is the big test and the 9th circle is where the door out of hell is at. You are mindful of suicide if you are depressed and thus you are mindful of death and that is a good indication so it is important you run with that mindset and seek the shadow of death and then fear not. Shadow being the operative word. Tracks off fell.

Now another aspect of this "conduct disorder" is antisocial behavior.
Society = left brain influenced containers
So anyone in society who tries to wake their self up, unveil right brain, is deemed bad because misery loves company. So antisocial behavior is simply a "sheep" that has left the herd and that being has a chance to be "found". The lost sheep is a person who is a left brain influenced container who is trying to find the "light" and the herd, society, does not take kindly to that prospect so they will give

that being all the psychological drugs in the universe to make sure that being gets back in with the herd because misery loves company. The darkness hates the light so any being seeking the light is deemed bad and the darkness will do anything to bring that being back into the darkness. So society perceives antisocial behavior is bad, but in reality world that is a being that is blessed because they are mindful they no longer wish to associate with the herd, the darkness, society, the left brain influenced containers. Change is a mindset not a threat.

A left brain influenced container oft gets tied up in the web of rules they attempt to aspire to. Oft one will avoid change if it contradicts their rules.

8:13:11 PM – This is the situation I am in. My new found religion doctrine is that the tree of knowledge, written education veils the god image in man, right brain, and so that is my religious belief so I speak out against the tree of knowledge being taught improperly. So my religious beliefs are that the tree of knowledge when taught improperly is harmful. I live in a country that does not believe that. The country I live in denies my religious belief and that is evident because it pushes the tree of knowledge on children and has no idea of its harmful mental effects and has no clue it veils the god image in the children, right brain traits. Because I live in a democracy the majority has determined it is proper to veil the god image, right brain in the children using traditional education so I am not allowed to go against the majority on a scale of forcing the majority to do things my way. The problem is the majority expects me to pay taxes that support veiling children's right brain because the taxes support the majorities "brand" of education. So paying taxes that support the tree of knowledge which I am against when taught improperly goes against my religious beliefs. Now the majority, the left brain influenced containers, will say that is too bad you have to support our "brand " of education with your taxes or you will go to jail. So I can either support the left brain containers main goal to veil the god image in all the children via their "brand" of education and deny my religion or I can go to jail. So this is a form of religious prosecution, because I am mindful what that "education" did to me, it almost killed me.

[That whenever (any Form of Government)(other voters, government, any authority) becomes destructive of these ends (denies freedom of religion), it is the Right of the People to alter or to abolish it,] The deeper reality is, deny one's self and that means no rules and no morals and no class. Another way to look at it is "When in Rome." After one applies the remedy they lose ego and one of these traits of ego is pride. Now if I had even an ounce of pride I would go against the majority and not pay taxes that support the tree of knowledge, written education that veils the child's right brain, the god image in man. So this pride aspect is gone and that is a blessing because that way I can support the tree of knowledge education with my taxes and at the same time write books explaining its devastating mental effects on the minds of children. So instead of having a nervous breakdown I am looking at the fact I have to support something that goes against my own religious beliefs as a blessing and a situation that will assist me to concentrate and focus on the log in my eye even more. Once you apply the remedy if you attempt to have pride or ego you will destroy yourself. If you attempt to have morals you will destroy yourself because there are six billion mentally unsound beings that have no conscience at all, their right brain intuition is gone and that is conscience or soul, and they will see a being with a conscience as evil so no morals, no rules, and no pride, which means deny yourself.

There is no constitutional suggestion relative to education but it appears some believe there is, but there is not. There are two forms of education, written, which veils right brain, and oral which does not veil right brain, so it is purely the free choice of every parent to decide which education aspect they will teach their children but that right has been taken away not on the premise of constitutional aspects but just because someone voted to take that right away from the parent. My country only has one "brand" of education, written education and that "brand" goes against my religious beliefs because it veils right brain, the god image in man when taught to small children and taught improperly. It is not important if six billion people suggest my religious beliefs are stupid. Now you perhaps understand why Freud said this "America is a mistake, a giant mistake." I will remind you, if you are ever mentally capable of understanding how wise Freud was. Since you have been conditioned to believe every word you hear you will either be an emotional wreck and afraid after reading these last few thousand words or you will look at them as concepts to ponder. I prefer you become an emotional wreck and become afraid and perhaps get a little closer to the 9th circle, after all that's my purpose, to convince you to commit mental suicide so you will wake up and stop mentally raping innocent children into hell, even though that was done to you and your nature now is to abuse because you were abused.

Cyclothymic Disorder is a chronic bipolar disorder consisting of short periods of mild depression and short periods of hypomania. This is very similar to how one who unveils right brain is but the major difference is they never can get depressed and never can become manic for more than a few seconds because right brain ponders so fast and also ponders in random access so the thoughts are changing in the mind on a speed scale that one is only able to suggest they are in neutral or in nothingness. This disorder is a symptom this being has right brain unveil to a degree they are experiencing some random access thoughts but because they are still left brain influenced their emotions are very strong so they suffering greatly. It is one thing to have manic thoughts and depressed thoughts on a scale of seconds as in when right brain is unveiled, it is complex, one with no sense of time can never be manic they can just be hyper appearing to the slothful ones. It is another thing to have those thoughts in left brain influenced state because those thoughts control that being. The mind can never escape thoughts so everyone has manic thoughts and depressed thoughts; how long they linger is the key. One symptom of this disorder is addiction and so this being does drugs to escape this nightmare state of mind they are in, left brain influenced state. Because they have right brain veiled they only see these thoughts as problems because the thoughts linger and build up and before they know it they are consumed by the thoughts. When right brain is unveiled thoughts simply cannot linger for more than a few seconds relative to a clock. The mind is in the state of now so a thought enters the mind and then another thought unrelated enters the mind and the mind is simply going through this at lightning speed at all times so no one state of mind can be maintained and that is mentally healthy because one cannot stress out about one thought or another. In the left brain state of mind the thoughts are slothful so they linger and when the remedy is applied the right brain is unveiled and thoughts are quick. Some left brain influenced containers stress out about things simply because they cannot get that thought out of their mind and that is a symptom of the slothful, sequential thoughts. Think about a police officer. They see many traumatic things and stressful things and the images and thoughts of those events never leave their mind and sometimes they linger and over time that lingering thought starts to take a toll on that being and then they start to drink to escape that thought and that is a logical conclusion to make that thought go away, but if right brain was unveiled the most traumatic experience in the universe would be forgotten and pushed into the sea of thoughts and it would never be able to effect the being. Another way to look at it is right brain does not judge which thought is better or worse. Right brain see's every thought as a concept and ideal so it is not picky which thought to focus on. In the left brain state a person may have thoughts they perceive are worse than others and then start to focus on those thoughts and then those thoughts become obsessions. So a police officer may drink to escape a thought but in doing so they reinforce that traumatic thought because they acknowledge it by drinking to escape it. One complexity is when right brain is unveiled all memories are concepts so the time stamps and emotional tags are gone, so the traumatic memory is just like an image but without emotional baggage attached. A person may drink to forget and forgetting is what right brain does. It makes the thoughts random so no thought can linger and so this is why a police officer may drink to forget and that goes for anyone who does drugs to escape traumatic thoughts. The deeper reality is every left brain influenced container goes through this same principle and after a while it takes a toll on that being. Some snap sooner than others but they all snap. I am mindful psychologists are perhaps the most mentally damaged of them all because they perceive a pill will cure these disorders and not only that, they are mindful the pills do not solve these disorders, so they just prescribe one pill and then a new pill comes out and they prescribe that pill and pretty much they are no longer even concerned about anything but prescribing pills they already are mindful will not solve these disorders. They say this pill is good then in a month they say that last pill was not as good as this new pill and that cycle goes on for years and years and they never solve anything so they are very interesting to write about. They rely on left brain intellect, because they have no choice, and so they prescribe whatever the psychologist next to them prescribes and neither have a clue what they are doing, so they cannot think for their self, no right brain intuition, so they are just a herd following the herd off the cliff. I invite any psychologist on the planet to contact me and will convince them of what kind of pills they should prescribe their self in quantities of a thousand.

Delirium is a rapidly developing disorder of disturbed attention that fluctuates with time. This is associated with Alzheimer's. When a left brain influenced container gets older the effects of the written education start to wear off. This is why there is a concept among the ones who have applied the remedy to a degree that everyone will wake up eventually, of course I humbly remind them this being didn't wake up [D. K. (15) allegedly took his own life by an unknown method] so perhaps they should rethink their understandings. An old person will start to talk to their self and be unaware if anyone else is even watching them and appear rather carefree, showing no ego. That is a symptom their right brain is starting to unveil. Right brain once unveiled silences ego so this older person is starting to lose ego. Their thoughts are all over the place and that is simply random access thoughts which are a trait of right brain. The left brain influenced containers create these psychological signposts that are not valid and then when one shows symptoms of that sign post they assume they understand what is happening. A better way to look at it is, left brain always see's traits of right brain as bad because a left brain influenced containers hate right brain. Another way to look at it is I exhibit every single known psychological disorder not relative to physiological disease but that is not because I have a psychological disorder it is just society has determined right brain traits are disorders and anyone who exhibits them must be psychologically out of whack.

I exhibit every psychological disorder you can come up with but that is only because you see right brain as evil so the only one with a true psychological self hating disorder is you because you have right brain and you can't stand its characteristics. So you are a house divided against itself. Anytime you show symptoms of right brain you take a bunch of pills to silence those traits. You avoid ever making a contradiction because you are not even mentally functioning enough to understand that is just right brain trying to throw out one of its complex paradox observations. I am not suggesting you hate the complex aspect of your mind naturally I am suggesting this society you love so much has conditioned you to hate right brain and so it has conditioned you to hate the better half of your own mind so you are essentially screwed as far as being a mentally viable at this point in your "life".

Dementia tends to happen to older beings or beings with some sort of physiological disease but on a scale of a being that has their right brain veiled to the degree they sense time they are also in dementia because they cannot concentrate. Their mind is so full of all these powerful emotions they can concentrate for an hour or so but then they start to get tired and fatigued and start to ponder they need a drug like coffee to help them escape the stress they perceive they are under. I write a novel a month and I never sense fatigue or stress or even sense it takes any effort at all and I never break a sweat and I am mindful no being on this planet that has a sense of time can even dream of that kind of concentration so that means relative to me they are all unable to concentrate and thus have concentration deficit disorders to just name one of their infinite disorders in the neurosis they are in. It's best to just use neurosis to explain your infinite disorders. Never underestimate how powerful right brain is when it is unveiled.

10:38:30 PM – I will explain this movie Avatar. I am not suggesting the director had this in mind when they created the movie but perhaps they did perhaps. First off, substitute the humans in the movie for civilization, the ones that sense time, the left brain influenced containers. Substitute the alien race for the ones with no sense of time, the right brain influenced containers. To make it easier, look at the humans as the "white man" and look at the aliens as the Native Americans. The white man saw the natural resources and saw they could make lots of money from them. At the beginning of the movie in one exchange a white man said something along the lines of , "We offered them education and they just want to sit in the mud." This is a classic example of how the left brain influenced beings assume anyone who does want their "brand" of education certainly must be stupid. So the "white men" saw the "Native Americans " had resources they could make lots of money off of and so they had to find a way to take it from them. Now the aliens, "Native Americans", lived in harmony with nature, this is a holistic right brain trait. So they respected nature more than money which is a symptom of sanity since once nature is destroyed the beings that rely on nature are destroyed. This movie is essentially a repeat of dances with wolves movie. The main character meets the "natives" and starts to understand their ways and then turns on civilization, the white men, and fights against them. That of course is a repeat of the story of Moses. He was in civilization, applied the fear not remedy and then fought against civilization, the left brain influenced ones that veil the god image in man, right brain. One of the early scenes in the movie the main character, a "white man", meets the "spiritual leader" of the Aliens, and that spiritual leader says something along the lines of "We will train you and see if we can cure your insanity." So this is a deep reality. First off is seeing holistically, a right brain trait, sanity or is seeing parts, a left brain trait, sanity? The truth is seeing holistically is a symptom of sanity because when the mind is sound and at 50/50 right brain traits shine through because right brain has complexity and left brain is linear in complexity or simple minded. So holistically is a symptom of right brain being at 50% and thus proof one is of sound mind and one who see's parts has left brain dominate traits and that is only possible when the mind is unsound or out of 50/50 harmony. So this alien religious leader who's tribe lived in harmony and saw holistically was saying to this being from civilization, who was only interested in the "gold" no matter how many tree's they had to cut down, "We will see if your insanity can be cured." The point is if you will destroy a forest just for some money you are insane. If you will risk harming nature for a few dollars you are insane. If you will risk destroying nature for a barrel of oil you are insane. If you will kill other people just to get some "gold" you are insane. Of course you do not believe that because you are insane. As the move goes on there is a final battle. This is like Armageddon. The ones that sense time, the beast, against the angels, the ones that don't sense time, the sane beings, and so the beast has many armies and many great weapons but the angels have courage to stand against the firepower of Goliath and they prevail in the end. Of course that is just fantasy land or wishful thinking. There is always this concept that the ones that don't sense time will finally prevail over the ones that sense time but the truth is the ones that sense time are never ever going to rethink their "brand" of education and so they will continue to veil the right brain god image in the children until the species eventually kills itself off because a species divided mindfully against itself cannot stand. So the best one can do is focus on the log in their eye and apply the remedy for their self with the understanding the "curse" on the species is fatal and unstoppable. Star wars is also a conflict of the ones with no sense of time, the ones with the force, right brain, against the dark side, the ones that do sense time and have right brain veiled.

12:58:15 AM – The spirit of these four lines is so indicative of this battle between the left brain influenced containers and the right brain influenced containers.

[Exodus 2:14 And he said, Who made thee a prince and a judge over us? intendest thou to kill me, as thou killedst the Egyptian? And Moses feared, and said, Surely this thing is known.]
[Who made thee a prince and a judge over us?] On one hand this comment is like a little child saying "You aren't the boss of me." On another hand this comment is like a person saying "Who died and made you ruler?" So Moses is speaking to the ruler of the left brain influenced beings and saying, "You're a human being and so you are not better than any other human being so how are you able to assume control over everyone when we are all equal?" Now a left brain influenced ruler today would see that as a revolutionary type comment because they are control freaks and left brain is all about

control, control is a form of coveting. So Moses is challenging the control structure of civilization. Civilizations control structure is broken down like this. The rich left brain influenced containers have the control. The poor left brain influenced containers are controlled by the rich rulers. Anytime a poor left brain influenced container's attempts to buck the establishment an example is made of them, they are demonized they are shown to be evil and bad and that way the rest of the poor left brain influenced containers stay in line.

[And Moses feared, and said, Surely this thing is known.] This is an interesting comment because it is saying Moses was mindful the crosshairs where going to be on his head, so to speak. Moses was standing up to the bully, the ruler left brain influenced container and so Moses was standing up to Goliath.

[Exodus 2:15 Now when Pharaoh heard this thing, he sought to slay Moses. But Moses fled from the face of Pharaoh, and dwelt in the land of Midian: and he sat down by a well.]
This comment is simply the left brain influenced ruler is aware Moses' argument is flawless and that means if Moses keeps talking and it gets around the rulers slaves may revolt so this ruler must kill Moses. Now contrast this comment with this comment.
[Mark 6:20 For Herod feared John, knowing that he was a just man and holy man, and observed him; and when he heard him, he did many things, and heard him gladly.]
[Mark 11:18 And the scribes and chief priests heard it, and sought how they might destroy him: for they feared him, because all the people was astonished at his doctrine.]

[Now when Pharaoh heard this thing, he sought to slay Moses.] = [For Herod feared John, knowing that he was a just man and holy man] = [And the scribes and chief priests heard it, and sought how they might destroy him: for they feared him,]

So why did all these left brain influenced rulers want to kill Moses, John the Baptist and Jesus? = [because all the people was astonished at his doctrine.] And the doctrine was the tree of knowledge, written education veiled the right brain and made them all mentally slothful and easy to control. So Moses understood the remedy, the fear not remedy to negate this mental sloth and unveil right brain, John the Baptist had his Baptism aspect of that same remedy and Jesus had the "those who lose their life mindfully will preserve it" remedy. So not only were these three beings explaining the situation they also had the remedy to the mental slavery the people were put in and that is a huge threat to a left brain influenced ruler, control freak. Some side notes on these comments.

[the scribes and chief priests heard it] A scribe is one who gets the written education and does not apply the remedy and the chief priests are scribes who are also religious leaders, but they are false teachers because they never applied the fear not remedy, so they are simply control freaks on the "religious" front, they seek money and control not righteousness.

Thursday, January 21, 2010 - Although I started this poorly disguised thick pamphlet diary on this date : 12/25/2009 10:04:39 PM I assure you it has been infinity. You can go on into infinity explaining how it has not been infinity but I assure you it has been infinity. I am mindful now that my sense of time is completely gone I am operating in some sort of speed world you are not even capable of understanding let alone believing. I am starting to lean on the fence towards the side that I am the only human being on the planet with absolutely no sense of time. I have not been able to convince anyone to apply the remedy successfully but I have convinced a few that the premise of the mental effects of the written education on the mind is potentially valid. I have a one percent sensation that I just tricked my mind into thinking I died and that is what the accident really was. That is very healthy to keep that one percent sensation alive because it keeps me honest. The simple fact is, I am underestimating the damage the written education has on the mind. The ones I have spoken to are mentally ruined from all that left brain education in a permanent way. I still have this mindset that I must do everything properly to increase my chances in convincing them but I am underestimating how mentally ruined they are and I am in denial they can never be recovered or cured, ever. They have been mentally killed and thus are mentally dead. It would be wonderful if I would have been aware of that before I agreed to the "write infinite books" idea. I am pleased there is no law against writing infinite books. I am pleased with the prospect that if I write enough books I will perhaps start to show signs of the curse again and then I can use the patented fear not remedy to assist myself to break the curse and then I can write infinite books and attempt to get the curse again. All I detect at this stage is a species that has invented a tool and that tool has ruined the species mentally. I detect I woke up to the fact a tool has mentally ruined our species. I do not see the point in rules or morals since we are mentally ruined as a species. We continue to ruin the offspring with the tool because the species is no longer able to even mentally understand the tool mentally ruined them. I am open minded to the reality I am the single human being on the planet that accidentally negated the mental damage caused by the tool fully and I at least have the presence of mind to explain what I discovered with the understanding it is going to have no impact relative to stopping the tool and thus mental damage being pushed on the offspring. Because of that understanding there is no special thing I am required to say. There is special deed I am required to do because I escaped the mental damage and that is as good as it perhaps ever will get. I escaped the mental damage but that does not mean any other human being on this planet will be able to. I am mindful I am attempting to under estimate exactly what I did in that den fourteen months ago. I am mindful I am being far too humble relative to what I accomplished by accident in that den. I perhaps did something no other human being on this planet has done for at least a thousand years and I did it accidentally. I continue to try and convince myself many people have done this but it is not true. I try to convince myself many people alive today must certainly be able to understand the ancient texts like I do but it is not true. My mind is in a state of optimism relative to being able to convince others to apply this fear not remedy but my intuition is suggesting I am not going to be able to convince any meaningful amount of people to apply it. So I arrive at the final conclusion that written language was fatal to our species. We as a species have inadvertently killed our self with this tool and I am included in that subset. You know not about moments of doubt.- 3:00:54 PM

Friday, January 22, 2010 – This is relative to the reverse thing. Essentially ones with a sense of time are always trying to live as long as they can, they never want to let go. It is understood on Einstein's last few days alive his doctors suggested they could give him an operation on his heart so he would live longer and he said something along the lines of "I have accomplished everything I can accomplish." So he could have lived longer if he got that operation but the truth is due to the location, death to ones who have applied the remedy or have right brain unveiled is a release from this location and from the heightened awareness. A release from watching what is happening to the children, relative to traditional education veiling right brain, is another way to look at it. One way to look at it is with no sense of time life is infinitely long and attempting to convince a blind man blindness is abnormal along with the fact life is infinitely long, one is very open minded to impermanence when its appears, so to speak. So the reverse thing is, one is accepting of impermanence when it arrives and is not doing everything in their power to stave it off. To one of sound mind death is expected and understood so there is no emotional hesitation and in some ways it's a blessing considering the situation relative to what is being done to the children. So ones that sense time perceive death is a tragedy and ones with no sense of time perceive death is a blessing. I do not want to sit here for infinity and watch you do to the children what you did to me so death is my only release and I will not deny it when it arrives, and that is as simple as it is. And now you know why Buddha said "Health is important.", and Einstein said to that comment, "No thanks I've seen enough. No heart repair surgery for me.", so to speak. The grief caused by being aware of needless suffering is quite intense, but I doubt it.

1/22/2010 3:29:28 PM – So looking at this Moses story relative to some of these movies one will see there is a common thread.
[Exodus 2:11 And it came to pass in those days, when Moses was grown, that he went out unto his brethren, and looked on their

burdens: and he spied an Egyptian smiting an Hebrew, one of his brethren.]

[when Moses was grown] means Moses applied the remedy. In Dances with Wolves the main character rides in front of a firing line in a suicide attempt but does not get killed so he applied the remedy, he did not know he would not be killed, so he faced the shadow of death, for example. Moses applies the remedy and then confronts the left brain influenced rulers who gave him the education that veiled his right brain and he is challenging them. [Who made thee a prince and a judge over us?]

[Exodus 2:14 And he said, Who made thee a prince and a judge over us? intendest thou to kill me, as thou killedst the Egyptian? And Moses feared, and said, Surely this thing is known.]

After Moses challenges the left brain influenced rulers he is mindful they want him dead because they understand he is a threat to their control and power so Moses leaves civilization, the left brain influenced ones. Moses joins the tribes which are the ones who live outside of civilization. They are either beings who never got the education or ones who applied the remedy after getting civilizations "brand" of education. So naturally civilization sees them as bad or evil because it sees anything that is not like it as bad or evil. A deeper reality is the left brain influence always see's right brain influence as bad or evil because right brain aspects are contrary to left brain aspects. In Dances with Wolves for example the main character applies the remedy and then decides to leave civilization and goes to an outpost on the edge of civilization.

[Exodus 2:16 Now the priest of Midian had seven daughters: and they came and drew water, and filled the troughs to water their father's flock.]

Priest of Midian, is simply a Master or Lord. So these beings that are not of civilization are simply getting some water that is in the wilderness and so it is every one's water and they are not attempting to control it they are just using it. This is similar to how Native Americans were, never controlling the land or natural resources they were living in harmony with them, everything depending on everything else, so to speak.

[Exodus 2:17 And the shepherds came and drove them away: but Moses stood up and helped them, and watered their flock.]

[And the shepherds came and drove them away] But then civilization, the left brain influenced containers showed up and determined all natural resources were theirs and that is a symptom of left brain. It covets and controls everything and will take things because it perceives it has might and thus has a right to take everything. Left brain containers cannot share ever, they can only take and control and they do it by force so they perceive that gives them the right. A real life example is the tribes in the Amazon have oil on their land, and the left brain influenced ones only care about money and so they tricked the tribes out of their oil and they did it under the guise of their own laws and morals, which they have none of. They just steal and take from anyone because they can, so they have no conscience. Civilization mentally rapes their own children under the guise of educating them and that is done for the prospect and promise of a few silver pieces.

[Moses stood up and helped them] This suggests Moses fought against the left brain influenced control freaks, civilization. Moses saw an injustice was being done to the tribes at the hands of civilization, the ones that sense time and although he was greatly outnumbered he still stood up to them so Moses faced goliath. In the movie Avatar the main character left civilization and joined the tribes, and then fought against civilization to protect the tribes. This is just a reoccurring theme in many movies, David against Goliath. Goliath being civilization, the left brain influenced beings, the ones that sense time, the ones that mentally rape their children into hell under the guise of education. The education itself is just a tool but when taught improperly and to a child the age of six it ruins the mind of that child. Although you do not have the mental capacity to understand that is truth that is not your fault because you were mentally raped into hell by civilization under the guise of educating you. Education is not a noun it is a verb although in your hallucination world it is not a verb. This spirit of the above lines is simply a repeating theme in history. A being is in civilization and gets the written education and in one way or another applies the fear not remedy and negates the mental neurosis the education causes and then that being turns against civilization and its "education" methods and is always very outnumbered and deemed an outcast in civilization. That is essentially the scenario that plays out in all the ancient texts in the east and the west.

1/23/2010 2:13:19 PM -
Change is a mindset not an aspiration. The truth has always been the same, only ones ability to see it changes. Out of the ashes a new palace is built. Without doubt one oft runs into dead ends. Tolerating neurosis requires ambiguity. Change is a mindset not a profession.

[Psalms 141:10 Let the wicked fall into their own nets, whilst that I withal escape.] This comment is a repeat of the comment a house divided cannot stand. A left brain influenced container has an unsound mind and so they are in disharmony mindfully and are in turn self defeating and that gives more credence to this comment [Luke 17:2 It were better for him that a millstone were hanged about his neck, and he cast into the sea, than that he should offend one of these little ones.] So the traditional education applied to a child veils that child's right brain and leaves that child with a house, mind, divided so all one has really done is destroyed that child and since the remedy is so difficult to apply relative to ones who has the curse, one has killed that child's potential. Another way to look at it is one has destroyed a universe unto itself. I am mindful, ones that sense time, will not be able to grasp that reality and that in fact is no surprise. You follow the herd, you drown with the herd. There are varying degrees of love and most of them lead to suffering. Illusions rarely need help they just need a little bending. The only thing more powerful than hate is indifference.

[Philippians 4:7 And the peace of God, which passeth all understanding, shall keep your hearts and minds through Christ Jesus.]
This comment is a very accurate description of the traits of right brain and also the word mind is mentioned in this comment.

[And the peace of God] = the image of god in man, right brain. The word peace denotes with right brain unveiled one is unable to stress out and become scared or afraid so they are at peace even in the largest storm. [which passeth all understanding] This is a very accurate explanation of right brain or the mind when right brain is unveiled. One understands things they never understood before they applied the remedy, so one's eyes are opened up.

[shall keep your hearts and minds through Christ Jesus.] Through Jesus Christ denotes if one applies what Jesus suggested which is to deny one's self and those who lose their life mindfully will preserve their life, applies the remedy, they [shall keep your hearts and minds] So after one gets the traditional education they lose their life, heart, conscience, and their mind, and then one applies the fear not remedy they preserve or regain their heart and mind, conscience.

It is important to understand the fear not remedy was still mentioned in the New Testament.

[Luke 1:13 But the angel said unto him, Fear not, Zacharias: for thy prayer is heard; and thy wife Elisabeth shall bear thee a son, and thou shalt call his name John.]

So the ones in the New testament were simply rephrasing the fear not remedy suggested in the Torah and this is because no matter what happens eventually the "curse" caused by written education gets out of hand after a time, so to speak. If one single parent gets the education and does not apply the remedy then their child will not apply the remedy and before you know it the world will [Leviticus 19:29 Do not prostitute thy daughter, to cause her to be a whore; lest the land fall to whoredom, and the land become full of wickedness.] become a land fall to whoredom and full of wickedness, which means everyone will have the curse. So one can look at it like the beings in the Torah had an excellent understanding of how to counter the "curse" but after a while, several hundred years, the curse got out of control again, and people stopped applying the remedy, then the beings in the New Testament came along and attempted to convince everyone to apply the remedy because they were mindful civilization stopped applying the remedy but were still using written language and of course they were slaughtered for their efforts. So Zacharias applied the fear not remedy on John the Baptist and then John the

Baptist gave his own version of the fear not remedy, baptism, which is to dunk a person under water until their hypothalamus gives the death signal and then that person , fears not. There is something about the version of the remedy that is very advanced because going under water is a certain way to get that hypothalamus to give the death signal but it is also rather delicate because one could literally drown. It perhaps goes beyond just being dunked under water until one perceives the desire to surface it is more along the line of being dunked by someone you do not trust and then being held under the water so one's mind perceives they will drown and then at that stage they do not fight it, so they fear not.

[Romans 1:14 I am debtor both to the Greeks, and to the Barbarians; both to the wise, and to the unwise.]
Socrates was from Greece his version of the remedy in principle was no true philosopher fears death. A Barbarian is a being who never gets the written education, a tribe. Civilization looks at these beings that never got the written education as savages, which makes perfect sense relative to the fact the darkness see's the light as darkness. Another way to look at it is, if civilization, which pushes the written "brand" of education on everyone ever suggested human being's that do not get our "brand" of education are equal then it would bring up the question that there may be a flaw in written education. If it is even suggested a human being that does not get written education is the same as a human being that does then the question of what is the point of written education comes to the surface. If any doubts that written education is not as good as oral education, relative to side effects on the mind of a child, then law suits would fly from every angle towards civilization. So this comment is suggesting the Greeks were wise, relative to Socrates and the Barbarians were unwise. But this wise and unwise is only relative to the ones that sense time. The barbarians are in fact wise because they never got written education so they never got the curse, and Socrates was wise because he got written education and then applied the remedy, no true philosopher fears death. Of course Socrates was killed by civilization because the darkness hates the light. Perhaps a being with a sense of time cannot see that is what that line is saying and that is understandable

because they are mentally unviable and their sense of time proves that, so in that respect I just validated the theme of all my texts so I am pleased that worked out.

[Luke 6:22 Blessed are ye, when men shall hate you, and when they shall separate you from their company, and shall reproach you, and cast out your name as evil, for the Son of
man's sake.]
There is some humor in this comment. After you apply the remedy it is best you look at when the men, ones who sense time, spit on you for explaining the dangers of written language, the tree of knowledge, as a blessing because if not you perhaps will not last mentally very long in "this kitchen" so to speak. Reproach means to criticize someone for doing something wrong. This means the ones that sense time will criticize you for speaking poorly about the mental effects of written language because they perceive it is not possible years of left brain education will ever effect the mind of a child, so they are out of touch with reality but relative to their perception and the fact they only see truth as lies, it is perfectly logical to them, years of left brain education does not alter the mind of a child at all. If the ones that sense time believed all the left brain favoring education bent their mind even one degree to the left they would apply the remedy, so they do not believe it did. In reality the written education bends the mind a gargantuan degree to the left so they are not even able to distinguish reality from hallucination anymore because their perception is totally obliterated. One cannot be any more mentally obliterated than if one senses time because right brain paradox does not even factor into ones perception anymore because right brain mental aspects are reduced to subconscious which means they are not even mentally there anymore.
<Eps> ever heard of punctuation?

"What it comes down to is that modern society discriminates against the right hemisphere." - Roger Sperry (1973)

[Matthew 7:5 Thou hypocrite, first cast out the beam out of thine own eye(first apply the remedy); and then shalt thou see clearly(have the brain function) to cast(to assist others with the remedy) out the mote out of thy brother's eye.]

Being recognized by an important being is a treasure beyond value.

"I prefer peace. But if trouble must come, let it come in my time, so that my children can live in peace(with sound minds)."
Thomas Payne

[Psalms 120:7 I am for peace: but when I speak, they(the ones that veil the children's right brain, the ones that sense time) are for war.]

Bloodbaths like sacrifices have certain restorative properties.

Please be mindful the ones that sense time are in a deep neurosis and know not what they do.

Perhaps my genes kicked in when I was forty.

Do you perceive I stutter?

Begun the process has. Tis well.

1/23/2010 4:15:21 PM